Roger V

BARDOT: "She had a
suffered if
than one ma...

DENEUVE: "Catherine was 17, and I was 32. Society
passes severe judgment on women who
sleep with a man less than 24 hours after
meeting him. On the contrary, I
respected Catherine."

FONDA: "When I made love to another woman, I
talked to Jane about it. With time, I went
further. I brought home some of my
conquests—sometimes even into our bed."

**"He likes his women young, nubile, innocent and
hot. . . .** He wants to tell us of his life behind the
scenes and under the covers with each of them."
—*San Francisco Chronicle*

**"This memoir has the same brash charm that has
made Vadim so demonstrably popular...** a skillful
raconteur."
—Janet Maslin, *Vogue*

"It's how I like my movie books. . . . We learn *much*
about three sex goddesses."
—Rhoda Koenig, *New York Magazine*

**"Loaded with fond recollections of the steamier
episodes of his life."**
—*Women's Wear Daily*

"Seems to enjoy the telling as much as the kissing . . .
surprisingly gallant."
—*People*

Also by Roger Vadim

FICTION

The Hungry Angel
Memories of the Devil

BARDOT DENEUVE FONDA

ROGER VADIM

Translated from the French by Melinda Camber Porter

WARNER BOOKS

A Warner Communications Company

☆ *Preface* ☆

This book is dedicated to my future grandchildren. If one day they should feel the impulse to discover what their grandfather or grandmother was like, I shudder to think of the image they would piece together from the thousands of articles, stories and biographies that have appeared in more than fifty countries over the past three decades.

What has been published about Brigitte Bardot, Catherine Deneuve, Jane Fonda and Roger Vadim isn't always inaccurate; it's that the spotlight often distorts the truth. Even worse is the distortion caused by our gluttonous, information-stuffed society's habit of labeling or pigeonholing everyone. I don't like the idea of being buried in a mask that is not of my own face.

But there is one other reason for this book: the need to speak of the joys, the pleasures, the sorrows and the wild times I have known at the sides of three remarkable women. I was unable to resist the desire to open the coffer of the past in which so many unique treasures have been stored. I didn't want to end my life as a miser hoarding these wonderful memories and images—fairy-tale images which will, one day, have vanished with me to the land where all is erased.

Brigitte, Catherine and Jane: three modern fairy-tale princesses. But fairy tales are also tales of cruelty, although fortunately they usually have happy endings. I want to speak of these adolescents, these young girls, and who they were before they became fairy-tale princesses.

I knew them well, these future stars with whom I shared life before they went on to sparkle on screens all over the world.

It is their astonishing transformations—often painful, always fascinating—that I am going to tell you about.

ONE

B·A·R·D·O·T

*T*HE goddess of love had not been seen emerging from the sea since Botticelli painted Venus floating on a mother-of-pearl shell.

But this was the spectacle that two thousand American marines witnessed on May 12, 1953, at 11:30 A.M. from the aircraft carrier *Enterprise,* anchored in the Bay of Cannes.

First they saw her long tresses floating on the surface of the water; then her face, streaming with drops of water, glistening in the sun like so many diamonds. Her innocent, sensual mouth and perfect oval eyes, her delicate nose, her cheeks as round as a child's, were made for pleasure and laughter. Two hands with aristocratic wrists gripped the edge of the Chris-Craft and the apparition hoisted herself on board: a delicate neck, a thin waist that a man could encircle with two hands; a round, provocative and tender derriere that would have been the envy of Adonis and Aphrodite; perfectly curved hips, long, firm thighs, charming ankles, and the arched feet of a dancer. A little bikini, a shadow rather than a garment, hid nothing of this sensual, glorious body.

The sailors of the *Enterprise* knew a goddess when they saw one even if they didn't know her name. Their whistles and applause could be heard as far as the steps of the Palais du Festival, on the Croisette. They ran to the portside railings jostling each other for a better look.

Standing up in the Chris-Craft, Brigitte burst out laughing.

"They'll make the aircraft carrier capsize," she cried out.

An officer walked down the gangway ladder and motioned to her to come aboard. It was against the rules, but he preferred to bend them rather than cause a riot or general mutiny.

With her natural spontaneity, Brigitte accepted the invitation. On the bridge, she shook hands, made everyone laugh with her few words of English and let amateur photographers take as many photos as they wished. It was a change from the visits of Bob Hope or the made-in-Hollywood prefabricated pinups that the marines were used to seeing.

When she left the ship, Brigitte had made two thousand friends.

Before arriving at the boat dock of the Carlton Hotel, she slipped into her blue jeans. It took her over half an hour to make her way past the photographers to the hotel and another half hour to cross the lobby. Finally she managed to disappear into the elevator, but other photographers were waiting for her in the corridor of the third floor where her room was.

The Cannes Festival was at its peak. It was a time of madness and gaiety. Stars didn't know then that they had been sent to earth, like the Messiah, to guide humanity, and journalists didn't judge them by their social conscience or political commitments. Brigitte Bardot had already made two films, but since she wasn't yet a star she hadn't been invited by the management of the Festival. She was in Cannes to accompany her husband, a young reporter from *Paris-Match* named Roger Vadim.

Brigitte and I had only been married four months, and she didn't want to remain alone in Paris.

Despite Brigitte's aversion to official receptions and press conferences, and despite the fact that none of her films was being presented at the Festival, a strange phenomenon had occurred on the very evening we arrived at the Carlton. Photographers abandoned their usual prey—international stars of both sexes—to pursue Brigitte. It became a real epidemic. They followed her everywhere—in restaurants, at the beach, in shops and even in our room.

I remember one afternoon when I was one of the few journalists interviewing Lollobrigida, Kim Novak and Kirk Douglas in a conference hall of the Palais du Festival. All the other journalists were out chasing after my wife, from the shops on the rue d'Antibes to the palm trees of the Croisette.

The Bardot "phenomenon": the incredible fascination that a young girl of eighteen exercised over the French media, was nothing new. But it was at Cannes, that year, that it took on international proportions.

In the evening after Brigitte's visit to the *Enterprise*, we were dining with some friends in a small inn in La Napoule. We had managed to lose the journalists (strange for a journalist to have to hide from his colleagues) when a man came up to our table. He introduced himself as one of Onassis's private secretaries.

"How did you find me?" asked Brigitte.

"I never reveal my sources, mademoiselle. It's a matter of principle."

"Your boss has a good organization," remarked Brigitte.

"Yes, you could say that. He has asked me to invite you tomorrow evening to a reception he is giving on board the *Christina*. All the stars of the Festival will be there. Mr. Onassis asked me to tell you that the evening wouldn't be a success without your presence."

"He's absolutely right," said Brigitte. "But unfortunately I'm busy tomorrow. I'm dining with my husband."

And, as the secretary turned toward me to extend the invitation, she added, "In private."

Brigitte's beauty and unashamed sensuality are well known. She exemplified the eroticism and love of life of a bygone era. But little is known of the anguish, the fears and the talent for unhappiness that often took her to the edge of tragedy.

Lovers who walk and kiss under the silver light of the moon never think about the dark side, the side that never sees the sun. It's the same with Brigitte: only one side of her is known.

Who was really hiding behind the radiant image of the last of the sex symbols?

☆ 2 ☆

*T*HE number 92 bus was going down Avenue
Paul Doumer, headed for the Bois de Boulogne.
The weather had been gloomy during the first
weeks of October; then suddenly one morning it brightened.
The autumn sun finally showed itself and lavished its most
beautiful light on Paris. The air was mild, the trees all gold
and russet. Brigitte was standing on the open platform of the
bus, rummaging through the jumbled mess of leotards,
ballet shoes, notebooks and textbooks in her large canvas
bag, and murmuring, "*Merde, merde, merde....*" She had
just turned fifteen.

The bus conductor admired the delicate nape of her neck
and the full breasts under her half-open blouse. "Has the
young lady lost something?"

"My algebra book. It must have fallen out of my bag
when I was at Boris's place."

The conductor envied Boris, whoever he was. How could
he know that Boris Kniaseff, who had been ballet master at
the court of Czar Nicholas II, was now Brigitte's ballet
teacher. Three times a week after school she went to this
brilliant tyrant at the Studio Walker, Place Pigalle. *Enlevé!*

Attitude! Pirouette! Entrechat! Jeté battu! ... One, two, three. *Head up! Grand saut, déboulé.* ... Boris had no time for amateurs or sloggers. After Brigitte's audition, he had said, "Fine. But you will have to vorrrk." And this meant, quite simply, that he was certain she would become a prima ballerina.

Brigitte got off the bus at Place de la Muette and walked with her usual quick and airy gait to 1 bis rue de la Pompe. In the ancient hydraulic elevator, perched on its column like a mushroom, she thought about the best tactic to convince her parents to let her go to the movies with a girlfriend. At the fifth and last floor of the building, she got out of the elevator and gave the bell to her apartment three short rings. The maid opened the door.

A surprise was waiting for her in the living room. Her mother was talking with Hélène Lazareff, editor-in-chief of *Elle.* Hélène was looking for a new face to illustrate an article on the young modern Frenchwoman. She was a friend of Mrs. Bardot's, and she knew Brigitte. "She's the one, I tell you. She's the one," she repeated as the young girl entered the room. Mrs. Bardot, "Toti" to her friends, was wary of newspapers and publicity. To please Hélène Lazareff, she finally agreed. "As long as she doesn't miss any classes," she specified.

Brigitte, always agreeable to anything that disrupted the family routine, was delighted.

*I*N those days (autumn 1949), I was living with Danielle Delorme and Daniel Gélin, both of whom were film stars in France. I often looked after their three-year-old son, Zazi. Since I have always loved children, the role of baby-sitter suited me. One day, after having pretended we were barracudas in the bathtub, fired blanks from a revolver at passersby on the Avenue Wagram and made a Roman toga from an old bed sheet, Zazi and I ran out of ideas.

"Make me a plane," he said. I tore a page from the last issue of *Elle* and was folding it diagonally when a certain face caught my attention. Zazi was becoming impatient waiting for his plane. "What are you doing?"

"I'm looking at a photo."

"Who is it?"

"Her name is Brigitte," I said.

Zazi took the page from my hands. "I don't know who she is, but she's pretty." Zazi had good taste.

The next day I showed the magazine to Marc Allégret. He had decided to film my screenplay *Les Lauriers sont coupés*, and was immediately convinced that Brigitte was the perfect incarnation of the heroine of my story. He wrote to Mr. and Mrs. Bardot expressing his wish to meet their daughter with the intention of arranging a screen test for her.

It was five years after World War II, and the film industry was not yet open to young directors. Marcel Carné, René Clair, Henri-Georges Clouzot, René Clément, Jean Renoir, Julien Duvivier and Marc Allégret—who, on the average, were just under fifty—reigned supreme over the cinema in France. Marc was reputed to have discovered an impressive number of stars. He had a unique gift for detecting talent. We had met three years earlier.

One day, during the shooting of his film *Petrus,* in which I had a walk-on role, he had to leave the set suddenly because his daughter had been involved in a small accident at school. I was in the courtyard of the studio when I saw him get into his car and race off at top speed. I returned to the set where the distressed producer was biting his nails. Time was expensive that day. We were shooting a festival scene with three hundred extras. I went over to the poor man and told him that Marc Allégret had given me instructions for the next shot. Not for one minute did the producer imagine that a seventeen-year-old would have the nerve to direct a complicated sequence with tracking shots and long shots of wooden horses, ending with a close-up of Fernandel, the star. He believed me.

We rehearsed, and two hours later the scene was in the can. When Allégret returned, the producer thanked him warmly. ''I know what it is to be a father,'' he said. ''You could easily have gone off without leaving instructions.''

I was ready to disappear like a coward, but instead of losing his temper, Allégret played along. He observed me out of the corner of his eye, and at the end of the day's shooting he called me to his dressing room. This was the first time he had ever spoken to me. ''The shot was good,'' he said. ''What an amusing idea, moving the camera from the horse's head to Fernandel.'' (Fernandel had a rather horsey face.) ''I hadn't thought of that. Are you free for dinner?'' he added.

Marc Allégret became my mentor, my friend and accomplice in certain situations that might be characterized as rather piquant, and in a way, my third father. My real father, Igor Plemiannikov, a French consul, had died of a heart attack in 1937 at the age of thirty-four. My stepfather, Gerald Hanning, an urban planner and collaborator of Le Corbusier's, was a remarkable man. He was ten years younger than my mother, and I admired and loved him as one might an older brother. Unfortunately, he and my mother had just separated. Although I was very independent, having fended for myself since the age of fifteen, I realized when I met Marc that I missed having a father.

I began my apprenticeship as an assistant director in London on *Blanche Fury*, a film starring Valerie Hobson and Stewart Granger that Allégret was making for Sir Alexander Korda. The British unions were very protectionist, so I, a foreigner, could not be paid a salary. I didn't care. I was living in a suite reserved for the director in the Dorchester Hotel and making love to the charming young actresses I met at the studio. I was studying both the English language and the English themselves.

A year later (still in London), I worked with Marc on the screenplay for a detective film, *Blackmail*. I had to rewrite scenes in the Hammersmith studio every night or morning.

There was still a supporting role that had not been cast. Marc took me to a private club (everything was private in London) to see the act of a young woman who opened the show dressed in a silver-sequined swimsuit, decorated with three ostrich feathers attached to the base of her spine. She was ravishing and she delivered her introduction with charm and humor. "She would be perfect for Polly," Marc said to me. For two weeks he fought to cast her in the role.

The producer, whose name I will not mention out of Christian charity, wouldn't hear of it. "She's already done three screen tests," he said. "Nobody wants her. She has an impossible nose. There's no hope of a career for that girl."

"That girl" was Audrey Hepburn. The mistress of one of the film's backers got the part.

*O*N my return to France, I finished *Les Lauriers sont coupés*. Not one of the leading characters in the story was an adult. At the time, the average age of the film-going public was between twenty-five and fifty, and films about teenagers were not yet in vogue. But since Allégret had agreed to direct my screenplay, a producer friend of his, Pierre Braunberger, paid 80,000 francs ($200 U.S. dollars) for the rights to the story. It was neither fame nor fortune, but *Cinémonde*, a film magazine, devoted a brief article to me entitled "Roger Vadim, the Youngest Screenwriter in Europe."

On the train from London to Paris, Marc and I had met the Ballet de Paris' youngest and most talented star. Her name was Leslie Caron. Marc had her do a screen test for the part of Sophie, and I played opposite her. But the producer wanted no part of it. Nevertheless, thanks to this screen test, Leslie was featured on the cover of *Paris-Match*, and soon afterward Gene Kelly signed her for the lead role in *An American in Paris*.

What Leslie and I felt for each other was more than mere

affection. We spent three weeks together on a skiing holiday in the French Alps. We were walking the tightrope of love, and neither of us dared to take the first step. I was shy, and she was having difficulty recovering from a tumultuous affair with one of her co-stars at the Ballet de Paris. Chiefly to save money, we shared the same room at the Hotel du Mont Blanc, in Megève. Leslie slept on a mattress on the floor. Feeling guilty about spending nights without making love in a room with the man whom she had encouraged, she punished herself by letting me sleep in the comfort of the bed. She slept with black velvet pads over her eyes like an old woman or a prewar Hollywood star.

A FTER a few months in Hollywood, where she was preparing to film *An American in Paris,* Leslie was very lonely and wrote me a long letter that ended with "Why don't you come? You would be able to write in peace. I am sure that you could sell your ideas for screenplays here. It makes me very sad to know that you are so far away. The more I think of it, the sadder I become. . . ."

I would undoubtedly have accepted her invitation if it had not been for an important event that had occurred in my life; about a month before receiving Leslie's letter, I had met Brigitte Bardot. I knew now that the fondness, the friendship and physical attraction that I felt for Leslie (we had never done anything more than kiss) was not love.

T HE chances that the Bardot family would respond to Marc's letter were slim, considering the type of future they envisioned for their daughter: a sensible marriage to a banker, industrialist or, *faute de mieux,* a government official. But since she did not take this audition seriously and was interested in meeting a famous film director, Mrs. Bardot gave in to Brigitte's insistence. She told herself that nothing would come of the meeting, and that by allowing it she would avoid Brigitte's reproaches and bad moods. The meeting took place at Marc Allégret's home, 11 bis rue Lord Byron, in the late afternoon, after school.

Brigitte never expected in the least to be actually cast in a film. Besides, acting didn't interest her. She intended to pursue a career as a classical ballet dancer. On the other hand, she was always open to meeting people who would provide a welcome change from her mother's and father's friends and from schoolmates who met with her parents' approval. Like her mother, she was interested in meeting a celebrity whom she imagined reigning over a court of stars and celebrities.

Neither Mrs. Bardot nor her daughter dreamed that this meeting would change the course of their lives.

☆ 3 ☆

WHEN I met Brigitte for the first time I was immediately struck by her posture, her bearing and her curved waist. She held her head like a queen. I was also impressed by her way of seeing things. Many people look but do not know how to see.

Her mother had light chestnut hair cut rather short, beautiful almond-shaped eyes, a rather long, fine nose, a delicately shaped mouth rendered unjustly severe by a constantly repressed smile and just a hint of worldliness. All this gave her smooth face a youthfulness rarely found in a Parisian of her class who was only two years short of forty. She did not resemble her daughter at all. Her nature had been stifled by her upbringing and the marks of her class; her daughter, on the contrary, was all spontaneity, like a running brook.

In Marc Allégret's sun-filled seventh-floor apartment, I listened to Mrs. Bardot explain to the director that, although she had given in to her daughter's whims and to her own desire to meet a man of such great talent, she did not see a film career in store for Brigitte. As she chatted away, she became aware that Marc was the exact opposite of the image that she and her friends had of people in the world of entertainment. Marc's good manners and elegant diction made one think more of a diplomat than of an inspired director possessed by his art who shouted commands on a film set. His culture, which he never flaunted, was deeper than Mrs. Bardot's veneer. ("Culture is like jam, the less one has the more one spreads it," said President Poincaré.)

Charmed by Marc, Mrs. Bardot allowed herself to be won over. "Brigitte is at an age when one loves new experiences," he said. "A test doesn't commit her to anything."

While this conversation was going on, Brigitte kept eying the young man whom Marc had introduced wryly as his collaborator. "Roger Vadim . . . he wrote the screenplay. He's lazy, always late and much too talented for his age." Brigitte burst out with a spontaneous and infectious giggle that immediately captivated me. Later she confessed that she too had been seized with a "serious attack of love at first sight."

It was decided that I would help Brigitte rehearse her lines after class on the days when she didn't go to the Studio Walker.

*O*N the way home Mrs. Bardot regretted having said yes to Marc Allégret. But she was a woman of her word; she would never go back on a promise. All she had to do was convince her husband.

Fifteen years older than his wife, Mr. Bardot ("Pilou" to his friends) was an eccentric but with all the traits of the traditional French middle class. He had a large forehead, salt-and-pepper hair—more salt than pepper—thin, fleshless lips, a determined, pointed chin and an intense look in his eyes that sometimes became a stare and was rendered even more intense by thick-lensed glasses. He could have been taken for the head of a psychiatric hospital, a retired colonel or the inventor of the gas mask. In reality, he was the president and managing director of a factory that produced liquid air.

Always precise, even in the midst of disorder, he was the type of man who would plan a car trip to the minute, replete with stops for refreshments and the average speed to be maintained down to the exact kilometer per hour. If along the way he fell in love with the sight of a cow grazing in a field, he would take photos of it for an hour; then, in order to keep to his timetable, he would drive like a maniac, risking the lives of his family at each bend, although the only appointment he had to keep was the arrival time he had written down in his logbook. Mr. Bardot loved puns and jokes; he always carried a notebook in which he wrote down funny stories. He would interrupt a conversation to open his notebook, read a joke, make a mess of the punchline and then laugh so hard that he would fail to notice that his audience was embarrassed. He was convinced that he made all the decisions in the household, but it was actually Toti who ran things.

His first reaction to the news that his daughter was going to have a screen test was: "I won't have any gypsies in my family." He added, "She'll have to climb over my dead body before she sets foot in a studio."

"Papa, you seem to be the one who's theatrical at the moment," Brigitte said. Toti added that she had already agreed.

"You agreed?" Pilou asked.

"Yes."

Mr. Bardot was faced with a classical dilemma: Should his wife break her word or should their daughter dishonor her family? He chose the second alternative, telling himself that after all a screen test was not a commitment. So he lifted his veto.

BRIGITTE arrived in the Gélins' apartment at 44 Avenue de Wagram one Monday in late afternoon. She put her schoolbooks on one of the chairs in the hallway and followed me into the living room.

"You remind me of Sophie," I said to her.

Sophie was the name of the heroine of a novel that I had written when I was still an adolescent. She resembled Brigitte like a sister. She was vulnerable and dynamic, romantic, terribly sentimental and very modern in her ideas about sex and her aversion to the rules of middle-class morality. She talked like Brigitte. Her conversation full of imagery was impertinent and spiced with crude words, but never vulgar. Later, when Brigitte read my novel, Sophie became her code name. For years, she signed all her love letters "Sophie."

She sank into one of the armchairs in the living room and we began working on the scene that I had asked her to learn. I owed my theatrical training to Charles Dullin, whose student I had been between the ages of fifteen and eighteen. I didn't have my illustrious teacher's experience, but I understood immediately that Brigitte was inimitable and that her faults might sometimes be qualities. She needed a gardener more than a professor. She was the type of flower that one waters but does not cut. It would have been an act of vandalism to train her whimsical voice. She was totally uninterested in discussing a character's psychology or motivation. She understood instinctively or not at all. When she digested the character and made it real through her own emotions, the miracle occurred.

Brigitte had a very peculiar memory. She could remember an entire scene just a few minutes before having to play it, but she would forget completely a text learned the day before if, meanwhile, she happened to be preoccupied or upset by something. When we said goodbye after our first week's session, she knew her lines by heart. Two days later, she couldn't remember a word. "My father's breaking all the dinner plates," was her excuse. Whenever she mentioned me at the dinner table, Pilou would pick up his silver knife and start banging on his fragile porcelain plate, usually until it broke. "Mother thinks that you're costing us a lot," she told me.

Bergson wrote that laughter is man's special gift. I've always thought that it was one of Brigitte's special qualities.

One day she was sitting on the floor dressed in a skirt and cardigan, with her back against the wall, clasping her knees. I made an effort to look only at her eyes, but she knew that I was aroused and that I wanted her. She said, "How about saying *tu* to each other?" English does not permit delicate nuances by the use of different forms for "you," but in French this familiar form of "you" is reserved for family, friends and lovers. I took her request for what it was, a veiled declaration of love. But I didn't take advantage of the situation. We met in order to work, and I was careful not to let our rehearsals degenerate into flirting sessions. I have always detested the idea of using the advantages of my profession for personal reasons. I was neither a celebrity nor a director at the time, but the fact that I was a screenwriter and Marc Allégret's assistant could not fail to make an impression on a young girl of fifteen. In all my career, I have never started an affair on the set of a film. I have made it a strict rule not to sleep with one of my actresses during the shooting of a film—unless, of course, I was already living with the actress, as was often the case.

In spite of everything, the sessions with Brigitte on the Avenue de Wagram, filled as they were with laughter and suppressed feelings, were not without charm.

*T*HE day of the screen test arrived.

Brigitte showed great ability. She had no acting experience but she gave the impression that she had been in front of a camera all her life. I was proud of my student and Marc was thrilled.

It was dark when I took her home by taxi. She held my hand. We had no idea what the producer's verdict would be. Would this trip through the streets of Paris be our last moment together? Before getting out of the taxi, she gave me a quick kiss (the first) on the mouth.

The producer was not convinced that Brigitte was right for the part. He didn't like her teeth; he thought she opened her mouth too much when she laughed. Like Leslie Caron, Brigitte Bardot was rejected, and the filming of *Les Lauriers sont coupés* was postponed indefinitely. I did not see Brigitte again for several weeks.

I hadn't forgotten her, but our lifestyles were so different that I didn't see how they could be compatible. I lived like a bird on the wing, sleeping here and there according to my mood or encounters during the day. Although 44 Avenue de Wagram was a haven for me, it was not really my home. I hung out a great deal in Saint-Germain-des-Prés, which was a sort of village in the midst of the big city. My friends were anonymous young people, some of whom would become famous, and already famous people such as Jean Cocteau, Jacques Prévert, Boris Vian, Jean Genet, and assorted stage and screen stars. I also knew Colette, Edith Piaf, Maurice Chevalier, Jean-Paul Sartre, Albert Camus, André Gide, Salvador Dali and some great jazz musicians.

Evenings in Saint-Germain were much talked about. The fashionable set flocked there for amusement or debauchery. It didn't matter whether or not one was broke. If one of us had a dime, we paid for our friends. The bistros and discotheques gave us credit—and for good reason. It was people like me and Christian Marquand, the avant-garde director Michel de Ré, Juliette Greco and the singer Annabel—now married to Bernard Buffet and mother of a family—who created a new style and launched the idea of basement clubs. It was I who coined the term "discotheque." One journalist dubbed us "existentialists." The beatniks and hippies would come later. We were often on the front page of tabloids like *Samedi Soir* and *France Dimanche*.

The eagerness of the media and local merchants to turn to

their advantage a spontaneous movement, which was more a lifestyle of peaceful anarchy than a political or intellectual attitude based on Jean-Paul Sartre's philosophy, didn't bother us at all. However, it was not long before the real postwar Saint-Germain was killed by this verbal pollution and turned into the amusement park that it is today. But at the time I met Brigitte, I was living an easy existence in Saint-Germain, a life of one adventure after another that enabled me to rub shoulders with some of the most cultured and interesting people of the day.

Sometimes I took a role as an extra, occasionally I sold a screenplay or worked as Marc Allégret's assistant for the duration of a film; but I refused to take a full-time job—I learned more by doing nothing. I felt that this period of great freedom following four dark years of Nazi occupation was an accident of history that would not last long, and I decided to make the most of it.

Under those conditions it was impossible for me to consider a relationship with a strictly brought up girl who was allowed to stay out until midnight only once a month. But the heart has its own logic, which the mind does not understand. I could not forget Brigitte, and I kept remembering the soft sensation of her lips touching mine.

One Saturday afternoon, coming out of a movie, I noticed that I had only a few francs left in my pocket. I had a choice between buying a subway token or using the money for a phone call. I decided to call Brigitte. Why I called that day rather than another, I'll never know. It wasn't a sudden inspiration but a necessity. It was a command from my subconscious which I could not disobey.

I am rather forgetful by nature. I have forgotten to turn up at appointments crucial to my career, forgotten what day it was, and even been known to turn up at the wrong studio for a film I was directing. But I have a mind like a computer for telephone numbers—luckily, because I always lose my address books. I remembered Brigitte's number although I had called her only once, one month earlier.

Contrary to my expectation, it was Brigitte who picked up the phone. She had found an excuse to avoid spending the weekend at Louvecienne with her parents. I knew by the tone of her voice that she was immensely pleased to hear from me. "Come over immediately," she said. "I'm with a friend and my grandmother. She's on guard duty here until Monday." Congratulating myself for having spent the money for my subway token wisely, I walked from the Boulevard des Italiens to the rue de la Pompe, a distance of about three kilometers.

Brigitte knew my weakness for chocolate with milk and had prepared a cup of hot, creamy Ovaltine for me. We sat in the Louis XVI-style living room and discussed boring subjects with her friend. I was only some five years older then they, but I felt myself a total stranger to their concerns. A whole world separated me from these adolescents who had never really known the war and who lived a well-ordered existence, relying on their parents for everything.

When her friend left, we were able to talk about more personal things, but Granny, who took her role as chaperone very seriously, appeared in the living room every three minutes, making any intimacy impossible. At 7:30, Granny made clear that it was time for me to leave. I caught her making a discreet sign to Brigitte, who disappeared with her for a moment into an adjoining room. As she said goodbye to me on the landing, Brigitte was biting her lips to hold back her laughter. "Granny asked me to take a look at your pockets to make sure you didn't steal the little silver spoons."

I took her in my arms and we kissed. It was a long, passionate kiss, interrupted only too soon by her grandmother's footsteps nearing down the hall.

Grandmother Bardot's opinion of me illustrated perfectly the still very reactionary attitude of the French bourgeoisie during the fifties. Just as royalty in the past delighted in court jesters, fashionable society hostesses prided themselves on entertaining famous singers and actors. They found them charming, sometimes dazzling, but always suspect—especially film people. Things have changed now, but not as much as one might expect. For example, in France, it is still unthinkable for an ex-actor to become prime minister or to be elected president of the Republic.

Given such an atmosphere, one can imagine how Grandmother Bardot panicked when this strangely dressed young man, who was in films and had almost dragged poor Brigitte into his bohemian world, turned up in her house.

Mr. and Mrs. Bardot were more broad-minded. They had a few friends who were in journalism, fashion and the theater. They liked the arts. They were not frightened by my plaid shirts, unpressed trousers and longish hair. They thought that my manners indicated a good upbringing. They were also favorably impressed by the fact that my father had been a French consul and had fought against the Bolsheviks at the age of fourteen. Pressed by Mr. Bardot's questions about my family's origins, I resigned myself to relating its history.

In fact, my real name was Roger Vadim Plemiannikov. Vadim was the name my parents chose for me and Roger was added because French law required one to have an officially approved name, and unfortunately, my godfather's name was Roger. Plemiannikov, my father's family name, means nephew in Russian. At this point in my story, I invited the Bardots to journey with me back in time to the thirteenth century, when the great Genghis Khan was raging. On his deathbed, Genghis Khan divided his empire, which extended from China to the frontiers of Europe, between his sons. One of them received a region comprising part of Poland and the Ukraine. At the end of his reign, it was not his eldest son but his nephew who inherited the crown. From that time on, the name Plemiannikov (the nephew) remained attached to this family, even after it had ceased to rule.

When my father was chased out of Russia by the 1917 revolution and arrived in France, he became a naturalized

French citizen. Like all the children of Russian aristocrats, he already spoke French fluently. After graduating in political science, he took the civil service examination and passed with flying colors. Named consul at the age of twenty-eight, he married a French woman, Marie-Antoinette Ardilouze. His first post was the consulate in Alexandria, Egypt.

I never imagined that I would owe my acceptance in a twentieth-century French middle-class salon to my distant ancestor who had razed cities and slaughtered his enemies. At the beginning I made a few faux pas in this milieu. Among other things, I had the habit of using a knife rather than a small spoon to cut off the top of my boiled eggs. That shocked Toti. I seemed to have a problem with small spoons in the Bardot household. In spite of the concern they felt as they observed Brigitte's growing attachment to me, Toti and Pilou liked me. With a certain resignation they accepted me as an honorary member of the family; but this did not happen overnight, of course.

At first I visited rue de la Pompe once a week. After a month I was allowed to take Brigitte to an eight o'clock film. Meanwhile we had perfected a system of secret meetings. Our headquarters was a small furnished studio on the second floor of 15 rue de Bassano (three hundred meters from the Champs-Élysées), which had been lent to my best friend, Christian Marquand, by his father. Mr. Marquand published a directory for businessmen, and Christian had to pay him rent for the studio by putting stamps on thousands of envelopes. Sometimes I helped him with this dreadful task, which occupied us for a few hours each month.

The only furniture in the room was a large divan, a chair and a small table. To chat we either stretched out on the divan or sat on the floor. The shade of our bedside lamp had been decorated in pen and colored crayon by Jean Genet. Christian allowed me to use the studio whenever I needed it.

It was three o'clock when Brigitte arrived for our first secret rendezvous.

"I should be in algebra class, but I have chosen freedom," she said.

She snuggled up to me and offered me her lips. We kissed and made for the divan. Brigitte had warned me that she was a virgin. The pill didn't exist yet, and in order not to frighten her I didn't tell her that I had never made love to a virgin before. I had a few ideas as to how to go about it, but as everyone knows it is a big step from theory to practice.

We had never gone beyond flirting. It was also the first time that I undressed her. What bowled me over when I saw her naked was the extraordinary mixture of innocence and femininity, of immodesty and timidity.

She knew absolutely nothing about lovemaking, yet she seemed to be a fully developed woman. She took me in her arms, and very gently I began making love to her.

The moments that we were able to steal passed quickly. It was already time to part.

While getting dressed Brigitte asked, "Am I a real woman now?"

"Not quite," I said. "Only twenty-five percent."

She looked at me with a Mona Lisa half-smile, dreaming of the 75 percent that was in store. I helped her forge her mother's signature on a note excusing her from the algebra class. Then I took her to the bus stop.

When I returned to rue de Bassano, I was cornered by Mlle. Marie, the concierge. Fifty years old and weighing two hundred pounds, she was the terror of the building. During the Nazi occupation she had been on the best of terms with the German authorities—at the cost of the lives of Jews and Resistance workers whom she denounced. On the liberation of France, she got on the right side of General de Gaulle's provisional government by denouncing collaborators.

"Who is that girl?" she asked in her heavy Parisian accent. She had seen Brigitte leaving.

"A friend," I said. "A very nice girl."

"This is a respectable building," Mlle. Marie muttered. "You're not going to turn it into a brothel."

I had a thousand-franc note in my pocket and I slipped it into her hand. Money always had a calming effect on her. If I wished to continue seeing Brigitte, I had no other choice than to pay off this watchdog. Satisfied, she went back to her lair—or rather, her cubbyhole.

On her second visit to the rue de Bassano, it was Brigitte who undressed me. She had learned the rules of the game quickly and was already applying them in her own way.

After making love to her, I rested my head on her chest. She asked me again, "Am I a real woman now?"

"About fifty-five percent," I told her.

On her third visit, I announced, "One hundred percent."

Brigitte clapped her hands, ran to the window and opened it as wide as she could. "I'm a real woman," she yelled to passersby in the street below, who stared up at her in shock.

In her enthusiasm, she had forgotten one detail: She was completely naked.

☆ *4* ☆

*N*OTHING fosters passion more than secrecy. Mr. and Mrs. Bardot's intransigent behavior transformed their daughter's first love affair into an epic drama. Brigitte was Juliet and I was Romeo.

For us to be able to steal away together for just two hours demanded all the ingenuity of a secret agent. We had our accomplices: Marc Allégret, my mother, Christian Marquand.

There were also enemy spies for whom we had to be on the lookout: her younger sister, friends of the Bardots and anyone who, intentionally or without meaning to, might mention having seen us here or there. In this atmosphere, making love was not only a pleasure but an adventure.

Brigitte did not consider sex synonymous with sin. She had no psychological traumas about making love, no mystical or religious anxieties and none of the Judeo-Christian mishmash attached to the notion of pleasure. She was Eve before God lost his temper in the Garden. She was an Eve particularly talented at making love, who seemed to know everything about it without ever having had to learn. She never thought of nudity as a secret weapon that enabled women to seduce men. Nudity was nothing more or less than a smile or the color of a flower. In this sense she was more painter than model—or rather, both painter and model.

Nevertheless, there were contradictions in her nature. This woman, so free of problems concerning sex or her own body, was, above all, a romantic. Feelings, atmosphere and decor were as important to her as sexual pleasure. She needed words for reassurance and soft lighting or candles to make her orgasm poetic.

Although she had a gift for infidelity, she always suffered if she had an affair with more than one man at a time. She never resolved the conflict between fidelity and the desire to follow the promptings of her body and her heart. More than once she nearly died from the conflict.

It was the same on the social level. There were two Brigittes. One was attached to bourgeois values—thrift, fear of adventure, preference for modest-size dwellings, a definite taste for ornate furniture and knickknacks. The other was modern, ahead of her time, independent to the point of scandalizing France and five continents. She was not equipped to deal with her own genius.

At the age of fifteen she could not have been aware of the impact she was to make on her contemporaries through film and other media. If she had been forewarned by some oracle or magic mirror, she would have been horrified and would not have become an actress.

If you get away with something for too long, you can become too confident. That's exactly what happened to Brigitte and me. We took more and more risks. Caresses sneaked in a corridor, an elevator or the back seat of Pilou's car when he was driving were nothing—mere provocations at the beginning of the bull-fight. More risky were certain nights. During the school holidays, when I could afford it I rented a room in a hotel that Brigitte's parents were staying in. At night Brigitte would tiptoe barefoot to my bedroom.

The winter of 1950–51, in Megève, a winter resort, was almost disastrous for us. The scene of the crime was Le Megevan, a pleasant hotel built completely out of wood.

The floors creaked terribly, and unfortunately my bedroom was just above Mr. and Mrs. Bardot's, a geographical detail I was completely unaware of.

Awakened by creaking floorboards overhead, Pilou thought he recognized his daughter's laughter and raced up to my room. Alerted in time by the sound of his footsteps, we had a split second to jump out of the window into the cool snow two floors below. Ten minutes completely nude in snow up to your neck is an interesting experience, but not one that I would recommend. Only youth and the heat of our emotions prevented us from getting pneumonia.

Brigitte and I continued to be rash. One day, when I arrived at the rue de la Pompe for my official biweekly visit, Brigitte announced, "My parents have gone. Mijanou is at Granny's." A mischievous fairy gave us the idea of remaining in the living room instead of playing it safe in Brigitte's bedroom. I made love to her on a Louis XVI chair. We moved from chair to sofa, strewing our clothes around the room. The French poet Lamartine, once cried, "O Time, arrest your flight." We had arrested it a little too long that day. When the front door opened we had just enough time to pick up our clothes and hide behind the curtains of the French windows that opened onto a balcony.

Mr. Bardot walked into the living room, accompanied by an important banker, his wife and their son, who had once made a vague attempt to woo Brigitte. Mrs. Bardot went to the kitchen to give orders for dinner.

Getting dressed behind a curtain without being noticed is not easy.

The banker's son began talking about Brigitte's innocence and good upbringing, rare qualities in today's young girls. The two fathers changed the topic to a less frivolous subject: the dangers of communism in France. The banker's wife asked whether the furniture was authentic Louis XVI or good copies. "Where is this darling little Brigitte?" she asked suddenly.

"No doubt in her room. I'll go and get her," Mr. Bardot replied.

Brigitte, now dressed, displayed great self-control. With the assurance of an actress coming on stage, she threw back the curtains and walked to the center of the room.

"Hello," she said.

Once the shock had worn off, Pilou asked, "What were you doing behind the curtains?"

"I was hiding. I didn't want you to see me with my hair in a mess. You would have scolded me."

The banker's son was much amused, and Mr. Bardot pretended to be delighted by this surprising aspect of his daughter's character. Brigitte ushered them into her bedroom to show off her collection of stuffed animals, while I managed to leave the apartment without being seen.

Mr. and Mrs. Bardot owned a little house in Saint-Tropez at the end of a narrow street of walls covered with Virginia creeper. This lovely port in the south of France, noted for its charm, fine sand beaches and the house of Colette and the painter Dunoyer de Segonzac, had not yet been invaded by tourists and vacationers. (Cannes, Antibes, Juan-les-Pins, Monaco and the Promenade des Anglais at Nice were the fashionable places.) I had discovered this pocket-size paradise when I was still a young boy on a bicycle escapade during the war. I went back every year.

During the summer of 1950, Brigitte and I met under parasol pine trees near a tiny deserted creek. She was suspicious of the cicada that stopped singing when we made love. These large-winged insects simply might have been respectful to the music of lovemaking, but Brigitte claimed that they were actually paid by her father to spy on us.

We caught two cicadas and baptized them Spy Number One and Spy Number Two. I promised I would never part with Spy Number Two, whom Brigitte interrogated every time we met. She put on a great show of jealousy, pretending that Spy Number Two had caught me in the arms of a Swedish girl or the dentist's daughter.

I must admit that Brigitte's jealousy was quite justified. I didn't lead an exactly monastic life in Paris. I traveled a great deal, sometimes in order to be on the set when Allégret was shooting a film, but often just because I felt like it. I honestly loved Brigitte, but I didn't intend to give up my freedom. She was her parents' prisoner and could do nothing but wait.

She took to lovemaking with extraordinary intensity. Sometimes she held up a mirror so she could see me making love to her, as though touching wasn't enough. Before I went off on trips, she asked me to take photos of her, dressed and naked. She wanted me to carry her with me—her face, her body, her sex. She was completely physical, and, at the same time, the most emotional woman I have ever met.

Brigitte wrote to me every day. Her letters were a mixture of childishness, passionate declarations of love, erotic fantasies, romantic dreams about our future and rebellion against her parents who didn't understand her. The same question cropped up each time: "You will always love me, won't you?"

I did not yet realize that women, obsessed with eternal love, are most susceptible to new relationships. "You will always love me?" really means: "Please don't allow me to fall in love with someone else." Most men consider these words proof that they are the one and only. In reality, it's exactly the opposite. Romantic women seek the absolute. They don't find it in *any* man. They talk about forever, but they run from present to present.

Brigitte wanted a sacred bond. She wanted life to be inscribed in a heavenly circle. She would be the sun, radiating life and warmth, with satellites circling in accordance with the dictates of her heart.

Our main problem occurred every month. It's hard to imagine today the absolute terror that young girls felt when they had no form of legal contraception. In some families a girl who got pregnant was cursed, dishonored and often thrown into the streets. People thought it more acceptable to choose an unhappy and doomed marriage. Pregnancy was always a nightmare. Unmarried mothers got almost no government assistance. Things were not much better for women then than in the time of Christ when the adulteress was stoned.

Every thirty days Brigitte's existence hung by a thread. She had a code name for her period: the Russians. Each month I waited for the sense of relief I would feel when she'd say, "The Russians have come."

A year after meeting Brigitte, I was living with Christian Marquand in the Ile Saint-Louis, Quai d'Orléans, in one of the most beautiful apartments in Paris. From my eighth-floor window I could see the flying buttresses of Notre-Dame, the dome of the Panthéon, the Seine and the rooftops of the houses of Sainte-Geneviève.

Evelyne Vidal, the owner, who had recently separated from her husband, rented us two rooms overlooking the rooftops. Evelyne was a ravishingly beautiful woman with short dark hair who had a sense of humor and of fun. Her marriage had made her rich and her divorce had made her happy. Everyone thought that she took us in because we were lovers. It was flattering but not true. Christian and I won her over after an evening of listening to Dave Brubeck, Thelonious Monk and the MJQ. We ended up painting the leaves of her ugly rubber plant in the hallway pink and violet. In the morning, Christian had said to her, "Damn it, Evelyne, we completely forgot to make love to you."

She needed friends, so we stayed on. The rent was only seventy-five dollars a month, but we never paid it.

Brigitte often came to see me at the Quai d'Orléans. One day we were standing at the window looking out at the Seine flowing by when she said, "You know, the Russians haven't arrived. I'm a day late."

She had a headache and an upset stomach, and she was

convinced she was pregnant. I reassured her. She had all the symptoms of a flu going around Paris. Christian and Evelyne had caught it the week before and gotten over it very quickly, thanks to massive shots of vitamin C I had given them. (I had learned to give injections during the war, when I had lived in an isolated house in the French Alps with no doctor anywhere near.) Brigitte agreed to a shot. She waited in the living room while I went to prepare some hot lemonade. Shortly after, Evelyne burst into the kitchen, screaming that Brigitte had turned green and that she was dying.

We ran to the living room where Brigitte was lying flat on the divan. Her left cheek, part of her mouth and the fingers on her right hand were indeed greenish.

"I can't breathe," she said. "I'm going to die. I'm already turning green. Look at me." She took my hand and clutched it against her chest. "I don't want to die, Vadim."

I had always thought that people turned green *after* they died. But I kept this notion to myself. I said, "It's nothing, darling. It must be an insect bite." I was, of course, terrified. Evelyne had already called Dr. Lefranc, whose office was on the second floor of our building.

Brigitte kept my hand on her chest. "Don't tell my parents that I'm dead. They wouldn't be able to take it." I couldn't see myself carrying Brigitte in my arms to the rue de la Pompe and telling her parents, "She's not breathing. Her heart's not beating. She's green. But it's not serious. She's not dead."

Dr. Lefranc walked in and knelt by Brigitte. He stroked her forehead, lifted up an eyelid, took her pulse and stood up. He looked at his fingers, held them to his lips and said, "It's paint."

Now that she knew she was not going to die, Brigitte suddenly remembered that she had gone to the lavatory after leaving me. The bathroom had been repainted that morning, and the green on her face and hands came from the walls and the door that she had touched without noticing.

* * *

*O*N the international level, the Russian alerts were much less colorful. The Cold War was at its height, the American army was in Korea, and the expeditionary French forces had met their first defeat at Lang Son in Indochina. There was social unrest throughout France, and demonstrations against the war in Indochina. The happy post-World War II interlude had come to an end. I was aware of both the domestic and foreign events that were taking the world into an era of uncertainty and danger, but this didn't prevent me from enjoying life and feeling optimistic. After all, I was only twenty. Despite Brigitte's monthly alerts and the fear of being caught in the act by her parents, I was happy.

Brigitte had stopped going to school and was now taking courses privately so that she could devote more time to her dance lessons. Sometimes I went along to her ballet class at the Studio Walker, and I was amazed by her graceful, sylphlike performance. She gave herself, body and soul, to her art. I have never seen her so perfectly in harmony with herself on a stage or in front of the camera. If she hadn't decided to give up dancing (for reasons I shall go into later), she would certainly have become one of the greatest ballerinas of her time.

After her unsuccessful audition for *Les Lauriers sont coupés,* she never imagined she would have a career as a film actress. She had only one vocation: dancing.

Nothing in Brigitte's milieu or heredity destined her for an artistic career. Nothing in her education encouraged her independent, nonconformist nature, her need to assert herself without regard for a morality that she felt was outmoded. She always said of her parents, "They're still living in the age of dinosaurs."

One childhood memory made a deep impression on her. She was nine years old and Mijanou was seven. One Sunday the two sisters were alone in the apartment. To amuse themselves they decided to use the net curtains from their bedroom to make nightgowns. When their parents came home, they flew into a rage. One can imagine and understand their anger, but the punishment they meted out was disproportionate to the mischievousness of two little girls who had been left to their own devices for a day.

"We can't trust you any longer," announced Mr. and Mrs. Bardot. "From now on you will no longer have the right to say *tu* when you address us. You will use *vous*."

"You know," Brigitte told me, "that day I really felt that I'd lost my parents and was living with strangers."

I am sure that Toti and Pilou didn't realize the traumatic effect their punishment would have on Brigitte. I suspect that because they admired it as elegant, they wanted to copy the tradition in certain aristocratic and upper-middle-class families which dictated that children use *vous* when addressing their parents. The curtains were only a pretext. It's one thing for parents to use *vous* with their children when they're beginning to talk; it's a completely different matter when you spring it on a child who's already nine years old.

Also, Brigitte had to go to Mass every Sunday, without question. Because church was forced on her, she began to develop virulently anticlerical feelings when she was very young. At the age of twelve, when she went to confession, she would admit to the most awful sins simply because she wanted to shock the priest, who was a friend of the Bardots. Since he had to observe the secrecy of confession, he could not breathe a word of it to her parents.

WE had known each other for over a year. Mr. Bardot was not always suspicious of my relationship with Brigitte, but he was becoming more and more nervous. When we were given permission to go to the cinema, Mijanou was sent along to chaperone us. One day

Mijanou told her parents that I had kissed her sister in the subway. Pilou summoned me to his study. He sat there deathly pale, his lips pursed. "I am waiting," he said.

"I'm sorry, but I don't understand," I said, to gain time.

"You kissed my daughter in the subway. I am waiting for an explanation."

I noticed that the date on his calendar was June 21, so I said, "It was to celebrate the beginning of summer."

He thought for a moment. "One celebrates with a kiss on the thirty-first of December at midnight. Not the first day of summer."

"I wanted to start a new fashion," I said.

He could not help smiling. But for two weeks Brigitte and I were not allowed to go to the movies together.

Brigitte was finding it more and more difficult to stand the constraints that her parents imposed on her. She became nervous, anxious and terribly frustrated. She saw no end to her suffering. She lost hope and cried a lot. I couldn't reason with her.

One evening I took her back to the rue de la Pompe three hours late. Mr. Bardot was watching for us from the balcony. Waiting had made him almost hysterical. While I was saying goodbye to Brigitte in front of the building, Pilou began throwing coins at us from the fifth floor.

"Ow!" Brigitte screamed. Two coins had hit her on the back of the head. "That'll pay for the subway tomorrow," she added.

When she left she didn't dare kiss me because her father was still watching.

He opened the door of the apartment and created a terrible scene. "I can't trust you any more," he said. "You will *never* see Vadim again."

The next day, unaware of Mr. Bardot's ban, I rang the doorbell. Brigitte opened the door, put a finger to her lips and told me that I couldn't come in.

I wanted to leave Paris for a while. In a whisper, I explained that I was finding it difficult to work on Quai

D'Orléans, where an endless stream of friends was coming and going all day long. I would be able to finish the screenplay promised to Marc Allégret at my mother's house in Nice, away from the temptations of Paris. In three weeks, I would be back.

Brigitte looked at me, her eyes brimming with sadness. She gave me a long kiss on the mouth and then, leaning over the banister of the staircase, watched the elevator slowly descend five floors. If she had told me then about the scene with her father the night before, I would not have left. But in blowing me a final kiss, she had simply cried out, "Don't ever forget poor Sophie!"

At the very hour of my departure on the train for Nice, Mijanou, Toti and Pilou were preparing to go out to see the monuments of Paris. For the first time in eleven years, projectors would bathe the jewels of the capital—the Arc de Triomphe, the Obelisk of the Place de la Concorde, the Opéra, Notre-Dame and the Panthéon—in light until midnight. This "premiere" symbolically marked the end of the postwar period. Paris was once again the City of Light.

"Hurry," Mijanou cried out to her sister. "You haven't even done your hair."

"I'm not going," Brigitte said. "I don't feel very well."

When her parents had left, Brigitte went back to her room.

Seated on her narrow bed, she caressed the furry head of the old teddy bear that she had had since she was five years old. She looked at the wall on which were hung a few family photographs and her ballet student's tutu framed by an old pair of ballet shoes and the program from the Rennes Opéra, where she had danced in public for the first time. Her collection of small stuffed animals shared the cherrywood table with a pad of writing paper, a music box and a few dried flowers.

She got up and walked over to the oval mirror that had been bought at a flea market. She liked old things. New objects frightened her. "Poor Sophie..." she said to her reflection.

Taking a sheet of paper and a pen, she left the room and went down the long corridor to the kitchen. Saturday was the maid's day off.

She sat down on a wooden chair, placed the paper on the table and wrote: "To Toti and Pilou. Forgive me, but I can't stand it any more. It's too hard. You don't understand that I really love Vadim and don't want to live without him."

She went over to the gas range, turned on a burner, knelt and placed her head on the cast-iron plate inside the oven. The odor was disagreeable but she hoped that it wouldn't be long. Soon a feeling of light-headedness came over her. She closed her eyes and waited for imminent death.

At that very moment, in the sleeping car that was taking me to Nice, I was overcome with a sudden, irrational anxiety. I put my book down. I couldn't understand the sudden attack of uneasiness that made my heart pound. The highly polished wooden walls seemed to close in on me. I felt as though I was locked up, a prisoner. I thought of Brigitte. I wanted to go back in time. I wanted to be back in Paris. I wanted to take her in my arms. I had never before felt torture that was both physical and mental at the same time.

After having admired the Arc de Triomphe and the Place de la Concorde, Mijanou began sneezing. The night was cool. A little annoyed, Mr. Bardot decided they would go home and get a coat for his youngest daughter. If Mijanou had put on something warm before leaving, Brigitte would never have become a legend. She was already unconscious when her parents, alarmed by the smell of gas, came into the kitchen.

"Ten minutes later, she would have been lost," said the fire chief, relieved to see a little color returning to the young girl's cheeks under the oxygen mask. Mr. Bardot was not heartless—but the habits of class and upbringing were so strong that his first words to Brigitte, when she was able to listen and understand, were "How could you have done that to us?" His second words were "Tomorrow you're leaving for boarding school in England." Mrs. Bardot, who was more pragmatic, asked him to be quiet and leave her alone with her daughter. "Darling," she said, "you know Pilou, you mustn't always take his threats seriously. You'll see Vadim again."

I remember the urgent, perfectly illogical desire I felt to leave my train and return to Paris. But there was no train to Paris till morning. I hadn't been able to sleep all night. I saw the sun rise over the cypress and olive trees in the Vaucluse. My anxieties drowned in the blue Mediterranean, after the cliffs of Cassis.

I know that twins sometimes experience telepathic communication. I have had this experience several times, but only with Brigitte.

In the days that followed, when sixteen-year-old Brigitte had regained her zest for life, her mother said to her, "If two years from now, you still love Vadim and he still loves you, we will allow you to marry him."

THERE was no telephone in my mother's villa in Nice, so I called Brigitte from the post office. She told me about her fit of depression. "I love you. Work fast. Come back quickly, my darling. I have difficulty living without you."

It was in a letter from Mrs. Bardot that I guessed the truth. "Brigitte has done something foolish. She is all right. We hope to see you soon."

My mother liked Brigitte very much but she always said, "I feel sorry for her." She found her too hungry for happiness to ever be satisfied. "She'll never learn to grow up. I think she'll always be a child. To be happy you must know how to love. She has a passion for love but doesn't know how to love."

I think she meant that by expecting too much from life and love, Brigitte would only know brief moments of happiness. I called that the "happiness disease."

I compared her to Lancelot pursuing the impossible dream, the overly gifted youth who went in search of the unattainable.

Brigitte's Grail was not only man's salvation but her own happiness. Unconsciously, she knew it: This magic stone, this perfect diamond could not exist on earth.

*O*N my return from Nice, Brigitte told me about her attempted suicide. She said that she didn't want to wait until she was eighteen to live with me. She had read that in Scotland one could get married without parental consent before coming of age. I had a difficult time getting her to see that this type of marriage, no matter how romantic and picturesque it might appear, would not be accepted legally in France. I hated the idea of being sent to prison by Mr. Bardot for corruption of a minor. The thought of her lover languishing behind bars convinced Brigitte. She decided to wait out patiently the two fateful years.

☆ 5 ☆

*O*UR engagement was officially announced. The wedding was set for December 1952, after Brigitte's eighteenth birthday.

For the first time she was permitted to spend a week with me during the Christmas holidays. My mother, who had given up her villa in Nice and rented a small house about a mile from Saint-Tropez, was to put us up and act as chaperone. After having given her a long lecture, Mr. Bardot presented her with a list of rules to be observed.

—Brigitte and Vadim will not leave the house without giving a precise timetable and itinerary of their activities.

—No more than two dinners alone together during the week.

—Be home no later than midnight.

—Keep an eye on Brigitte's appearance. She must never have breakfast in her nightgown.

My mother promised to follow these instructions, and she kept her word.

Pilou neglected to mention one important point, however. It seemed obvious to him that we would have separate rooms, so he gave no instructions as to where we should sleep. For the first time Brigitte and I shared the same bed without fear of being found out.

Brigitte and I went for drives along the port in an old Bugatti convertible that I had bought for my mother for $180. We played "baby foot" (a table soccer game) with the local youths in cafés now famous: le Gorille, l'Escale, le Café des Arts. We took the back roads of the hinterland. Sometimes, when the Bugatti jolted to a halt, it had to be pushed, like an obstinate old donkey. On our way home, we would fill the back with dead branches gathered in the woods for the fireplace in our bedroom. And at night we would make love by the glowing light of the wood fire.

Our idyll ended more quickly than we would have liked. Brigitte was shocked. She didn't want to go back to Paris.

"Let's elope," she suggested.

"Where to?"

"Italy or Spain... or even Tahiti. If you take me back to my parents, we'll never be as happy as we are now."

It seemed childish and unreasonable, but in a sense she was right. I should have risked her parents' anger and threats. Brigitte was just seventeen. When all is said and done, I don't believe that I would have been sent to prison for corrupting a minor. I was very young myself. Reason prevailed, however. But was it reason?

Back in Paris, Brigitte underwent subtle changes. She wasn't aware of it, but something inside her had been crushed.

Every time Pilou slackened his leash on us, he immediately regretted it and made up for his leniency with an outburst that terrified Brigitte.

One morning she rang me at the Quai d'Orléans. She was whispering, and I sensed that something serious had occurred.

"I must see you right now."

"Come on over. I'll be waiting," I said.

"Not at your place. It would be too dangerous."

"Place Saint-Michel, at the subway entrance. All right?"

When we met half an hour later at the place agreed upon,

I could see that she was pale. She threw herself into my arms.

"Do you have a revolver?" she asked.

"You know very well that I don't. Why?"

"You must get one. Right away."

After five minutes of confused explanations, I was able to reconstruct what had actually taken place. Her father had summoned her to his study, opened a desk drawer and said, "Do you see this?"

Brigitte bent over and took a look.

"What is it?" Pilou asked her.

"It's . . . a piece . . ." Brigitte had replied, using the slang word.

"One does not say a 'piece' . . . one says a 'revolver,'" Pilou corrected. "Now take a good look at this revolver. If I ever learn that you have been Vadim's mistress, I will shoot him without a moment's hesitation."

Too stunned to take the threat seriously, Brigitte ran to her mother, who was sitting at her dressing table putting on makeup.

"Mummy, I think Pilou's had sunstroke."

"That would surprise me," replied Toti. "It's been raining for a week."

"Then we have to put him away."

Brigitte recounted the scene in Pilou's study.

"I approve wholeheartedly of your father's decision," Toti replied calmly. "In fact, if you ever take it into your head to sleep with Vadim before your marriage, I myself will use the revolver, should Pilou change his mind."

"You must be joking."

"No. I am absolutely serious."

I was sure that neither Toti nor Pilou would have risked the scandal of a court trial to preserve their daughter's chastity. They wanted to frighten her. They didn't realize that it was too late.

We had left Place Saint-Michel and were walking along

the banks of the Seine. My attempts to calm Brigitte had failed.

"As far as Mummy's concerned, you're probably right," she said. "But I know Pilou. He's capable of anything."

Brigitte told me that Pilou had once locked himself in the attic of their country house after a row with his wife. Three hours later, he had still not come down, so Toti went up to find out what he was doing. When she opened the door . . . a shot went off. Pilou was seated in a chair. He had placed a shotgun on the table in front of him and attached it to the door by a series of pulleys. The trigger was attached to the door handle so that it would fire when the door was opened.

The shot had missed him by a few feet.

"Let's say that I get a gun," I said to Brigitte, "and that your father comes here with his revolver. You don't expect me to kill him, do you?"

"I don't see any other solution. I'd rather be an orphan than a widow."

"You can't be a widow. You're not married."

"Stop harping on silly details," said Brigitte, losing her temper. "Whether we're married or not, if you died I would be a widow."

I had only one argument left. "What would you say to our children when they grew up? Would you tell them that Daddy killed their grandfather?"

"I don't want to have children," said Brigitte.

I tried to reassure her by telephoning a friend, Jean-Paul Faure, whose brother had a collection of war weapons. He lent me an American army Colt, but I didn't have any cartridges to slip into the magazine.

Fortunately, Brigitte was not interested in such details.

*I*N order to be worthy of the princess's hand in marriage, I had to perform two tasks. The first was to get a steady job. The other was to pass my catechism.

My parents were freethinkers, but to please my grandmother I had been plunged into water by a priest when I was three months old and declared Russian Orthodox, so I didn't need a Roman Catholic baptism. To be married in church, however, and raise my future children in their mother's religion, I had to learn the Old and New Testaments, Lutheran and Calvinist heresies (to protect my hypothetical children from the temptations of Satan), and about twenty prayers to be said on waking, at mealtimes, on dying, for repentance, and I forget the rest. I also had to go to confession.

Brigitte found all of this amusing, especially since the priest responsible for my religious education was the same one she had tried to shock by confessing abominable sins. The priest was actually a man of the world. He was also sincere, and I learned many things from him that could not help but satisfy my curious nature.

Finding a regular job was more difficult. Unlike Hollywood, France does not have film studios that give yearly contracts. I would not have accepted that kind of slavery anyway. So what was left? Work in the postal service? In a bank? That was not exactly my style. But journalism was a possibility.

Herve Mille, then editor in chief of *Paris-Match*, was one of the most brilliant Parisian personalities of the day. He and his brother Gerard, a talented interior designer, entertained everybody in their mansion at 72 rue de Varenne. Theirs was both the most open and most closed house in Paris; open in the sense that one could gain admittance without age, wealth, fame, closed because only talent, intelligence and boldness were welcomed. The habitués of the rue de Varenne were often unknown young men and women, some of whom were to become famous: reporters, photographers, disco dancers, actors and brilliant spongers who had elevated refusal to work to a fine art. Also among the regulars were Marie Hélène de Rothschild, the Princess de Savoie, Aly Khan, Jean Genet, Jean Cocteau and Marlon Brando.

Gerard and Herve Mille adored Brigitte. On the evening I

introduced her to my friends, her father accompanied us. After having shaken hands with Marie Laure de Noailles, General Corniglion-Molinier, Juliette Greco and a young American senator named John F. Kennedy, Pilou left us, his mind at ease.

Among the guests was a woman whose amorous adventures had been the talk of Paris for more than thirty years. Simone Beriau, now a theater director, had been a great courtesan. Now over fifty, she had become subdued, but she remained notorious for her immoderate language. She decided to get a laugh by attacking Brigitte.

"Are you a virgin?" she asked her point-blank. She expected to upset the young girl and make her blush.

But without becoming flustered, Brigitte replied, "No, madam. Are you?"

Every one laughed with Brigitte, and she won the first round by a knockout.

The house on the rue de Varenne became one of the places where Brigitte and I could meet without fear. Little did Mr. Bardot suspect that guests there did not just discuss art and politics. Evenings on this very official street with its row of government ministries and embassies were often fun and quite wild.

In any case, Brigitte had to be home by midnight.

Herve Mille gave me a job at *Paris-Match*. I became a journalist willingly. My salary was modest: two hundred dollars a month (plus bonuses and expenses), but it represented a regular job.

Before the reign of television one kept up with current events through magazines, and *Paris-Match* was one of Europe's most prestigious weeklies. We were twenty or so reporters and photographers, much envied by our colleagues. Ready for anything and capable of anything, with means at our disposal enjoyed by few journalists today, we were a gang with our own rules and vocabulary. (Many expressions and slang words invented in *Paris-Match*'s editorial offices have become part of the French language.) We created our own style of reportage.

We covered a very wide field—arts, sports, revolutions, wars, accidents and natural disasters. We were everywhere. Kings and princesses, paratroopers from Indochina, mercenaries, film stars and politicians talked to us, though they would close the door to many of our colleagues.

I was accepted immediately by this private club of journalists because I knew most of the reporters and photographers who were members. But above all, we were kindred spirits. I belonged to the same race of shrewd, warmhearted and cynical kids educated by the harsh realities of the Nazi occupation.

The price of adventure was terribly high. Within ten years over half of my friends had died in automobile or plane accidents—and in one way or another in Indochina, Africa, Budapest, Suez or Cuba.

It was always I who was going on a trip, but once the roles were reversed. With permission from her parents, who knew one of the ship's managers, Brigitte accepted an invitation to dance for the passengers on a cruise of the *Ile de France*. A friend named Capucine accompanied her. Capucine was not a professional chaperone or baby-sitter, but one of the most famous models of the early fifties.

Capucine promised Pilou that she would keep an eye on Brigitte. In spite of a few unexpected slips and slides due to the rolling of the ship, the *Ile de France*'s star dancer enjoyed herself immensely and was a great success. Nevertheless, it was on her return from the cruise that she decided to give up dancing.

"I can't be a dancer and remain with you. We would be apart all the time."

It was not a lighthearted decision. She knew that she would be denying herself the realization of her childhood and adolescent dream, her only true ambition, which was to be a prima ballerina. However, she never reproached me for the sacrifice she had made, not even during our worst fights. Having turned over a new page in her life, she decided to take sole responsibility for the future she had chosen.

For Brigitte, love came before vocation.

*O*NCE she had decided to forget dancing, the idea of becoming a screen actress didn't seem so incongruous. She knew that my ambition was to direct films, so if she became an actress, she could work and be with me at the same time.

Brigitte often caught the attention of producers and directors when we went out, particularly at Marc Allégret's home. She had always turned down proposals to act in films. Now, having changed her mind, she decided to accept the part of an ingenue in a sentimental comedy, fortunately destined to be forgotten.

Her male co-star was Bourvil, a genial actor who was not yet a big star. One evening when we were discussing Brigitte, he said, "She'll be a star. But it's a shame that she doesn't really like the profession."

It was neither the title of the film, *Crazy for Love (Le Trou Normand)* nor the screenplay nor the director that attracted Brigitte to the project. Rather, it was the fact that it would be filmed only eighty kilometers from Paris. The location had the double advantage of shielding her from constant contact with her family and at the same time putting her within an hour's drive of her lover. Since going to work for *Paris-Match,* I had bought a Simca Aronde which, although not as quaint as the Bugatti, was faster and in better condition.

Brigitte's first experience in films brought her no revelations. She took up her new profession willingly and diligently. She also counted the hours that were bringing her closer to December 20, the date her parents had chosen for our marriage.

"People always count the minutes separating them from a happy event," she said. "But they forget that death stops the clock. Death is the only banker who gets rich as he loses his capital."

A few years later, still on the subject of death, she said, "Death drives me crazy. I sometimes feel like messing up his plans and arriving early, without warning, just to infuriate him, so that I can say 'I got the best of you.' "

*T*O the surprise of Jean Boyer, director of *Crazy for Love*, a number of journalists turned up on the set asking for Brigitte. I had helped this young actress to become known, but I certainly had no power to influence the press. The unexpected attraction Brigitte held for them could not be explained by the fact that my name had been listed on *Paris-Match*'s masthead for two months. I had been the first to succumb to her charm and didn't need a drawing to understand that my romantic little dancer was a siren. Her voice, her body or her singing—who knows which—were luring sailors to the reefs of modernity.

She became a celebrity before people knew who she was.

There was the "Bardot mystery," but Brigitte was never mysterious. "Journalists are such a drag," she said.

She was still a brunette.

*T*WO weeks after she finished working on *Crazy for Love*, Brigitte left for Corsica to make another film called *The Girl in the Bikini (Manina, Fille sans voiles)*. The director of this dreadful piece thought he knew something about eroticism.

Censorship being what it was in the fifties, we were only permitted to see Brigitte emerging from an ocean wave in a bikini. People began talking about the young Bardot's explosive charm.

Although Pilou and Toti were sticklers for decorum, they were not offended when they saw photos of Brigitte in a swimsuit the size of a postage stamp. They were people of quality. Though ill-adapted to modern life and the changing morality, they showed that they were capable of progressing in their ideas.

I had advised Brigitte to work in films that were, to say the least, unlikely to be shown at Henri Langlois's Cinémathèque.

"You decided to act in film, fine. Start off with unambitious projects. You lack experience, but no one will judge you as long as you appear in minor ventures. After all, you don't criticize an amateur painter as long as he doesn't start exhibiting in fashionable galleries," I said to her.

I mentioned several very gifted young actors whose careers had ended abruptly although their first films had been made with great directors. People expected too much from their second films, and they weren't ready. They either started over again or were soon forgotten.

"Don't listen to people who tell you to turn down every offer until you get that phone call from René Clément or Henri-Georges Clouzot. They don't know what they're talking about."

It takes time to learn how to express talent. There are few Mayakovskys, Raymond Radiguets or Rimbauds. In any case, they died young. I don't recommend that at all to actors.

I N September, Mrs. Bardot bought a little apartment with a bedroom, living room, dining room and kitchen.

"I don't want to encourage your tendency to be lazy," she said to me, "but you need a little nest so that you can change your bad habits. After you get married you can have the apartment for three years."

Pilou was still watching over his daughter's chastity.

"Vadim," he said to me, "for a while I misjudged you. You're an honorable man, I might be old-fashioned and a little naive, but I am happy that my daughter will be a virgin when she goes to her husband's bed on her wedding night. Here, let me embrace you." He kissed me on both cheeks.

I was fond of this old-fashioned man "from the days of the dinosaurs," as Brigitte so often characterized him. We had practically nothing in common, yet I understood him.

Over twenty years later, they laid him to rest in a pretty cemetery in Saint-Tropez. I arrived from the United States, widowed by another divorce; Brigitte had not asked me to come to the funeral. I slipped into the crowd of faithful friends and curious spectators and followed them to the mausoleum. I had come to say goodbye to Pilou. The coffin was lowered into the crypt, which would never know sunlight. There was the sound that separates future death from death in the present. And there was the silence of reflection and meditation. Brigitte turned around, saw me and said, "Do you see what he has done to me?"

I thought of the kitchen scene in the apartment on the rue de la Pompe. Brigitte had just escaped death by a hair's breadth, and Pilou was saying, "How could you do this to us?"

*B*RIGITTE had waited so long and placed so much hope in our marriage that it had become a sort of daydream, an abstraction for me. I didn't see it as the beginning of a different life, but rather as the end of a state of anxiety, nervousness and daily frustration.

One night, after dinner on the rue de la Pompe, they made up my bed on the sofa in the dining room, and I slept over.

The next morning, half awake, I was trying to find my way to the bathroom when I heard Brigitte's voice. She and her mother were discussing the color of the curtains for our future apartment. In an instant I realized that I was a stranger, an unlikely graft on this family tree. I was not their kind.

I walked into the bathroom and brushed my teeth. Brigitte joined me almost immediately. She pressed herself against me and kissed me on the mouth, not caring that there was toothpaste all over it.

"Oh, Vadim!" she said. "We've only eight days left. I'm so happy."

☆ 6 ☆

*B*RIGITTE designed and chose the material for the white, hand-sewn wedding dress from Madame Ogive, the dressmaker on the rue de Passy. It was the equal of the most stylish models in the collections of Chanel or Balenciaga and would be worn Sunday in the church at Auteuil.

The civil ceremony was celebrated the day before at the *mairie* of the XVI arrondissement.* The bride wore a blouse and skirt, and the bridegroom a navy blue suit with matching blue tie.

The mayor, perturbed by my family name, made a speech on the importance of international marriages that encourage peace in the world and hailed our union as a "symbol of Franco-Russian friendship." Brigitte had great difficulty controlling her giggles.

When we left the city hall office, she threw herself into my arms. "It's done. I'm Mrs. Plemiannikov!"

The dinner, at the rue de la Pompe, was restricted to

*Since Marie Antoinette was guillotined, a religious marriage is no longer considered legal in France. A couple must perform a civil ceremony.

family and close friends. Around eleven o'clock I went up to see Brigitte, who had retired to her bedroom. Already in bed and naked under a very romantic, slightly transparent nightgown, she radiated happiness. I sat down on the edge of the bed.

Half an hour later, Pilou walked into the bedroom. "My dear Vadim," he said, "I believe it's about time for you to leave."

"Leave? Where to?" asked Brigitte.

"We have prepared his bed in the dining room," said Pilou.

"But we're married, Papa. Don't you remember? You signed, and Mummy signed, and the witnesses signed. I said 'I do' and Vadim said 'I do.' I'm married, Papa . . . *married . . . a married woman. . . .*"

"You will be married tomorrow after the religious ceremony," said Pilou, unshakable.

"He's crazy!" Brigitte cried, sitting up in the bed. "Papa has gone mad. Help! Pilou's mad."

"Don't behave like a child," said Mr. Bardot. His face was becoming dangerously tense; the mouth was just a thin, straight line. "This morning was a formality that we had to go through. Nothing more. Vadim will become your husband *tomorrow,* at the church."

Brigitte's face was flushed with anger. She was on the verge of exploding.

"I will sleep with my husband tonight—in the streets, on the sidewalk, if necessary!"

The scene that I had found amusing at the beginning was now becoming serious. I asked Pilou to leave me alone with Brigitte for a moment.

"That's too much!" cried Brigitte, still seething. "I've been waiting for three years for the right to sleep with you. I'm married. I'm legal. I'm going to sleep and make love with my husband in *my* bed. Or in his, or in the Pope's bed . . . I don't care. But I'm not going to sleep all alone tonight!"

She took off her nightgown and ran to the closet. "I'll get dressed and then we'll get out of here."

I grabbed her as she went by and held her in my arms. After a few kicks, she stopped struggling. I explained to her that this was not the time to fight with her parents. The situation was somewhat ridiculous, but it was up to us to show good sense. I didn't want her to regret one day having cut herself off from her family on a sudden impulse.

She finally calmed down and even began to laugh.

"So you're going to spend your wedding night all alone, in the dining room? It could only happen to you."

So, I spent my wedding night on a narrow sofa after having married the most beautiful of Parisians, whom the newspapers would one day describe as every married man's impossible dream.

*B*RIGITTE and I had agreed to a religious ceremony to please her parents. We were both surprised by the emotion we felt during the service in the church filled with friends. The organ, the priest's voice echoing under the vault, the light filtering through the stained-glass windows, the magic of chandeliers glowing with candles, the respectful silence of the guests—there is no doubt that it was all theater, but it was theater that touched the soul.

Marc Allégret, my best man, seemed very moved. I remember that my mother and my sister Hélène, whom I considered hardly vulnerable to this sort of atmosphere, cried.

Brigitte looked at me. Her parted lips were trembling and tears were running down her cheeks.

After the ceremony, the daylight outside, the photographers and our applauding friends brought us down to earth. The reception in the Bardot apartment was a great success.

At nightfall, Brigitte and I took the old open-top hydraulic elevator, which had so often separated us, down the five flights. Our suitcases were in the trunk of my Simca Aronde. In keeping with tradition, we went off on our honeymoon.

Near Fontainebleau (about thirty-seven miles from Paris),

Brigitte asked me to stop the car at the roadside.

"I'm frightened," she said.

"Of what?"

"Of everything. I want to go home, back to Paris."

I refrained from reminding her that only the day before she had almost fled her apartment in the middle of the night. I knew that this sudden mood was neither a game nor a whim. The future and distant places had always frightened Brigitte. Megève, our destination, was only two hundred and fifty miles away, but she couldn't imagine where the path her life had just taken would lead.

She cried for half an hour with her head on my shoulder, and then calmed down. She never again spoke of going back to her parents.

*A*T the end of 1952, no one knew who Roger Vadim was. I doubt that anyone at all remembered the article in the film magazine three years earlier that had named Europe's youngest screenwriter. As for Brigitte, she was often photographed by the press, but was by no means a star. Consequently we were rather surprised to find our wedding photos widely published and given a four-page spread in *Paris-Match*, coverage usually reserved for royalty or stars. I had thought that the photos taken by friends from the magazine during the wedding would end up in our family album, not in the newspapers.

Again, this was part of the Bardot mystery. Some great actors wait all their lives for media attention. Brigitte got married and, without even trying, created an event.

We had reserved a room in a cozy, comfortable little hotel called La Gerentière, which was awarded a star in the Michelin guide after our stay.

Our first serious arguments occurred during stormy games of Monopoly. I'm very calm in life's important moments, but losing at this childish game made me fume.

"You just lost the rue de la Paix. You owe me thirty thousand francs."

"I drew six. I have another turn."

"You drew five. You're stuck at rue de la Paix."

I am an expert skier, so Brigitte didn't try to follow me on the slopes. She just sat on the terraces of restaurants and sunbathed. The only sport she had ever practiced or been interested in was swimming. When she went to a soccer match she was surprised to see the players running after a ball. "They ought to give them several. Then they would stop fighting," she once said to me.

We spent lively, happy nights in Megève, but Brigitte couldn't wait to get back to Paris. Her dearest wish was to furnish and decorate our apartment.

For the young women who long to know the recipe for success, and for readers intrigued or fascinated by the paths leading to fame, I must admit that the future international star didn't care at all about her photos in *Paris-Match*. or future film contracts. Her thoughts were for the color of the carpet in the living room and the possibility of borrowing her mother's set of pink Limoges porcelain.

*T*HE apartment on rue Chardon-Lagache was small but sunny. A balcony, large enough to put flowerpots on, overlooked the police station. Since there was no elevator, we had to take a very narrow staircase up three flights. Mme. Ledieu, the concierge, was very old, very gentle and very sentimental. Her best friend and companion, Tino, was gray, measured a few inches from beak to tail and lived in a cage. He was a nightingale and, like all nightingales, subject to depression. When Tino stopped chirping, Mme. Ledieu stopped distributing the mail and wouldn't sweep the stairs. I never knew whether the bird's volatile moods were psychosomatic or linked to changes in the weather, but they had a direct influence on the comfort of the tenants of 79 rue Chardon-Lagache.

Some mornings Mme. Ledieu would exclaim joyfully, "He's singing." And we knew that for a week all would be well.

Brigitte took her role as housewife very seriously. Her parents had lent us the apartment, but we didn't have a single piece of furniture. For the first weeks we slept on a mattress on the floor. I should be able to describe many touching scenes of the couple building their nest day by day. Actually, furniture, curtains and kitchen equipment were of little interest to me. I can't even remember when the bed arrived. I just found having to take the garbage down the stairs every evening rather annoying. Also I wished we had a telephone.

Brigitte had a strange attitude toward saving money. She would spend a fortune on taxis, traveling all over Paris to save thirty cents on a roll of fabric. I pointed out that her economizing was expensive. "You don't understand," she replied. "It's a question of principle. There's no reason to pay six francs forty a yard for velvet when you can get exactly the same thing for six francs ten centimes."

I let Brigitte economize in her own way. My salary was enough for us to live on, but we couldn't afford to buy furniture.

The offer of a part in a film to be shot in Nice put Brigitte in a double bind. She needed money to decorate the apartment but wouldn't be able to do it if she left Paris. That was undoubtedly what persuaded her to accept a role in Jean Anouilh's play *An Invitation to the Castle*. Brigitte was taking on a tough job. The very best actors fought for the honor of acting in an Anouilh play, and it was only reluctantly that the director, André Barsacq, had given in to what he thought was one of the author's whims. How could this beginner with no theatrical experience hold the stage? Jean Anouilh rarely went to films, but he had seen ten minutes of *Crazy for Love* because of Bourvil. It was Brigitte who amazed and captivated him.

From the very first rehearsals at the Atelier Theater she was aware of the difficult chance she had just agreed to take. "I must be mad," she told me. "We can wait for the sofa and the carpet. I'm going to get out of it."

I managed to persuade her not to jump off a moving train and helped her to discover the character she was interpreting by rehearsing with her at home. I made her swear not to breathe a word about this to André Barsacq, one of the most highly regarded stage directors in France. The pride of great men is as easily irritated as the skin of a newborn baby's bottom.

Brigitte's performance was miraculous. On opening night, she astounded not only the audience but also her fellow actors. Her voice carried and she provoked laughter from the audience at exactly the right moment. The charm, self-assurance and genuineness of her performance helped the audience to forget her lack of professional training. The critics didn't hail her as the new Sarah Bernhardt, but they were favorably impressed. It was a master stroke in the career of a young beginner whose talent, malicious gossip said, was due to the small of her back.

Success didn't go to Brigitte's head. She realized that although she had come off with flying colors this time, she wasn't ready for a career in the theater. Besides, she didn't like the idea of having to play the same character every evening, day after day, week after week. "That's proof enough for me that I'm not cut out for the stage," she said to me.

*T*HE apartment was now very comfortable and we often invited friends over for dinner. Brigitte cooked, but she was not exactly a cordon bleu chef. One evening when Lilou, Christian Marquand's sister, was at our place, we were alarmed by a thick plume of smoke coming from the kitchen. Grease from the lamb Brigitte was roasting had caught fire and great flames were pouring out of the oven. Lilou rushed to try to put out the fire by throwing water on it, which only added to the damage. Terrified, Brigitte shut the door on her friend. Lilou began banging on it, but Brigitte kept her hand firmly on the door knob and wouldn't open it.

"You're crazy," I said. "Open it, right now."

"If I open the door," replied Brigitte, "all my furniture will go up in flames." I pushed Brigitte aside and saved Lilou from being burned alive. Using towels, I managed to control the beginnings of a conflagration.

Our frequent and sometimes rather violent quarrels were always provoked by something childish. I remember our rages and mutual insults, but I have absolutely no memory of what caused them. On the other hand, I will never forget the business with the door.

A heated argument begun in bed after dinner degenerated into a quarrel in the living room and reached a climax in the kitchen. Suddenly, without any apparent reason, Brigitte calmed down. That was not like her, and I should have been suspicious.

"You forgot to take down the rubbish," she said. "Go on, darling. Be a sweetheart. I'll wait for you in bed."

I picked up the garbage can and went out. The moment I set foot on the landing, I realized that I had made a mistake. But it was too late. Brigitte had just closed the door behind me, and I could hear her bolting it. I was in my pajama bottoms. Dressed like that, it would be difficult to get in my car and drive to a friend's house. Besides, I didn't have the keys to the car. Sleeping on the landing in pajama bottoms with the garbage can didn't seem to be a good idea either.

I tried to knock down the door by throwing my shoulders against it—a trick that apparently only works in films. Then I thought of another way. The landing was very narrow. If I pressed my back against the banister, I could push against the door with my feet. Anger had evidently given me added strength because the door collapsed almost immediately. Brigitte looked terrified and ran to the bedroom to hide. I followed her. I can't remember ever feeling as angry as I did then. I wanted to hit her, but I have never lifted a finger against a woman in my whole life, and I couldn't do it then, despite the rage I felt. It was terribly frustrating. I then had an idea which now seems a little extravagant but struck me as inspired at the time. I managed to force Brigitte down on the thick wool carpet, tore the mattress from the bed and threw it over her. Then I began to jump up and down on the mattress with both feet, restricting myself to the area covering her bottom.

Suddenly all my anger disappeared. Brigitte held a grudge against me for a long time, however. Not because I jumped up and down on the mattress (I didn't hurt her much), but because of the door. The wood had splintered and we had to get a new one.

Four years later when we decided to get a divorce, Brigitte's lawyer asked her to list her complaints against me.

"I have nothing to say against him," said Brigitte.

"Surely, if you want a divorce it is because there is something you reproach him for."

"No. We often quarreled, but it was my fault as much as his."

"But, madame, I must establish a file for the judge. Try to remember something. Find something for me."

"Oh...well, yes..." said Brigitte. "There was something—and I'll never forgive him for it."

"Very good. Tell me about it."

"It was the door. One day he broke down my door. I had just had it revarnished."

J UST as Brigitte could not provide her lawyer with material for his file, I was unable to find a complaint to lodge against her. She loved me. She was faithful— or at least, I thought she was. Besides, if I had discovered that she'd been unfaithful during a trip, I would undoubtedly have been a little upset, but I wouldn't have felt betrayed. We knew how to laugh and amuse ourselves. We had good times in bed—and elsewhere. There were, of course, the frequent quarrels, the spats of unruly children and unbridled lovers, but they were the froth on the wave, not the storm. They were the sound of two strong personalities clashing without destroying each other. On the contrary, we gave each other a great deal.

It was probably Brigitte's profoundly childlike nature (a point to which I will return often since it is essential if one hopes to understand her) which made our marriage difficult in the end. Like a child, she demanded too much from those she loved. If one failed to pay attention to her for one moment, she would be filled with anxiety. "I'm unhappy. I'm frightened," she would say. Work forced me to take frequent trips, and that destroyed something in her. She needed me with her in order to breathe easily. Day or night in Paris, or during a filming in the country or abroad, she would call for help and I had to come running. By the time I arrived, sometimes having left important work hanging in midair, her mood would have changed. Everything was fine, as happens with children who forget all about a nightmare the following morning. In this sense she was very egotistical. There were also the long hours between sunset and sunrise when I had to exorcise demons and reassure her.

"I'm frightened, Vadim. Tell me you'll always love me."

She changed her mind just as she changed her moods. At the last minute she would cancel a dinner invitation that she had accepted a week before. She would refuse to speak to journalists who had come from Rome or New York only because she had agreed to an interview. She hasn't changed much. I had dinner with her one year ago and she said, "You were the only one who would let me change my mind. Now I no longer have the right to change my mind. It's hard."

It's true that I put up with many of her whims, as I would do later with my children. But a child grows up and adapts to a new stage, called the age of reason. Brigitte didn't grow up. On the contrary—the more attention success brought her, the more personal devotion she demanded. It wasn't that, like certain domineering women, she wanted to control everything and make all the decisions; it was a much more subtle form of tyranny, an unquenchable thirst for love. This type of servitude began to weigh heavily on me.

On the other hand, Brigitte was more sensible than I when it came to material things—to money and to organizing our life. In fact, she was too sensible for my taste. Her discussions with the cook about the price of a cutlet, her obsession with knickknacks and furniture, reminded me too much of her bourgeois upbringing. I like money and luxury as long as I can enjoy them without being enslaved to them. Unlike most people, I have never been able to endow material things with moral value.

There was nothing predictable about Brigitte, however. I have seen her scold the maid for buying an expensive veal cutlet, and the very same day offer her understudy a car so she wouldn't have to get up at five o'clock the next morning to take the bus from her home in the suburbs.

Several years before *And God Created Woman* came out, Brigitte was in no way a star. But Warner Brothers offered her a fabulous contract. Olga Horstig, her agent, spoke of the money involved in a voice trembling with excitement: $1,500 per week for the first year, $3,000 per week for the second year and $5,000 per week for the third year. In addition, she would have a house with a swimming pool in Beverly Hills and a car.

"How much is that in francs?" asked Brigitte.

Olga did the calculation.

Brigitte could not help whistling in admiration. *"Merde,"* she said. "They're not stingy in Hollywood."

She asked me if I would come and live with her in America.

"Of course," I said.

The contract was duly signed and returned to Warner Brothers.

It was only then that Brigitte realized what she had really agreed to. Yes, she would have lots of money and fame in the center of the film world. But she would also have a new, completely different life, in a country where people didn't speak French. She was panic-stricken.

"I'll never be able to make a niche for myself there," she said. "I know it."

For Brigitte, "making a niche" meant recreating her existing environment in a new place. A fox chased from its hole, or a rabbit from its burrow, will die if it cannot recreate its niche. It was the same for Brigitte.

She cried every night for a week. Nothing I said reassured her. "It's hopeless," she said. "If I live there, I'll die. And if I stay here they'll sue, and I'll spend the rest of my life paying them."

I went to see Olga and told her that it was out of the question for Brigitte to go to Hollywood. Disappointed, the agent got Hollywood to cancel the contract.

Brigitte's smile returned and I was able to sleep again. To compound her happiness, someone gave my wife a black cocker spaniel puppy that she named Clown.

It was our first and, I must add, our only, child.

☆ 7 ☆

*O*NE of Brigitte's greatest qualities was that she was not a snob. We met many celebrities but she was never impressed by a name or a fortune. She was more likely to be suspicious of well-known personalities. She enjoyed going out and having a good time, but not to those fashionable gatherings where every face was that of someone famous. Getting her to go to an opening was quite a job. Nevertheless, we did have close friends who were famous. Above all there was Marlon Brando.

I met Marlon about the same time I met Brigitte. I was sitting with Christian Marquand on the terrace of a café in the Boulevard Montparnasse when an extraordinarily handsome young man at the next table caught our attention. He had taken off his shoes and was massaging his naked foot, which he had placed on the table between a glass of Perrier and an ashtray. Groaning with ecstasy, like a woman about to have an orgasm, he kept saying, "Shit . . . that feels good. . . . Shit . . . that feels good."

We started up a conversation and the Adonis explained that one of his greatest pleasures in life was massaging his feet after walking a long time. He introduced himself as Marlon Brando and told us that he was alone in Paris and living in a very uncomfortable little hotel on the Left Bank.

He had felt a sudden need to escape from New York and had come to France though he knew no one here. We felt an immediate rapport with him and invited him to share our small apartment in the rue Bassano.

The next day he told us that he was an actor and had just starred in Tennessee Williams's *A Streetcar Named Desire* on Broadway. Although he was already famous in New York, we had never heard of him. He became one of Christian's and my closest friends from the very beginning, and we are still a little like brothers.

For reasons I've never analyzed, Marlon and Brigitte never felt any real rapport. They liked each other and were quite friendly and cordial, but that's all. It seemed to me that two such spontaneous and profoundly sensual creatures would have understood each other. Brigitte was not at all dazzled by Marlon's physique; he found her charming but no more than that. Having never seen him act, she discovered his genius in a totally unexpected way.

Christian, Marlon, Brigitte and I had spent an amusing evening going from the Club Saint-Germain to Tabou, and from there to Les Halles. We'd had a few drinks but we weren't drunk; Brigitte never drank much. We were walking up the Champs-Élysées when, at the corner of Avenue Georges V, in front of Fouquet's, a tavern well known to film people, Marlon noticed the chairs and tables chained together so that they wouldn't have to be taken in at night. Without saying a word, he pulled on the chains and arranged the chairs on the sidewalk. Then he began reciting the opening lines of *A Streetcar Named Desire,* playing all the parts.

It was dawn. Soon we were no longer on the Champs-Élysées, but in a tiny, stifling apartment in New Orleans. Marlon had recreated the true magic of the theater with just a few chairs and two barroom tables. Grumpy men and women, half asleep on their way to catch the first subway train to work, stopped out of curiosity or amusement. But after watching Marlon for a moment, they were spellbound and fascinated. And yet, take my word for it, Parisians are rather blasé and not at all impressed by the antics of people partying in the early morning. But even if they didn't understand any English, they recognized pure talent.

*I*T'S generally believed that I invented Brigitte. But it is precisely because Brigitte was not the product of anyone's imagination that neither her parents or society nor her profession affected her deepest nature, and that she was able to shock, seduce, create a new style and finally explode in the world as a sex symbol. Nudity, more or less veiled, has always existed in film. Brigitte's joyful and innocent nudity excited and at the same time irritated some people. Besides, she didn't have to be naked to shock pharisees and moralists.

During one of my battles with the censors, after shooting *And God Created Woman,* one of them criticized me for a scene in which, according to him, Brigitte gets out of bed completely naked in front of her young brother-in-law. I had the scene projected for him. Brigitte was seen getting out of bed dressed in a pullover that half covered her thighs. The censor believed he had seen her naked and is convinced, to this day, that before the screening I replaced the scene showing Brigitte naked with one of her clothed.

I did not invent Brigitte Bardot. I simply helped her to blossom, to learn her craft, while remaining true to herself. I was able to shield her from the ossification of ready-made rules which in films, as in other professions, often destroy the most original talents by bringing them into line. Above all, I provided her with a role that was a perfect marriage between a fictional character and the person she was in real life. At some moment in the career of all great stars there is the miracle of a role which seems made for them. For Brigitte it was Juliette in *And God Created Woman*. She had already made sixteen films. Her seventeenth made her a star.

Brigitte had a tendency to close the door on reporters and photographers. She spent her life standing up journalists from all over the world. I fixed things up and helped her as best I could in her relations with the press.

She herself never sought publicity. But it is a fact that she always created an event.

Brigitte had accepted a secondary part in an English film, *Doctor at Sea*, starring Dirk Bogarde. It was a tasteful comedy, but certainly not the film event of the year. The production company had followed the usual procedure: a photo of the French starlet and a short biography had been sent to all the press. None of her films had been seen in London, but people there undoubtedly knew her name. The first surprise was to find, instead of the half-dozen or so journalists expected, more than thirty congregated in the Dorchester Hotel suite reserved for the press conference. Brigitte was late. I'd been unable to get her to leave her room that day (she was feeling "rotten"). By the time she made it to the conference room, the petits fours had disappeared and the few bottles of champagne had long been emptied. I could feel ill-temper in the air. But again a miracle occurred. Brigitte's magnetism took effect. She had put on a simple jersey sheath dress that fitted her like a glove. It was modest and indecent at the same time. The photographers used up their rolls of film. They forgot, or forgave, her for the fact that she was late and there was no more champagne.

A journalist asked her, "What was the best day of your life?"

"A night," she replied.

Another: "Who is the person you admire most?"

Reply: "Sir Isaac Newton."

"Why?"

"He discovered that bodies attract each other."

Laughter.

"Are there people that you detest?"

Reply: "Doctors who practice vivisection on animals and President Eisenhower for having sent the Rosenbergs to the electric chair."

She also had stock replies that hit home. For example: "When a man has many mistresses, people say he's a Don Juan. When a woman has many lovers, they say she's a whore."

The next day she was on the front page of the *Daily Telegraph*, the *Evening Express* and the *Guardian*. Ten other papers had published her photo and were talking of the "French kitten."

I took Brigitte to dinner at a very posh private club. She had been warned that the English like their meat over-done and she had looked up the translation of the word *saignant* (rare) in the dictionary. The translation given was "bloody."

A very British, very dignified maitre d'hotel took the order.

"I want a steak," said Brigitte. "But a bloody steak."

The maitre d'hotel didn't bat an eyelid. Leaning over towards Brigitte, he suggested, in an even tone, "With some fucking potatoes, perhaps?"

*B*ETWEEN the year we were married and the summer of 1954, Brigitte made a comedy with a French director and a spaghetti melodrama in Italy. She learned more about acting when she accepted two small parts in Anatole Litvak's *Act of Love*, with Kirk Douglas, and *Royal Affairs in Versailles* by Sacha Guitry.

She had now found her own style. She let her hair fall down her shoulders, or tied it in a pony tail, and wore a fringe, while decolleté blouses revealed the curves of her breasts and shoulders. She accentuated her tiny waist and wore her skirts just about the knee so that an edge of her frilly petticoat was showing. She wore no stockings with her casual flat sandals. In France, Italy and England, in fact in all the nonsocialist European countries, in the countryside and in the cities, there were thousands of copies of Brigitte.

In 1954 Brigitte and I went to Rome. Robert Wise had just chosen her to play Rosanna Podesta's confidante in *Helen of Troy*, an American-Italian superproduction. It was the Rome of *la dolce vita* that Fellini would immortalize a few years later. Stars from all over the world could be found in Cinecittà, the Hollywood on the Tiber. We lived in a room with a terrace on the seventh floor of the Hotel de la Ville, at the top of the Spanish Steps. From our windows we had a view of the beautiful rooftops of the sacred city, undulating like a sea of ochre and pink to the horizon.

It was a brief, happy period, which we shared with Italian, French, English and American friends. We went to nightclubs, of course, but I remember most the dinners, when we were serenaded by guitars, the long walks at night through the narrow streets of the Trastevere, the midnight dips at Ostia in the pure waters of the Mediterranean, not yet polluted by tar and chemical wastes. Drugs were not yet a ''must'' and there was nothing artificial about this Roman paradise.

Our friend Daniel Gélin had seduced and abducted a ravishing German-Swiss girl of seventeen from a Swiss boarding school near Geneva. This excessively romantic dream girl suffered because of her lover's eventful life and infidelities. She had left family and country and was running the risk of being picked up by the police because of her great love. In Rome, she quickly realized that she was part of Gélin's harem. One night she arrived in tears at the Hotel de la Ville with nothing except a small suitcase, and asked if we could put her up.

''My poor darling,'' said Brigitte, ''we would really like

you to stay, but we've only one bed. It's big, mind you. There's room for three in it."

And that was how I came to share my bed with Brigitte Bardot and Ursula Andress for a week. I know my readers will be disappointed, but the three of us didn't even flirt, let alone make love. Brigitte had never been drawn to group sex. I was actually rather frustrated—but what pleasure it was just looking at them! One morning, I remember, I was sitting on the terrace where breakfast had just been served. The French windows were wide open and the sun was streaming through to the bed where Brigitte and Ursula were resting their naked golden bodies unashamedly in the heat of summer. They were whispering secrets to each other and giggling. Neither in films nor in the presence of great masterpieces in museums have I ever felt such a rush of emotion for art as I felt then.

I had to leave Rome and Brigitte two weeks before the end of filming. Herve Mille at *Paris-Match* had noticed my absence.

I was driving along the Via Aurelia toward the French border when two young girls carrying heavy luggage thumbed a ride as I passed them. I stopped and asked where they were heading.

"Nice."

Maria was dark and voluptuous, not to say plump. A little common, she had fleshy lips, buttocks constantly moving under her clinging skirt and dark eyes that seemed to swallow what they saw. Her father owned a small bistro in Venice.

Francesca was a tall blonde with an oval face like a Botticelli and green eyes that were naive or perverse, depending on her mood. She was very beautiful. Her husband was a blower in the Murano glass factory.

One was running from her family, the other from her

husband. On Lido Beach in Venice they had met a fifty-year-old man who had claimed to be head of production at the Victorine film studios in Nice. They were expected in Nice by this "Mr. Robert" who was going to make film stars of them. With their savings they had paid for train fare and then for the bus to Pisa. They were exhausted, sweating and convinced that a dazzling film career awaited them. But first they had to get to Nice. There was one major problem: neither of them had a passport.

We stopped off at the best hotel in San Remo. (*Paris-Match* did not pay its journalists well, but the expense accounts were generous.) The receptionist turned up his nose when he saw my two hitchhikers, but fifty thousand lire slipped into his hand brought back the smile and unctuousness of his profession.

I had dinner and champagne sent up to my suite. Maria began talking about her life of poverty and her jealous father who would slip his hands between her thighs when she served drinks at the bar. She told me of her mother who thought that her breast cancer was God's punishment for the fact that she had not been a virgin when she married, and of her brothers who picked fights with any man who showed signs of an erection after dancing with her.

Francesca told me of her timid husband, who, before their marriage, would masturbate in the lavatory when he came to see her. One day when she walked into the bathroom to brush her hair, she caught him with his trousers open, his penis in his hand. Hearing loud laughter, her father went to the bathroom. Francesca was not responsible for the young man's indecent conduct, but in her father's eyes she was sullied. There was only one way to put things right: marriage. She didn't love Franco but she married him. The timid onanist turned out to be a jealous tyrant. He beat her when she wore makeup or when one of his friends looked at her at the dinner table. She was pregnant for two months and had a miscarriage. "God punished you because the child wasn't mine," he said. When she came home from the hospital, he beat her furiously. And since she was hemorrhaging, he forced her to drink her own blood. "Drink the blood of sin," he screamed, stuffing her bloodsoaked bandages in her mouth.

I was uneasy and yet fascinated listening to this angel-faced woman tell such horror stories as if they were everyday domestic problems. Maria found it all very amusing.

Later in the evening she began flicking through a copy of the magazine *Grazia,* which had been left on the table, and she noticed a picture of Brigitte Bardot and her husband that had been taken on the Via Veneto by a paparazzo. My social standing suddenly skyrocketed: they were in the presence of BB's husband!

Maria ran to the bathroom. Two minutes later she came back wearing only her bra and panties, her hair drawn back in a pony tail. She did a very good, but for me painful, imitation of La Bardot. The fleshy, common, sincere, grotesque Italian girl had chosen the wrong director to impress. She seemed to have walked straight out of a Fellini film. I don't have the cruelty of that hallucinatory Catholic genius. I didn't know how to tell Maria that she had chosen the wrong profession. She would not have believed me anyway.

Francesca sighed, "I'm not sexy" (she pronounced it "sexchy"). "I'll never make it."

After one glass of champagne they went to their room. They had left the door open, and I joined them. They were naked under the sheets. Suddenly they became shy, but they were nevertheless determined to repay the ride, the champagne and their first night in a palace with the only commodity they had: their bodies. Perhaps they were also stimulated by the thought of making love to Brigitte Bardot's husband. I sat on the edge of the bed, and we discussed the difficulty of getting across the border without a passport. I advised them to take a country lane north of the main highway. During the war I had helped Jews and Resistance fighters cross the Swiss frontier, so I had some experience in this domain. Maria didn't find the prospect of a fifteen- or twenty-kilometer walk appealing.

"Not with the suitcases," she said. "We'll swipe a boat in the port. And when we get to Nice we'll write to the owner of the boat to come and get it."

I offered to take the luggage in my car, but Maria clung to her idea of a boat.

In the morning, I took them to the port and watched them leave with their suitcases. They were so vulnerable, yet confident of a glorious future. They were victims of films and magazines. But, I thought to myself, above all they were victims of their backgrounds and a morality of bygone days.

*T*HE day after I returned to Paris, Gaston Bonheur, the poet, and an editor of *Match,* called me to his office.

"Mr. Roux questions the bill you ran up at the hotel in San Remo," he began. Mr. Roux was the accountant to whom we submitted our expense vouchers. He respected me the way a police officer respects a talented thief, but dreamed of catching me red-handed.

I began one of my mathematically unassailable explanations, much envied by my colleagues, but Gaston Bonheur interrupted my very first words: "Save your imagination for Mr. Roux. I've called you here for another reason. I think you might have put your finger on an international story. Perhaps a scoop."

He had just received a call from the DST (the French secret service). The day before, a Riva, which had been stolen in San Remo, had been caught in a storm and had been shipwrecked on the rocky coast between Menton and Nice. It would have been a rather ordinary incident if the owner of the boat hadn't been a Yugoslav believed to be working for Marshal Tito's secret police. The bodies of two young Italian girls, whose suitcases had been found on the boat, had been recovered by the police, not far from the shipwreck. In one girl's bag they had found a name and address: Roger Vadim, 79, rue Chardon-Lagache.

I told the whole story to Gaston Bonheur, who agreed that it was highly unlikely that my hitchhikers were really new Mata Haris.

Nevertheless I had to go to Nice to give a report to the police and to identify the bodies. The young girls were almost unrecognizable, but I had no doubt as to their identity. One was the Botticelli whom I had held in my arms; the other was Brigitte Bardot's fan.

That incident had a direct influence on Brigitte's and my career. The moment I got back to Paris I asked for an indefinite leave from the magazine, without pay.

The main reason for my decision was Maria and her sudden admiration for me on learning that I was BB's husband. I now felt an urgent need to make a name for myself. My cocker spaniel, Clown, who only had his shiny coat and charming nature to recommend him, was better known than I was. I often dined with Brigitte at the Élysée-Matignon, where the show-business elite congregated. One evening Brigitte rang me there to say that she would be going directly home from the theater. I left my table to go to the coatroom. Since no one was there, I decided to collect my own coat and noticed the label that had been attached to the lining. "Mr. Clown," it said. The checkroom girl knew Brigitte's name and her dog's name, but not mine. "Mr. Bardot" would not have upset me; "Mr. Clown" amused me. But the incident, no doubt, remained in my subconscious, and Maria had activated a release mechanism. The title of Prince Consort suddenly seemed intolerable. I was not cut out merely to observe and report on events, but to create stories.

The time had come to begin serious work.

☆ *8* ☆

*B*RIGITTE seemed to be in danger of becoming an eternal starlet. She could only find lead roles in mediocre films directed by mediocre directors. Two of these productions, however, were box-office hits in Europe. But if they made money for the producers, they did little to enhance Brigitte's image as an actress. The great directors, Marc Allégret, of *The Future Stars* with Jean Marais, and René Clair, of *The Great Maneuver* with Gérard Philipe, offered her only small parts.

Having left *Paris-Match,* I devoted all my time to writing screenplays. Stubbornness and talent always pay off in the long run. I owed my first success to Jean Cocteau. Marc Allégret was going to direct a film based on Louise Vilmorin's charming novel *Julietta* for Pierre Braunberger, the producer who had rejected Brigitte after her first screen test. The deal was built around the name of Jean Marais, who was very close to Jean Cocteau. A week before shooting, however, Jean Marais turned down the screenplay. This was a catastrophe for the producer, who had already sold the film. Allégret asked me to help him out and rewrite the screenplay. Jean Marais asked Jean Cocteau if he could trust Marc

Allégret's young screenwriter. Cocteau said, "Vadim? You can say yes. With your eyes closed." I modified and rewrote the dialogue within a few days. The film was a big success. I had suggested Brigitte for the female lead. But despite Marc Allégret's support, they used a star of the day named Dany Robin.

In the film world everything soon is common knowledge. When Mr. Senamaud, a producer of B films, heard about my miraculous intervention, he asked me to rewrite the screenplay of a project which had already been sold in Italy, but which Jean Bretonnière (an operetta singer in vogue in 1955), the star they had in mind for the lead, didn't like. I agreed to do it under two conditions: Brigitte Bardot would play the principal character, and the director would be Michel Boisrond, René Clair's first assistant director. It was not yet the era of the inspired children of the *nouvelle vague*. Michel Boisrond was halfway between an established filmmaker and an unknown. If they couldn't have the master, they would accept his pupil.

For the first time, Brigitte played a character written for her, in modern language; and she had a classically trained director who was making his first film. *Mam'zelle Pigalle* was a success. One might say that it was the French equivalent of a Doris Day film, but with a bolder, more liberated edge.

Then I wrote another comedy for Marc Allégret called *Please, Mr. Balzac*. It was a hack job, based on an "original idea" by the producer, which was anything but original. A young well-bred girl, chased out of the house by her parents, arrives in Paris without a dime and gets a job as a stripper in a night club. I changed the plot and wrote a rather amusing, romantic and sexy story. Our friend, the remarkable actor Daniel Gélin, played the male lead.

For the third time I won a silver medal. In Hollywood this would have assured me a screenwriting career. In France, screenwriters didn't have the same prestige, and they weren't even reasonably paid. But Brigitte moved from the rank of starlet to the more honorable status of a "bankable" actress. I had won my first battle.

People in the film business knew that I was more than just Allégret's or Boisrond's screenwriter. I took part in conceptualizing and in the direction and often rehearsed the actors. The moment had come for me to move from pen to camera. I was ready. All I needed was opportunity and luck. Opportunity came in the form of Raoul Lévy. A few years older than I, this man, who had charm to spare, exhausted everyone around him with his unusual nervous and intellectual energy. When there was nobody left, he wore himself out. He always knew where to find money and was perhaps the only man who would steal it from his own pocket. One night when he was drunk and knew that he would remember nothing the next day, he opened his safe and took out all the money, about three thousand dollars, which we lost before dawn playing three games of banco against King Farouk at the Aviation Club. The next day Raoul found his safe empty and registered a complaint with the police.

A Belgian of Russian origin, Raoul Lévy had enlisted in the RAF in 1943 and rapidly earned the reputation as the worst navigator in the air force. Thanks to his lack of talent for reading maps and plotting positions, European cows suffered more damage than the Third Reich's war factories. On his last mission he outdid himself. After having dropped bombs a few hundred kilometers from the supposed target, the flying fortress in his care got lost in the fog and soon ran out of fuel. Then Raoul noticed a runway below, and gave the pilot the green light for landing.

"It's Dover," he said. "There's something wrong with the radio. I can't understand what those guys in the control towers are saying."

It was not Dover, but Stuttgart, Germany. Since this exploit occurred only a few weeks before the German surrender, he didn't remain a war prisoner for long.

Raoul Lévy belonged to the vanished race of adventurous producers who loved and understood movies. He didn't have the means to finance a big-budget picture, so he decided to gamble. His two trumps were a young screenwriter named Roger Vadim, and his wife, Brigitte Bardot. He proposed that I write and direct a film starring Brigitte. He had bought the rights to *The Little Genius*, a novel by the nephew of France's greatest lawyer, Maurice Garçon. The story was not very inspiring and I couldn't do much with it. A little discouraged, I went to Rome with Brigitte, who had to meet a producer there to discuss an important project. At least, that is what her agent, Olga Horstig, had told her. But I knew that for Italians everything is always "important."

Now, a year later, we were back in our room in the Hotel de la Ville. Nothing had changed, except that passion had left us. The deterioration of our love had nothing to do with Brigitte's professional success. Fame hadn't changed her. My lack of passion worried her, and she was already seeking the intensity of new and violent desire in other men's eyes. She was horribly tormented by this need. Some nights she would cling to me with desperation in her eyes, troubled by fear and pain at the thought of what was going to happen to our relationship. I knew what she was thinking: Keep me. Don't let me fall in love with someone else. I don't want to. It would be like dying. She was suffering from the happiness disease again. She always wanted everything and more, immediately. Passion was a drug to her. And, as with any drug, she would be enslaved by it all her life.

But I loved her. She was my wife, my daughter and my mistress. We had moments of intense sexual pleasure, but I couldn't be the Grail she wanted. I knew that if she didn't follow her endless search through other men, she would die.

At the Casa del Orso, she met a very seductive Italian guitarist. From our table, I watched her dance. She was radiant and dazzling, exuding that incredible sensuality; she was a woman, animal and a work of art. I was reminded of the young Brigitte from the Studio Walker, doing her enlévés and pirouettes, stretching, sweating and regal.

She remained on the dance floor for more than two hours.

It was then that I remembered an unusual story I had read in the papers about the trial of a young girl who had been the mistress of three brothers, one after the other. She had killed one of them. What struck me was not the murder, but the young criminal's personality, her attitude toward the jury, and the way she replied to the lawyers and the judge. In a flash of inspiration, I had found the subject of my film for Brigitte. I asked for some paper and for the rest of the evening I took notes. When I finished I had my screenplay— ten pages scribbled in haste, as though I had succumbed to automatic writing.

We returned to the hotel around three in the morning. All night Brigitte clung to me like a shipwrecked person to a lifebuoy.

The next day I decided to return to Paris. I knew Brigitte was going to see her guitarist again. It was inevitable. I didn't want lies, false remorse or tears. And I didn't want to suffer needlessly. I drove twenty hours without stopping to Fouquet's, where I found Raoul Lévy.

"Forget about *The Little Genius*," I said, "I have our story."

I spoke for an hour about my ideas. He was convinced.

"Okay," he said. "Do you have a title?"

I didn't find the title until three months later. It was a good one, I think: *And God Created Woman*.

☆ *9* ☆

*B*RIGITTE wanted our marriage to survive, but her affair with the Italian guitarist would set in motion an irreversible chain of events. She started and couldn't stop. She fought with all her strength against this form of inebriation. Despite our breakups, there were rare and precious moments when we regained the ardor and tenderness of the past. But I was not taken in by the mirage. I accepted the end of our marriage as inevitable. Brigitte didn't understand this attitude, which she interpreted as abdication on my part.

There was also a problem about which, unfortunately, I could do nothing. Making love to Brigitte excited me less. I suddenly understood the meaning of the term "fulfilling one's marital duties." It might have been mutual, but weariness was inexcusable on my part when one remembers that at twenty-one Brigitte was at the height of her beauty. Any man would have sold his soul to take my place in bed with her. Some couples develop a new kind of love and harmony after the sexual intensity of their first years together. I knew that with Brigitte this type of shift to a more spiritual love was out of the question. It was all or nothing.

A few years later, she would tell an English magazine, "If only Vadim had been jealous, things might have worked out." Jealousy can serve as a crutch to love that is unsteady— but only for a while. Once the reprieve is over, the separation becomes painful and hostile. If the torments of divorce are drawn out, you part as enemies. I didn't want that at any price.

Indeed, I was jealous, but in my own way—that is, without showing it. I realize that in this domain I am not a good example to follow. I took the elegance of non-jealousy a little too far. This attitude, which springs from a sense of decency and not indifference, has often been taken as the height of cynicism or decadence. "How can a man who loves his wife undress her in full view of the whole world, and worse still, hand her over to other men, in front of the camera?"

I don't become jealous of a woman's physical or even sexual contact with another man. Complicity with another, lying, flirting and romance are what stir jealousy in me. I suffer if the woman I love smiles at another man, or if they touch hands, even if it doesn't lead anywhere, but I am not upset by another man looking at her taking a bath.

Nudity on a set doesn't embarrass me in the least. Many painters have painted nudes of the woman they adored and have exhibited the paintings with pride. What is the difference between a painter's brush and a camera lens? The technicians on the set? Well, there were often visitors in Rubens's or Renoir's studios.

Brigitte was undergoing the first "adult" crisis of her life. She sensed that our marriage was foundering. She held her fate in her hands and it terrified her.

We were stretched out on the sofa listening to "The Little Horse," a song of Brassens'. "You don't love me like you used to," she said abruptly. "What have I done to hurt you?"

I turned the question back to her. "You don't love me like you used to. What have I done to hurt you?"

She thought for a moment. "Perhaps it's no one's fault."

She added, "When Tino died, I knew something terrible would happen to me." Tino, the nightingale that belonged to Madame Ledieu, the concierge, had been eaten by the cat from the police station.

That kind of logic was beyond me, so I kept quiet.

She continued, "It's like your wedding ring. That, too, was a sign. I should have known it."

Brigitte was alluding to its mysterious disappearance. Not used to wearing a ring, I fell into the habit of taking it off and playing with it. One day, in the office of the producer of *Mam'zelle Pigalle,* the ring fell off my finger. For two hours the entire production staff looked for it on their hands and knees, to no avail. It had quite literally disappeared into thin air. A year later, on the eve of this very conversation with Brigitte, I found myself alone in Senamaud's office. Bored, I began fiddling with the key in the drawer of his cherrywood desk. And I found my wedding ring. As in a magic trick at a fair, the ring had slipped onto the key and around the keyhole of the desk. It was impossible to see the gold on the brass. The coincidence was extraordinary. But between saying that and claiming that it was a warning from heaven was a step that I would not have dared to take. Brigitte had no doubts about it.

"It was a sign," she repeated.

"The nightingale and the ring. It sounds like a Chinese tale," I said.

"Or Russian. I should have listened to Granny and been wary of Russians. Dirty Russians!"

She began laughing and kissed me.

We spent a lovely evening performing our "marital duties," which were, for once, conjugal pleasures.

"It's funny," she said suddenly. "We do things backward. Couples who have lived together too long invent games to excite each other. We did that at the beginning. We used to hide naked behind the curtains in the living room. We made love in the snow. Remember Megève? You gave me a little mirror so that I could watch myself making love. When you went away you used to take along nude photos of me. . . . As I grow older I'm becoming terribly normal."

"You just turned twenty-one," I reminded her.

"Yes. That's not too old. Even so, that old bourgeois side of me is taking over."

She sighed.

I didn't remind her that the "bourgeois" girl didn't seem so proper a few weeks earlier in Rome, dancing wildly with her guitarist.

At dawn (around nine o'clock, I mean), the telephone woke me. It was Raoul Lévy.

"Still sleeping?" he asked.

"Yes."

"Can you pack your bags when you're asleep?"

"I've never tried."

"Well, now's your chance. I'll be waiting for you at ten forty-two at the Gare de L'Est, platform twelve. The express for Munich."

A long silence followed.

"Repeat," Raoul said.

"Munich," I said.

"Perfect. Above all, don't be late." He hung up.

"What are you doing?" asked Brigitte, opening her eyes with difficulty.

"Packing a bag."

"A bag? What for? I was very nice last night."

"I'm not leaving. I'm going to Munich."

"If you're not leaving, how can you get to Munich?"

"Raoul's waiting for me at the station."

"What for?"

"I didn't ask him. I was too sleepy."

"You're leaving for Munich and you've no idea why? You guys are crazy."

She turned over and went back to sleep. I met Raoul at the station.

"What about making the film in color and CinemaScope?"

I couldn't believe what I had just heard. At that time in France, it was a sort of miracle that a young man of twenty-six would have the chance to make a feature film. To shoot his first film in color and wide screen seemed impossible. Nevertheless that was my secret ambition. I had ideas about how to use color and the big screen.

"Come on," he said. "I'll explain on the train."

He waited for it to move before he said anything else.

"Columbia is giving me the money to produce the film in color and Scope, on one condition." He hesitated. "They want Curt Jurgens. It's him we're going to see in Munich."

"For which role?" I asked. "The mother?"

The only other important parts in the story were the three brothers, aged 15, 20 and 25, and these had already been cast. Poujouly, who had played the young boy in *Forbidden Games (Les Jeux Interdits)*, was now a young adolescent and was to play the youngest brother. Jean-Louis Trintignant would play the middle brother and Christian Marquand the eldest.

Curt Jurgens was then a great international star but he was over forty. I couldn't see how, with his heavy German accent, he could play a young fisherman from Saint-Tropez.

"Unless we turn it into a slapstick comedy and get Laurel and Hardy for the two other brothers," I suggested.

"You're right," Raoul said. "Jurgens can't play any of the brothers."

He was disappointed, but he hadn't given up his dream. Just before we reached Saarbrücken, our first stop, I was trying to retrieve my suitcase from the luggage rack when Raoul caught my arm.

"I have a great idea. You'll develop the character of the rich arms dealer, with Jurgens in mind for the part."

"Impossible. He'll never accept a secondary role."

" 'Impossible' is not French."

"You're Belgian and I'm half Russian," I remarked.

He laughed, but we stayed on the train.

When we got to Munich, Raoul locked me up in a suite in the Four Seasons Hotel with caviar, smoked salmon and vodka whenever I wanted it. The best perk was Maria, a spectacular call girl who was also a typist. I finished the new version of my screenplay in two days.

Curt Jurgens welcomed us with characteristic elegance and kindness in his superb Bavarian villa on a lake not far from Munich.

He had just signed a four-film contract with a Hollywood studio, but he didn't intend to go to California before the summer.

"I'll read your screenplay this evening," he promised. "If I agree to do it, I can give you four weeks in May."

The next day he phoned us. "I'll do it."

"You see," said Raoul, "miracles do happen. You just have to believe in them—and make them happen!"

Few people have this gift.

When we were actually shooting the film in Nice, I asked Curt what had made him accept a secondary role, with a director who was just beginning his career, while the great masters of film were waiting for him in Hollywood.

"Several reasons," he said. "First, the script. The tone was fresh, very different from the screenplays normally offered me. Brigitte Bardot, of course, intrigues me. I can't quite manage to place her. She's a phenomenon that I wanted to observe at close range. And the Lévy-Vadim team. I had the feeling that it was going to make waves. It would be amusing to be part of the action."

☆ *10* ☆

*A*soft morning light filtered through the curtains. I looked at Brigitte sleeping. With her long golden hair flowing over the pillows and the childish pout of her lips distended by sleep, her face had an innocent, poetic quality.

"When you look at your mate sleeping at night and tears of joy come to your eyes, you know you're really in love," Brigitte had once said to me.

"Do I still love her?" I asked myself. "Yes," was the reply. But it was a different kind of love. I loved her like a daughter, like a child one had to protect. It's strange living with someone and following a daily routine while knowing all the time that the end of the road is at the next turn. Did you ever awaken in the morning in the middle of a fascinating dream and try to recapture it by closing your eyes? That's something of what I was experiencing.

I got out of bed and went to the kitchen to make breakfast: freshly squeezed oranges, tea and buttered toast. When I returned to our bedroom, Brigitte was just opening her eyes. She'd been awakened by Clown's licking her. He was much less respectful of her sleep than I was. I sat on the side of the bed and put the breakfast tray down on the patchwork cover.

"Oh, how nice," she said.

She drank the orange juice and ate the toast with her usual healthy appetite. I never knew her to worry about her diet. When she was hungry, she ate whatever she wanted. She had no concern for the cruel calories, proteins and carbohydrates that enslave the modern woman. She led an active life, but except for the cha-cha and the merengue, she no longer danced, and she had not replaced her abandoned exercises at the Studio Walker with gymnastics or sports. Yet her body remained supple and firm.

She pushed the breakfast tray aside and jumped out of bed. In the summer she slept in the nude, but it was early March, and she wore one of those "antique" nightgowns found in flea markets. Brigitte discovered the charm of nineteenth-century laces and fabrics long before the hippies. She played on the floor with the dog for a while.

I had disappeared into the living room to answer the telephone when she called out to me. "Vava!"

I hurried back to the room and found Brigitte looking at her reflection in the mirror on the door of the wardrobe. When she saw me, she lifted the hem of her nightgown above her breasts.

"Can you still get your hands around my waist?" she asked.

I tried and, by squeezing hard, managed to encircle her waist with my hands, bringing my fingertips together.

"It's still all right," she said.

And off she went to the bathroom, followed by the dog.

WE had a luncheon appointment with Raoul Lévy and Jean-Louis Trintignant at Fouquet's. Brigitte had not yet met the man engaged to play her husband on the screen, and Jean-Louis had never acted in films. I had discovered him in the theater. His rather shy charm, a certain physical magnetism camouflaged by clumsy mannerisms and, of course, his talent, had convinced me that he would be perfect for the role of Michel.

Brigitte stared at him with a critical eye all during the meal. This made him so uncomfortable that he left before coffee arrived. When he was barely out of earshot, Brigitte exclaimed, "He's a clod."

"He's no Brando, but he has a very winning smile," Raoul said.

"One doesn't go to bed with a smile," said Brigitte.

"No one's asking you to go to bed with him," I remarked.

"No. But to pretend to—that's even worse! I could never make anyone believe that I was in love with that guy. You could have found someone else."

Brigitte was headstrong, and you could never change her opinions by discussing them. Luckily, Juliette is not in love with Michel at the beginning of the film; it's only gradually that she gets to know him and becomes attached to him.

"Don't worry," I said to Raoul, who was dismayed by the outcome of the first meeting between Brigitte and Jean-Louis. "Jean-Louis has a lot of charm. I also think he's very shrewd. Brigitte will change her mind about him in time."

Little did I realize how prophetic my words would prove to be.

*T*HE camera first began to roll on *And God Created Woman* on a small beach on the bay of Cannoubiers, not far from Saint-Tropez. The weather was good. I knew exactly what I wanted, and I experienced none of the anxieties that one might expect of a director making his first film. In those days, color and CinemaScope presented technical problems which, far from frightening me, stimulated my imagination. I was surrounded by first-class technicians and by actors chosen in complete agreement with my producer. Like the young Bonaparte at the beginning of his Italian campaign, I felt certain of victory. The doubts that veteran technicians had about working with a novice and with new cinematographic standards were quickly dispelled. Strangely enough, it was Brigitte who gave me problems at the beginning.

Accustomed to playing in films that were amusing, erotic and always superficial, she didn't realize that I would demand a type of authenticity and sincerity that she had never had occasion to express on the screen. To become Juliette she would have to delve into the depths of her being. Undressing in front of a camera had never embarrassed her. But the thought of baring her soul and revealing her most intimate self terrified her. I would mess up her hair before each scene and forbid her to add makeup between shots. She felt naked and vulnerable. She was panic-stricken. I knew that no matter how unpleasant this "psychological strip-tease" might be, it was indispensable to the success of the film—and to her own success. She had grown used to being a starlet. I was creating a star.

It was a week before we could view the rushes in the Victorine studios in Nice. Brigitte was crying when we left the screening room. She thought she looked "ugly," and hated her hairstyle and makeup. We got into my car and drove to the seashore at the end of the Promenade des Anglais. It was late April and the beaches were still deserted. I made her sit down on the pebbles next to me. She had stopped crying, but she was complaining about the mascara stinging her eyes.

"I'm going to look just great this evening with eyes like an opossum."

"What are opossums' eyes like?"

"They are red!"

I had always imagined that opossums' eyes were blue, but I didn't comment.

"And I don't call this a beach. It's more a board with

nails for a fakir or old Englishwomen who never take off their shoes.''

She finally calmed down and even laughed at her temper tantrum.

''Do you remember how you used to feel about your parents?'' I asked her. ''You didn't believe me when I said that one day you'd be happy to have them as friends. But you trusted me.''

''And you were right.''

''Well, trust me now concerning the film. Have I ever harmed you in any way?''

''Yes, but without meaning to,'' she said.

I looked at her, a little shocked, and continued, ''Even if you don't understand why I am asking you to do something on the set, don't resist me. If you do, we'll both lose. And it'll be worse for me than for you. You are already signed up for another film after this one. Your career is not at stake. If I'm wrong, all it will mean for you is a third-rate film that will soon be forgotten. If I'm right, something very important will happen to us. Will you promise to trust me even if you don't agree with everything I ask of you?''

''Yes, I promise,'' Brigitte said.

Although she often changed her mind, Brigitte always kept her real promises.

After three weeks on location in Saint-Tropez, the crew left for Nice to continue shooting in the studios.

Brigitte became comfortable with my style of directing and began to identify more and more with her character to the point where she began to feel in reality Juliette's emotional change toward her husband, Michel, played by Jean-Louis Trintignant. I had tried as far as possible to shoot the script in chronological sequences. Reality caught up with fiction every day.

Brigitte was not yet in love with Jean-Louis, at least not consciously, but a kind of intimate understanding had grown up between them.

I wondered about the filming of the great love scene

between Brigitte and Jean-Louis. She would be naked on the bed. He, naked also, would join her and they would make love.

Brigitte, who had undressed in her dressing room and had slipped into a dressing gown, joined us on the set. She was completely relaxed and laughing with the crew. Jean-Louis seemed tense and ill at ease.

I tried to analyze my feelings objectively and discovered that I was not jealous. I made no connection between what was taking place on the set and reality. It was like leafing through a picture book.

Brigitte took off her dressing gown and stretched out naked on the bed. Jean-Louis, as called for in this scene, stretched out beside her and took her in his arms.

When I said "Cut," they remained motionless. A wardrobe woman covered them with a bathrobe.

Later in the day, I' was shooting another scene. The camera framed Brigitte in close-up as she was standing and kissing Jean-Louis. He knelt down in front of her and his head left the screen. The camera remained on Brigitte, who was supposed to pretend that she was being caressed offscreen (a euphemism for a more intimate place) by her husband. The way she moved her lips, held her breath, closed and opened her eyes, was so realistic that I asked her after the scene, "Were you thinking of Jean-Louis or of me?"

"Neither you nor him," she replied. "I was thinking of the pleasure."

*O*NE day, after lunch, I was strolling with Brigitte through one of the corridors of the Victorine studios when we saw the silhouette of a man walking toward us and treading heavily with the aid of a cane. At first I thought it was Orson Welles; but Welles was not that old, I remembered, changing my impression. When we got closer I recognized Sir Winston Churchill. He was accompanied by a man I knew well, General Corniglion-Molinier.

I greeted the general, who knew Brigitte from having met

her at the rue de Varenne. He introduced us to Churchill. Brigitte was always herself, whether in the presence of her wardrobe woman or the world's great personalities. After the usual exchange of polite formalities there was silence. Churchill's eyes sparkled as he looked at the young actress without speaking. He seemed to be wondering what platitude would come out of this sensual mouth made for love and the screen. By tacit agreement, Corniglion-Molinier and I were careful not to disturb the silence.

"When I was eight years old and heard you on the radio, you frightened me," said Brigitte. "But now you seem rather cute, considering you're a legend."

"Cute" was not a word people normally used to describe Churchill to his face! The great orator remained speechless.

"What are you doing in Nice?" Brigitte asked, in order to fill the silence.

"Painting," replied Churchill. "You are an actress, and I am a painter. We have art in common."

"My father bought one of your landscapes," said Brigitte.

"I don't sell my paintings."

"Well, then your friends do. The painting my father bought has a hill, a parasol pine in the foreground and the sea in the background. Do you remember it?"

"And on the right a broom bush in flower?"

"Yes. Do you like to paint?"

"I love painting. But I shall never go down in history with Cézanne."

"You know, my films are not nearly as good as your paintings. And I never won a war."

"That is no great loss," Churchill concluded.

With a smile resembling a friendly grimace, he went off toward the screening room.

Two days later, General Corniglion-Molinier telephoned me. Churchill had been greatly amused by Brigitte. He wished to see her again and had asked the general to invite her to dinner with mutual friends. At the very last moment,

Brigitte refused to go. I suspected that she had planned to meet Jean-Louis Trintignant that evening.

I am not exactly sure when Brigitte and Jean-Louis made love for the first time. But I realized that they had already become lovers when we were shooting one of the key scenes.

In the story, Juliette is physically in love with the eldest brother, Antoine (played by Christian Marquand). But she married the other brother, Michel, to avoid having to return to the orphanage. Just when she discovers her husband's profound qualities, she begins to love him. Antoine comes back to live with them. Juliette is torn between her desire for happiness and harmony with her husband and her visceral attraction for Antoine. She doesn't want to give in to her physical passion for Antoine, but she knows she will. One night Michel awakes and notices that his wife has left the bedroom. He finds her on the beach, near their home. Here is an extract from the scene:

MICHEL: You're not happy?

(Juliette smiles sadly. Michel caresses her cheek. Suddenly Juliette clutches Michel's shirt. Her face is filled with anguish.)

JULIETTE: You must love me a lot.

MICHEL: But I'm crazy about you.

(Close-up of Juliette.)

JULIETTE: Then tell me. Tell me you love me, say I'm yours, that you need me. Kiss me, Michel. Kiss me!

(Michel is shattered by the tragic intensity in her voice.)

JULIETTE: I'm frightened.

MICHEL: Of what, darling?

(Juliette does not reply. She lets herself slide down on the sand with extraordinary suppleness. Her body is fluid, like water. Her cheek and the corner of her mouth touch the sand.)

JULIETTE *(sweetly and almost calmly):* It's difficult to be happy.

Never before had Brigitte, the actress, been so profoundly honest and desperate. She was really Juliette, who wanted to love her husband and save her marriage but knew that she would never succeed. She was also Brigitte, still attached to her husband and terrified at the idea of leaving him for a man whom she had just met, and whom she could not resist. It was like a world of reflecting mirrors, with Pirandellian subtlety. Jean-Louis Trintignant, her husband in the film, began to represent her husband in real life. When she told him, for the camera, that she was frightened, Brigitte-Juliette was actually speaking to me.

In our bedroom in the Hotel Negresco, after the shoot, I asked her, "He's your lover, isn't he?"

"Yes," she said.

"Do you love him?"

"I'm frightened."

Before going to sleep she murmured, "It's difficult to be happy."

Even to this day, I am not sure whether she had deliberately repeated a phrase from the dialogue of the film, or whether she was saying what she felt.

Our suite in the Hotel Negresco looked onto the sea. Jean-Louis Trintignant, always secretive and slightly Machiavellian, had insisted on staying at an inn in La Colle sur Loup, a very romantic Provençal village in the hills, about fifteen kilometers from Nice. It was there that they had first made love, Brigitte later told me.

"There is nothing less aphrodisiac than making love in front of the camera," she explained to me. "It's like trying to make love with a policeman directing traffic in the Place de la Concorde. He's shouting, 'Move a little to the right; a little to the left; don't show your tongue so much. A little more feeling, please. Close your eyes. Open your eyes.

Don't dribble. For God's sake, don't groan so loudly!' It's horrible if you really like your co-star. So Jean-Louis said, 'We ought to rehearse for ourselves. For our own pleasure.' Talk of rehearsal. It was more like opening night! He had really kept quiet about his talents.''

One might imagine that I was going to take Jean-Louis by the collar and tell him to cool his passion. That was one of the solutions I considered, even though it made little sense. He caught me off guard, however, by threatening her: "If you don't leave your husband and come to live with me, I'll never see you again, ever, once the film is over.''

I found myself in our room in the Negresco with Brigitte, in tears (again!), pleading with me to save her life; that is to say, allow her to join her lover in La Colle sur Loup. It was a delicate situation.

On the one hand, I knew full well that our marriage had no future. So why not let her go with Trintignant, whom I was actually quite fond of, rather than with a guitarist? But, on the other hand, I was the captain of a team whose respect I had earned. What would they think of a director who handed over his wife to her leading man? I could already hear the comments: "It's not enough for him to let his wife be unfaithful. He has to hand her over with free delivery.''

I could understand how a young boy, driven wild by a love that he couldn't handle as a grown man, might lose his head. However, he placed me in an impossible position. If I asked Brigitte not to give in to Trintignant's threats, then the three weeks of shooting that remained would undoubtedly be hell. It was out of the question for me to put myself in the position of imploring my wife's lover to grant me a favor.

"I only ask you to continue living with me until the end of the film," I said to Brigitte.

"I understand," she said.

She spent the night in my arms but couldn't sleep. At eight o'clock in the morning our breakfast was brought in. Brigitte was very pale. She didn't eat.

I had thought things over. If Brigitte was willing to sacrifice her love to protect my image on the set, I should be able to sacrifice my pride.

"You can pack your bags," I told her. "I would always hate myself for having used my marital rights to protect my vanity."

"You've become very pompous," she said, trying to smile.

I took her on my knees and hugged her.

In the evening, after the day's filming, she left in Trintignant's car. I thought that there was little chance that a man who had to resort to Trintignant's manipulations to get a woman would keep her for long. But that idea was no comfort at all to me.

I hadn't spoken of my decision to anyone, not even to my best friend, Christian Marquand. I was to experience one of the greatest surprises of my life. On the set, everyone from the makeup man to the chief electrician, from the director of photography to the lowest member of the crew, every actor, workman and even the walk-ons—all of whom knew, of course—behaved with the most perfect discretion. Not only did they not laugh at me behind my back, but I acquired a flattering reputation as a knight of noble heart.

With the newspapers, it was different. I became a Machiavelli.

*B*RIGITTE was naked.

Trintignant entered the conjugal bedroom. She stood up on the bed, dragging the sheets behind her, opened her arms wide like a bird stretching its wings, and embraced her husband, enveloping him in a gesture of possessiveness. Scene number 152.

"Cut. Very good."

I was not jealous. I wasn't even suffering. On the contrary, the last few weeks of shooting had been a kind of exorcism for me. The deepest pain after separation comes from obsession about the unknown: What are they like together? What do they do when they make love? Does her face look different now when she has an orgasm? As a director, I "spied" legitimately on a love affair which lost all mystery for me because it was out in the open. I neither expected nor wished to get Brigitte back, but I was happy—and, I must admit, a little amused—by this unexpected therapy which spared me the bitterness that usually comes at the end of an affair.

We had returned to Saint-Tropez for the last day of shooting.

Brigitte was living with Jean-Louis, but in a way the umbilical cord between us had not yet been cut. On the set, I was still her older brother and her friend. She confided in me and asked me for advice. It was Jean-Louis who became jealous.

In a way, I had reversed roles with him. I was the conspirator, he the one conspired against. But once the film was over, he would carry off the spoils of war. How would I react at being alone after seven years with Brigitte?

I had rented a Chris-Craft, and I decided to go by sea to the beach where we were shooting. My mother, who had come down from Paris, was with me. In the middle of the bay we ran out of gas. It was an irritating hitch for me, but a disaster for the producer, who couldn't afford an extra day of shooting.

By a lucky coincidence, a fishing boat returning to port happened to notice my signals for help. His engine was too weak to tug the Chris-Craft to harbor. So I asked my mother to wait on the boat so that it would not be boarded and declared derelict.*

---

*French maritime law stipulates that any boat that has been abandoned more than five kilometers from the coast becomes the property of the person who finds it and brings it into port.

"I'll send a rescue boat for you within the hour," I promised her.

The fisherman dropped me off near the set. I asked my first assisant, Paul Feyder (son of the well-known director Jacques Feyder), to call the port authorities.

At 6:30, after the very last sequence had been filmed, I cried, "Cut!"

The umbilical cord binding Brigitte to me had been finally severed.

Brigitte looked at me. "I'd like to talk to you," she said.

"Fine."

"In an hour. At La Ponche. Okay?"

"Yes."

When I arrived in Saint-Tropez, I went straight to the headquarters of the harbor authorities. I was surprised that I hadn't seen my mother all day.

"Did you bring my boat into harbor?" I asked.

"What boat?"

My assistant had forgotten to call the authorities.

I telephoned a friend, Paul Albou, who lent me his boat, which had a powerful motor. At nightfall, I retrieved my mother, who had been stranded about ten kilometers from the coast. I didn't know how to apologize.

"I wasn't at all worried," she replied. "I'm not rich enough for you to hope to benefit from my will. I just did some yoga exercises while I was waiting for you."

We were moving along slowly, at barely five knots, because the Chris-Craft had to be towed behind us.

"I had an appointment with Brigitte at La Ponche," I told my mother. "She must have left Saint-Tropez by now. I wonder what she wanted to say to me."

"She didn't have anything to tell you."

I must have looked a little confused, for my mother added, "Brigitte, like all children, doesn't know what it is to feel remorse. She only wanted to be sure that you still love her."

☆ *11* ☆

*I*T was a surprise.
Instead of the horrible depression that I had
expected, I felt happy, liberated and carefree
once again. The vacations of the past returned, now flavored
with success. It was delightful.

Saint-Tropez was at its height. The beaches were ours.
The restaurants were waiting for us; the Esquinade, the only
nightclub there in those days, existed only for our wild
times. The yellow road of the Wizard of Oz was open. The
curtain rose on the fairy tale with the morning sun and
seemed never to drop. The young, celebrated, wild but very
wise Françoise Sagan once said to me, "You must celebrate
the end of a relationship as they celebrate death in New
Orleans, with singing, laughter and a lot of wine. Love, like
fire, is not meant to be hoarded. It is to be spent."

Sometimes, in the uncertain hours of dusk, I felt just a
touch of melancholy. But always waiting was the night full
of faces and short-lived promises.

It was at the Esquinade that I met a timid, sentimental
young German who was dazzled by our bunch and ready to
do anything to be accepted as one of us. I was the only one

who spoke to him. He said his name was Gunter Sachs von Opel. I think he would have died on the spot if anyone had told him that ten years later, to the very day, he would become Brigitte Bardot's third husband.

Where was Brigitte? What was she doing?

Every week I went to Nice to work on the editing of the film with Madame Victoria Spiri-Mercanton, known as Toto. This remarkable Russian-born woman was distinguished for having made nonflammable celluloid the standard of France. After two fires, during which she lost a director, who was burned alive, as well as part of her hair and her favorite coat, the government passed a law assuring safety in the editing rooms. "You understand," Toto said to me in her heavy Slavic accent, "I wanted to be able to smoke my Gauloises while working."

Feared by all of the directors, but much sought after because one can't dispense with genius, she reigned over her moviola like a queen. When people heard that a novice who had just directed his first film was going to fall under her iron rule, even those who envied me were worried. But it was love at first sight for me and Toto, even though she was twenty years older than me. Shouting matches were frequent, as she didn't mince words. But we loved and understood each other.

It was through Toto that I got news of Brigitte. "She came to the studios with that actor of hers to see some of the editing."

"Did you show her anything?"

"I said, Show me the authorization signed by the director."

"How did she seem?"

"I asked her how life was with her new plaything. She replied that she was wildly happy, and burst into tears."

"She's always crying. That means nothing."

"That means she loves you. And it's proof that she's a complete idiot. She wanted to know where you were living in Saint-Tropez. I gave her hell and told her to leave you alone, and that you'd find better women. She kissed me and ran to the actor, who'd been blowing the horn of his car for over ten minutes."

After sitting in front of the moviola for two hours screaming at each other and sulking, we finally agreed on the changes to be made in the scene on the beach. We went to the studio bar for a few drinks. Suddenly Toto handed me a piece of paper. "You're old enough to be responsible for your stupidity," she said.

I read the letter: "Vava, nothing's like it was before. But how was it before? I'm happy now. I don't cry any more. The stains you see on this note aren't tears. They're Charles Trenet's fault. Do you remember the song 'It's Raining on My Heart'?—I'm tired of the rain messing up my letters. I had problems at the hotel we're at in Italy because they still call me Madame Plemiannikov. When we're old we'll have gray hair and we'll listen to Piaf's song 'Padam, Padam.' —Clown sends you kisses. Sophie."

I ordered another whiskey.

"You're not going to become drunk or, even worse, sentimental," Toto said.

"I'm lucid when drunk and I'm cynical when sentimental," I replied.

"Tomorrow," said Toto, "they're moving the equipment. I'm going to finish the editing at Billancourt. And I'll need you."

"I'll be in Paris in a week."

"Meanwhile, don't play the fool with your Lancia. I have a beautiful film in the can, and it doesn't deserve to be an orphan."

It was the first compliment I'd received on the film. Coming from Toto, it was worth as much as an Oscar.

After my holiday, I returned to Paris. The rue Chardon-Lagache belonged to the past, so I rented a room on the third floor of the Hotel Bellman.

☆ *12* ☆

*T*HE rain was coming down so hard that I was forced to drive with low beams. At three in the morning, in early autumn, highway 7 was deserted, except for an occasional passing truck that blinded me with its headlights. I hadn't taken my foot off the accelerator since leaving Paris. I had already spent my salary for *And God Created Woman* (three thousand dollars) and even had to sell my little monster, the Lancia Sport 2000, the week before and was now driving my old Simca Aronde, which reached a maximum of 130 kilometers per hour. All the same, my speed was excessive at night on a road that was as slippery as a skating rink.

Thanks to having driven hundreds of thousands of miles all over Europe as a journalist for *Paris-Match*, I had the skills and reflexes of a race driver. I had escaped near-fatal situations hundreds of times, but on this particular night I was crazy. Only the instinct of survival and my conditioned reflexes kept me on the road. By continually tempting the devil, I discouraged my guardian angel, who abandoned me in the middle of a turn. I did a four-wheel skid. One, two, three spins. I didn't touch the brakes; the car slid sideways toward the ditch. I steered into the skid, hit the accelerator, straightened up at the last second, bounded over the ditch and shot between two trees at over eighty kilometers an hour. Bounding again into a field of alfalfa, I hit my head on the roof of the car. Suddenly all was quiet. The engine had stalled, though the headlights were still lit. I was bogged down in the mud, but there was no great damage. Taking a deep breath, I stretched my legs, rested my neck on the back of the seat and decided to go to sleep.

And then I "saw" myself.

It wasn't the first time that I'd experienced being split into two different selves. I could "see" myself inside the car, my head flung back, my eyes closed. The windshield wipers were still working. The rain blurred my image between each movement back and forth. That hallucination (I use the word "hallucination" so as not to irritate scientifically minded readers) lasted a little less than a minute. I opened my eyes, realizing that I should turn off the headlights and the windshield wipers so as not to run down the battery.

By now I was perfectly calm but bewildered by this sudden fit of madness—a sort of possession—that had brutally struck me like a thunderbolt from a cloudless sky. I didn't understand it then, nor do I understand it now.

I had made plans to meet Raoul Lévy at the Élysée-Matignon for dinner. I was in a relaxed, good mood, and we talked about my next film, *No Sun in Venice (Sait-on Jamais)*, based on an unpublished novel that I had written a few years earlier. It was a love story with a detective-story framework. Raoul insisted on changing the action, which in the novel took place in Paris, to Italy. He wanted Françoise Arnoul, a young French star much sought after at the time, to play the female lead.

"It's better for your career not to work exclusively with Brigitte," he said to me.

I wasn't taken in. I guessed his real motive. *And God Created Woman* had not yet come out, and Raoul, who was a shrewd producer, wanted to give us a second chance in case the film wasn't well received.

At that moment Brigitte and Trintignant entered the restaurant. It was an unexpected meeting because the two of them were rarely seen in public together. Since the end of the filming at Saint-Tropez, they had managed to keep their idyll hidden from the press. I had seen them again once before one afternoon in the studio when they came to dub the film, but in a purely professional context.

I kissed Brigitte on the cheeks and said hello to Jean-Louis. They withdrew to the table reserved for them.

At Raoul's invitation, they joined us for coffee. Jean-Louis was not very talkative. Brigitte was friendly and almost tender. I had the feeling that she wanted to talk and be alone with me. No doubt it was my imagination.

They left before ten o'clock.

I left the restaurant soon afterward, got in my Aronde, which I'd parked in true Parisian style with two wheels on the sidewalk, and headed for Saint-Germain-des-Prés, hoping to meet some friends at La Discothèque or Castel's. I don't know what demon prompted me but I did a U turn, drove along the banks of the Seine to the Boulevard Exelmans and stopped at the corner of the rue Chardon-Lagache. I wanted to see the windows of the apartment where I had lived with Brigitte for more than four years.

At that moment, the front door opened. Brigitte came out of the building holding Clown on a leash with one hand and leaning on Trintignant's shoulder with the other. They walked along the pavement talking. I couldn't make out what they were saying.

Through the window on the third floor I could see that the light in the bedroom had been left on. For the first time, I realized with a visceral, physical awareness that she was making love and, even worse, sleeping, with another man in our bed. Clown had perhaps smelled me because he was tugging at the leash. I was very fond of Clown; he was part of the family. I watched the couple and the little cocker spaniel. I felt as though I was the victim of a theft, a betrayal, a crime of injured love.

I snapped.

It was brutal, irrational and totally unexpected. I wasn't exactly sad, but I was dominated by a self that I had never met until then. My actions were dictated to me from then on; stripped of all willpower, I functioned on automatic pilot.

I drove to the Bellman at reasonable speed, stopping for red lights. At the hotel, I went up to my room and wrote two letters, one for Raoul, one for Brigitte. However, Raoul never gave Brigitte the letter I had written for her. He returned it to me unopened with a photocopy of my letter to him, to make me feel "ashamed." Poor Raoul. Fifteen years later he would shoot himself in the stomach with a hunting rifle because of a miserable love affair.

On rereading these letters, I am not ashamed, but I don't understand. Even my handwriting was different.

"Raoul: I'm very fond of you. I'm leaving this evening. I'll either end up dead under a tree or reach my destination by beating the automobile Tour de France's record." A page of extravagant sentimentality followed.

The letter to Brigitte wasn't dated. It ended as follows: "You can think of me as a stranger. I come from another country. You will never know that country. One goes there with the heart."

I went to 24 rue du Boccador where Raoul Lévy lived and put the two letters in his mailbox.

When I left the building, rain was pouring down on Paris as though it were the first day of the Great Flood. In the time it took me to run to my car (only a few meters away) I was completely soaked.

Ten minutes later, I passed the Porte d'Italie and took highway 7, the road to the sun.

In a field of alfalfa, twenty kilometers from Avallon, I stretched out on the imitation-leather seat and slept. The sun had been out for more than an hour when I awoke. I got out of the car and pissed on the clover, which steamed from the morning heat. A farmer on his way to work agreed to pull my stuck car back on the road with his tractor. I drove on a few kilometers and stopped at a village for a delicious breakfast: café au lait and buttered country bread. "Nevermore," I said to myself, like Edgar Allan Poe's raven. "Nevermore."

Since then I have suffered many heartaches. I have been bewildered, lonely and sometimes profoundly unhappy, but I have never allowed this unknown demon to take possession of my body and soul again. I became immune to the virus forever.

Everyone creates his own signposts. For me, the invisible frontier separating France from the Mediterranean runs through Montélimar, the city famous for its nougat, a candy of honey and almonds. Just before the first bakery-candy shop, a billboard caught my eye. Under the heading *France Soir* (the most important afternoon daily) I read, "Please send me news of you. Sophie." These electronic billboards were new to France. I wondered if it was an advertising slogan for a film or a best-seller. Twenty kilometers farther on, I read the same phrase, "Please send me news of you. Sophie."

Coming into Avallon, I saw a third message near the Shell station where I stopped to fill up.

"It's new, this advertising," I said to the attendant.

"It's not advertising," he replied. "It's a new idea from *France Soir* for notifying drivers when something has happened at home. Yesterday, it said, 'Armand. Come back. Urgent. Rose is worse.' Once it was a garage owner trying to warn a client that he had forgotten to fix the steering box. It was too late. The guy had already smashed into a tree while driving out of Cavaillon."

I suddenly understood: Sophie was Brigitte. She was sending me a message.

I called Raoul immediately.

"Are you okay?" he asked.

"Yes, I'm fine. Don't worry about your film. I was an ass. I'm sorry."

I had assumed that Raoul would find my letters in the morning when he got his mail. But instead of going home after dinner, as expected, he had stayed on late at Fouquet's with an American producer. Around midnight, out of habit, he opened his mailbox and found the two letters. Worried, with just cause, he called Brigitte, hoping that she would have news of me. Pierre Lazareff, the editor in chief of *France Soir*, was a friend of ours. Brigitte got him out of bed at one o'clock to order his paper to send her message to me on its two hundred billboards spread across France.

"I don't want to call Brigitte," I told Raoul. "Tell her immediately that the old Russian has survived his depression. And sing her an old Brassens song for me. You know the one: 'I'm a Bad Seed.' "

Raoul, who couldn't even sing "Frère Jacques" in tune, remained silent on the other end of the line.

I began again. "I'm going to stay with my mother in Toulon for a while. I'll finish the screenplay there."

"I'll need it in three weeks. Can you finish it by then?"

"I'll try," I replied.

MY mother is a feminist who has never marched in the streets and never insulted the oppressor sex with manifestos, newspaper articles or vituperations on television. She did better. Long before the various movements for women's liberation were organized and thrust into the limelight, she had practiced her own philosophy of equality. After my father's premature death in 1938, she found herself without money or professional skills. She had only herself to rely on. Yet, even though she was beautiful and didn't lack suitors, she never gave a moment's thought to remarrying just to assure her children of an education and material comforts. She took all sorts of jobs: worker in a chemical plant, weaver at home, farm worker, director of a youth hostel. When she married the architect Gerald Hanning during the German occupation, it was for love. At the time he was just another mouth to feed. She never sacrificed her love life for her children, nor her children for her love life.

She taught me to respect women without fearing them, and that love is the most important human quality. She was strong but she never tried to impose her ideas on others. She was also vulnerable and tender. It was from her that I acquired a taste for the independence and freedom that go along with respect for others. And it is due in part to my mother that I have always helped the women I loved to flower and fulfill themselves without fearing that their success would estrange them from me.

"You can't keep love in a prison," my mother always said to me.

A few years after the war, she and Gerald Hanning separated. He had become obsessed by his work. His projects in Algeria and other African countries forced him to travel continually, and, even though my mother loved him, she couldn't resign herself to being just part of an architect's luggage. Nevertheless, at the age of fifty a woman does not generally choose to live alone, unless she has considerable means. At that time, my sister and I were in no position to help her financially.

She found new jobs for herself such as antiques dealer and director of documentaries. At the end of 1956 she had just moved to Toulon, where she started up a business in prefabricated houses.

I hadn't told her of my arrival, since I didn't know myself that I would be fleeing Paris. It didn't surprise her too much to see me arrive without any luggage. She guessed the reason for my impromptu trip but didn't ask any questions. She knew that I would talk to her about it in time. If I felt the need to.

All she said was, "I've been worried about you for a few days. I've been using the darning egg." For my mother "using the darning egg" meant to project a thread of mental love to protect my sister and me whenever she thought we were in pain or in danger. It was a sort of spiritual cocoon.

I felt peaceful. My energy returned and I finished the screenplay for *No Sun in Venice* in three weeks.

The evening before I left, my mother read the cards for me: "I see a lot of happiness for you, dear. And a big success. Not immediately. But not too far off, either. I see a blonde. A stranger."

It wasn't a blonde who was waiting for me in Paris, however, but the film critics. On November 28, *And God Created Woman* was given an exclusive showing at the Cinéma Normandie on the Champs-Élysées.

☆ *13* ☆

I was sitting in the first row of the balcony. Brigitte was on my left and Raoul on my right. Trintignant and the other actors (except for Jurgens, who was filming in Hollywood) were there too, naturally.

When the lights came on again in the large theater, the public and the invited guests clapped. It was better than polite applause but not really enthusiastic. Many people who had enjoyed the film didn't know what to say, and they shook their heads when others spoke of pornography or an outrage to decency. But I was pleased by sincere and warm compliments from men like Jacques Prévert, Jean Cocteau and Boris Vian. Cocteau called Brigitte "the most feminine of androgynous beings."

Jacques Prévert, who had found the film enchanting, thought that it was precisely because of its qualities—a new, bold tone and a very free style, unusual on the screen—that the critics would try to demolish it. "Fools are predictable, but not really dangerous," he said to me. "They contradict themselves shamelessly at every change in fashion."

Brigitte, who had already seen the film, thought she was

"all right," but she never imagined for a moment that it would have an impact on her career.

Raoul Lévy's party to celebrate the premiere was very successful. Brigitte was at her best—charming and funny—and we had a pleasant chat. Before leaving, she kissed me and whispered, "Fool, you gave us a dreadful fright."

She was alluding to my stormy departure for Toulon.

I didn't read the critics' reviews in the days that followed—a habit I've kept to this day. I had no desire to allow myself to be pulled apart by hasty, rarely objective judgments. With distance, one can calmly read the reviews—the good, the bad and the malicious—and eventually get something positive out of them.

Raoul, however, had pounced on the papers.

"I've read eleven reviews," he said. "Not one that's really good. I don't have much faith in journalists, but this is disturbing."

He opened the newspaper *Combat*.

"Listen to this: ' . . . it would be better if you went to a striptease show in Pigalle. The girls are at least as delectable [as Miss Bardot] and often more so. They know how to move with subtlety. Eroticism is an art.' "

I quote that passage because it was typical. Nudity and eroticism were acceptable in a woman only if she was an object. A whore or a prostitute was even better. You paid her and she became your property. She wasn't dangerous. The writer of the article wouldn't be alarmed by a prostitute in Pigalle because she presented no challenge to his male prerogatives. But Brigitte frightened him. And since he couldn't bite, he barked. In conclusion he wrote, "Fortunately for the French reputation for charm, this film has no chance of ever being shown abroad."

A great prophet!

The next day a young film critic wrote a long article on *And God Created Woman* in one of the most respected art magazines of the day. He loved the film and predicted that it would leave its mark on its time and open up new horizons for French cinema, which was becoming fossilized. His name was François Truffaut.

At the beginning of January 1957, Raoul asked me to accompany him to the United States to meet some Columbia Pictures executives. Since the New York office was in no hurry to give a definite date for the film's American release, he decided to go to Hollywood first to visit Harry Cohn, the head of the studio.

Jet engines had not yet replaced propellers and so the journey lasted twenty-four hours, with stops in Greenland and Canada. Before landing at Winnipeg, two of the engines caught fire and the pilot had to land with half of his propellers feathered. The incident upset Raoul (even though he had been an RAF war hero), and he decided to take a sleeping pill for the rest of the journey. He had bought some Nembutal suppositories in Paris, but not realizing that they were to be taken rectally, he carefully sucked on three. They made him so ill that he couldn't close his eyes during the rest of the trip.

Harry Cohn had invited us to dinner at his home in Bel-Air. I knew the famous mogul's reputation as a tyrant and I was anxious to meet him. For me, Harry Cohn was the embodiment of legendary Hollywood, one of the last surviving pioneers of film's epic age. He proved to be charming. He was interested in the state of European cinema and sorry that Brigitte had not come.

"I can recognize a director when I see one. It doesn't happen often."

He predicted a great future for me. After the pettiness and insults from Parisian hack reviewers, these words from one of Hollywood's greats were heartening.

And God Created Woman had become Harry Cohn's baby. To counter those in the New York office who didn't want to distribute the film, saying that it didn't have a chance at the box office, he organized a series of private screenings to which he invited the biggest stars, a few producers and carefully chosen journalists. The enormous success of the screenings convinced Harry Cohn that he was right about the film.

"Tomorrow I'll order those pigheaded idiots to get on with the release," he told us.

At one o'clock in the morning we were still talking. He decided to give me a present to commemorate our meeting. He picked up the telephone and woke up the head of the prop department.

"Get a viewfinder," he said, "and have it engraved 'For Roger Vadim from Harry Cohn.' I'll be waiting for it at my house."

I can't imagine the president of Columbia getting one of his employees out of bed in the middle of the night today to satisfy a whim. He would have a strike on his hands the next day. But in 1957, Harry Cohn could still indulge in that kind of extravagant behavior. They brought him the view-finder, engraved in his own handwriting, at 2:30 A.M.

"It will bring you good luck, my friend," he said.

Harry Cohn himself never imagined that the film would be such an enormous success or that it would create the scandal that it did. Committees for the protection of morals were organized in more than a hundred cities to prevent the film from being shown. Sermons in churches and temples threatened Brigitte and those responsible for the "satanic" work with eternal fires of hell. Women were the most indignant. They were not defending sexual equality but protecting the traditional institutions of marriage and the weaker sex in society.

This violent reaction was not limited to America. It was widespread in Europe, Africa and Japan as well. The commotion that the film created abroad had a boomerang effect in France. A strange phenomenon occurred: six months after the opening in Paris, the movie houses which had been empty were now packed.

Nevertheless, the uproar was based on a misunderstanding. People pretended to be shocked by Brigitte's nudity and unabashed sensuality when, in fact, they were attacking a film that spoke without hypocrisy of a woman's right to enjoy sex, a right up to that point reserved for men. It wasn't Brigitte's sunbathing in the nude that enraged "decent" people. It was the scene where Brigitte makes love with her husband after the religious ceremony, while her parents and friends wait for her in the dining room. It was an amused Brigitte without complexes, appearing in her dressing gown, her lips puffy from lovemaking, picking a few apples and chicken legs to feed her lover—for even though married she treated her husband like her lover and not her master. And the mother asking, "How is he feeling?" and Brigitte's reply, "Not bad." And the mother, "Why doesn't he come down? Does he need anything?" And Brigitte, "I'm taking care of that." She went to the staircase with her tray and, even though the sun was still in mid-sky, said goodnight to the guests.

Films have always had more impact on people than the written word. Simone de Beauvoir's books never frightened anyone. Brigitte's appearance on-screen, embodying a woman judged "amoral," caused panic.

As a consequence of the excessive reactions, the film was a hit. In a few months Brigitte had become an international star.

People have often wondered why an actress who had attained that degree of celebrity never made a film in Hollywood. I have already told the story of Brigitte begging her agent to cancel the contract she had signed with Warner Brothers. Another example deserves mention.

In March 1958, Raoul and I met Frank Sinatra at the Fontainebleau Hotel in Miami to discuss doing a musical with him and Brigitte to be called *Paris by Night*. We had the outline of the story but the screenplay hadn't been written yet. Sinatra was interested and had agreed to let me tell him the story. Many people have talked of his capricious nature, his moodiness and violent outbursts; with us he was always courteous and friendly. He took us with him wherever he went. Unfortunately, between his bodyguards, lawyers, agents, pretty blondes, musicians, friends—among them Ella Fitzgerald, who was preparing for a concert—and a few mysterious people straight out of a Mario Puzo novel, it was difficult to find a moment when we could be alone. A week went by, a week of which I have wonderful memories, and I had still not been able to tell him the story of *Paris by Night*. He decided to leave Miami for Chicago, where he had to attend two major events: the funeral of Mike Todd, who had just been killed in a plane crash over Mexico; and the rematch between Carmen Basilio and Sugar Ray Robinson. We went with Sinatra to Chicago.

After the funeral we went back to his hotel suite with a Mafia "godfather" and a Chicago police chief. A limousine took us to the stadium where the boxing match was to take place. A police motorcycle escort cleared the way through traffic. I sat on a foldaway seat opposite the police chief. I forget his name but let's call him John. John had been to Paris several times. He liked the city and we got on well.

After the superb fifteen-round match, won by Robinson, Sinatra took us to a restaurant in Cicero where the godfather was giving a dinner to celebrate his daughter's engagement. Italian cooking, plenty of wine, spicy stories, general good humor—Coppola didn't make up anything. While waiting for the espresso, John took me aside. "Follow me," he said. "I'm going to show you something that you don't have in Paris."

We went out to the street and John took me to a café—a restaurant that had nothing special about it except that it seemed a little grimy. John pushed open a door behind the bar and we found ourselves in a small, smoke-filled room with about twenty male spectators watching with devouring eyes a stripper peel off her clothes without much conviction. She had a good body, but I told John that we had girls in Paris just as pretty.

"Wait," he said to me.

I waited, and indeed, something totally unimaginable for the United States in 1958 occurred: The girl took off everything. John was right: Even in Pigalle the dancers kept their G-strings on.

After a few leaps and an awkward split, the girl left the stage, making way for her friend.

Out of politeness, I made an exaggerated show of surprise. John was delighted.

"Naturally," he said, "this kind of show is completely illegal." He laughed and added, "But if you're with me, you have nothing to worry about."

Later he told me that it was not the mayor but the police who were responsible for censoring films in Chicago.

"I have had twelve minutes cut from *And God Created Woman*. I thought I'd keep the cuttings as a souvenir, but since you're a friend, I'm going to order the censored scenes restored and shown in all the movie houses."

That's how some people, at least in Chicago, got to see my film in its uncensored version.

The next day Frank Sinatra gave me a two-hour private interview. He liked my story. He decided to trust me and asked his agent to give me a letter of agreement, confirming his intention to make *Paris by Night* with Brigitte Bardot.

Everyone had told us that we'd get nothing from Sinatra, but once again Raoul had taken a chance and succeeded.

I began to work immediately with the screenwriter, Harry Kurnitz. The Sinatra-Bardot team was sure to be a hit, and Raoul had no difficulty financing the film. Unfortunately he hadn't foreseen one small detail. Brigitte demanded a contract stating that the film would be shot entirely in Paris. She wouldn't hear of Hollywood. Sinatra refused to spend four months in Paris. He, too, had his habits. So *Paris by Night* was never made.

☆ *14* ☆

*T*HE skeletal dogs that wandered around the studio canteen were hovering in the shade of the walls. The *policía* on duty, their revolvers in heavy holsters and rifles on their shoulders, were sweltering in weighty woolen uniforms. One of the electricians on the set, which was not air-conditioned, fainted, seriously burning himself on the white-hot metal of the arc lights. Since lunch, it had been necessary to redo Brigitte Bardot's makeup three times. At the beginning of August 1957, Madrid was experiencing its worst heat wave in this century.

Making a film under these conditions was agony, and the Spanish temperament, already fiery by nature, was near the danger level. The smallest incident turned into drama. Under Franco's iron dictatorship the workers were treated like serfs. Without a trace of humaneness, the Spanish production manager abused the rights conferred on him by statutes that benefited only those with power. When we had to shoot late into the night, on overtime, to finish a sequence, the workers and technicians, citing the infernal working conditions caused by the heat, asked for a second break for dinner and a bonus for night work. They were refused. As in the times of Roman galleys, revolt was simmering among the slaves. At two o'clock in the morning, with the last take done, we were about to leave the set when the production manager made a serious error. He called one of men, who was threatening to quit, ''a frail woman expecting her period''—a supreme insult for a race absurdly proud of its male prerogatives. The crew formed a semicircle and slowly advanced toward the production manager and his team.

Suddenly, the man panicked and made a sign to the *policía* on duty to call his colleagues. Half a dozen of them invaded the set, rifles aimed. Also overcome by the heat, these trigger-happy men were only waiting for an excuse to fire into the crowd. A single raised fist risked setting off a massacre. But we were still, according to the rules of their ritual, at the stage of verbal confrontation.

''*Que sí!*'' cried the workers.

''*Que no!*'' replied the production manager.

''*Que sí!*''

''*Que no!*''

I tried to intervene. I shook up the production manager. But nobody wanted to give in. I tried to talk to the highest-ranking police officer. He pushed me aside roughly.

Brigitte could have escaped and taken refuge in her dressing room, but she was incensed at the way the crew had been treated, and by remaining she showed support for the men. It was a courageous attitude which, unfortunately, would change nothing. Tempers were too high.

Then she had a stroke of genius. She began singing the tune of a then popular samba, imitating the adversaries: ''*Que sí, Que no. . . .*'' My assistant, Serge Marquand (Christian's brother), always quick-witted and funny, understood Brigitte's intentions immediately. He began a duet with her: ''*Que sí! Que no! Que sí! Que no. . . .*''

And Brigitte: ''*Que sí! Que no. . . .*''

Dancing the samba, they rushed into the midst of the workers and the police, whose rifles were already raised to their shoulders. After a moment of wavering, a few workers began to sing along with Brigitte. *"Que sí! Que no!"* They were soon followed by the others. The production manager and his team also played the game. *"Que sí. Que no!"*

The drama became a musical comedy. Since the honor of both sides was intact, there was no bloodshed. I gave my word that I would get their bonus from the producer, Raoul Lévy, who was expected in Madrid the next day.

These men, many of whom remembered the bloodbaths of the civil war, were not easily moved, but they were deeply impressed by Brigitte's courage and quick thinking. The next day, in her dressing room, she found a bouquet of flowers with a card signed by every member of the crew, from the sweeper to the first assistant, Pedro Vidal.

"Never have I found flowers so flattering," she said to me.

I had not made a film with Brigitte since our separation (we were still not legally divorced). At the beginning of the year I had directed *No Sun in Venice*, which for many film buffs was and has remained my best film. Jean-Luc Godard wrote that my second film had broken with tradition, which for him and others at that time was the highest possible compliment.

Having filled the coffers of the French treasury with dollars, made my producers rich, propelled Brigitte to stardom and opened studio doors to young directors, *And God Created Woman* produced an opportunity that Raoul Lévy was not going to let pass. Another Bardot-Vadim film was a must. He acquired the rights to a French novel entitled *The Night Heaven Fell*. It was a very beautiful love story of a highway robber and a young woman from a good family, set in nineteenth-century Auvergne. Raoul, now part of the envied group of producers with an international reputation, fell into the same trap as his colleagues, forgetting that one does not produce a film as one does automobiles or cans of beans. In order to use Columbia Pictures' pesetas (blocked in Spain by the Spanish government), he decided to transpose the story to present-day Andalusia. He hired a screenwriter named Remi because his detective film had just been a hit in Paris. Remi was a charming man who was behind the times and totally lacking in talent. But I gave in to Raoul. I was under exclusive contract to him, and I didn't want to declare war on this man whom I considered to be a loyal friend. I was convinced that in the course of shooting I could turn this banal script into a good film. Nothing of the sort happened; but I left some magnificent shots of the south of Spain on film. I should have remembered that I was a director, not a painter or photographer.

Meanwhile, Brigitte had gone back to the routine of harmless French comedies. She had made *The Bride Is Much Too Beautiful* and *A Parisienne*.

Her affair with Jean-Louis Trintignant was floundering. Stretched out on a mattress alongside the swimming pool at the Savoy Hotel, she confided to me, "I should have burst into tears when he left for military service. Instead, I thought 'Thank goodness.' "

She had met a famous French singer who was at the pinnacle of his career. (I'll call him X since his romance with Brigitte was not widely covered.) He was as nervous as Jean-Louis was calm, imaginative, a little crazy, with dark eyes and dark hair.

"I don't think I love him," Brigitte said to me. "But I can't live without passion. I need to wait at the end of the phone with my heart throbbing. My poor heart! It doesn't have enough to do pumping all that blood around my veins, it also has to get involved in my love affairs from morning to night."

She laughed rather sadly, as a way of mocking her excessive romanticism. She was alone and vulnerable.

"My Vava," she said, taking my hand, "you're the only one who really knows me." She usually called me Vava or

"You old Russian"; Vadim was reserved for important occasions.

At that moment, a woman whose radiant beauty commanded the attention of every man present walked toward us. She had sunflower-golden hair, eyes so blue that they challenged the blueness of the sky, luminous milk-white skin as soft to the eye as to the touch, a slightly aquiline nose, a mouth as luscious as a candy fruit drop, a body with full, rounded curves. She was the very essence of femininity, but more goddess than pinup, with not a hint of aggressive sexuality. She was wearing a crepe de chine blouse over her bathing suit to cover her stomach, for she was five months pregnant. The child was mine.

She kissed Brigitte and sat down next to us.

It was at the beginning of the year that I had met Annette and her sister, Merete, who was less beautiful but so dynamic and sexy that she scored as many points on the scale of success as her younger sister. The two Danish girls had just arrived in Paris and were driving all the playboys in town crazy. Their father, a country doctor, had committed suicide when his wife left him. At the time the girls were only eight and nine years old. Their mother, a nurse, lived with a strange, brilliant man, a scholar, a hero of the resistance against the Nazis. But the couple were poor, and as soon as the two girls were old enough they left Copenhagen to earn a living. Annette was a baby-sitter and a water-skiing instructor in England. Merete posed for fashion magazines. Although they arrived in Paris broke, they refused the advances of Aly Khan, the Maharajah of Baroda, Darryl Zanuck and other millionaires seeking glamorous mistresses. They said no to relationships based on money and no to marriages of convenience. That made them even more sought after.

One evening, I was at the discotheque in the rue Saint-Benoit with Annette and Merete. I got up to dance a "slow" with the eldest (we had been flirting for the last few days) when Annette said in her indescribable accent, "No, you're dancing with me."

The two sisters had already discussed which one would have me. I never learned what their criteria were, but Annette won. Convinced that women are always the ones who decide but allow men the illusion that they have won them over, I imagined that this Scandinavian transaction saved time for all three of us. I danced with Annette, took her home to the Bellman that very evening, made love to her and fell in love. We were together from then on. She accompanied me to Venice, where I was shooting *No Sun in Venice*.

On January 26, we celebrated my birthday with the crew at the Grappa di Uva. Afterward, in the elevator at the Hotel Bauer Grünwald, one of the palaces looking onto the Grand Canal, Annette took off her cashmere cardigan and began unbuttoning her blouse. She continued her striptease on the third floor, shedding right and left her shoes, skirt, bra and, finally, panties, as we walked along the corridor to our room. When we reached our door she was as naked as Eve in the Garden of Eden. She turned toward me and held out her open hands. A small serpent, a treasure, was coiled up in them. A fine gold chain and a plaque with the inscription "To my Pipfugl."

Pipfugl means sparrow in Danish. It was the nickname she had given me. "You're the richest and the poorest of men," she said. "Like a sparrow, you see everything and understand everything, but you have no bank account." Later I learned that she had sold her two Balenciaga dresses to buy that present for me.

I didn't have time to thank her, for people were already getting out of the elevator. "Where's the key?" screamed Annette.

I had forgotten to take it from the concierge. It was too late to collect the clothes strewn across the corridor. A couple of American tourists walked past us. Annette smiled at them with the graciousness of a woman in an evening gown returning from a ball apologizing for not recognizing fellow guests. I took off my jacket, and she put it around her shoulders.

And then I heard the laughter.

It was the full-blown, generous, apocalyptic laughter of Orson Welles, who was coming toward us followed by a bellboy carrying his luggage. On the way he had picked up the feminine garments scattered along the corridor that had caused him to burst out laughing. He recognized me and greeted me with a friendly nod, but he kept his eyes on Annette. This lover of beauty did not indulge in hollow compliments. His eyes squinting mischievously, he said to Annette, who was clutching my jacket to her breast to hide her nudity as best she could, "Please excuse my appearance. I've been driving since Milan, and I'm not very presentable."

"Our door's closed," stammered Annette. "We forgot the key."

"Please come and change in my room."

Without waiting for a response, Orson walked off to his suite.

While Annette was dressing, he opened a magnum of Dom Ruinart. We had already drunk quite a bit at the Grappa di Uva, and knowing Welles's capacity for drinking, I was preparing for a long night.

He was in Venice to meet an Italian producer about a project that seemed to excite him but which—again—never saw the light of day.

He asked Annette if she had a part in my film.

"I don't want to be in film," she said.

"One day," he told her, "you'll realize that life is really cinema. And cinema is an excellent way of getting back at life."

I was shooting early the next morning, but Orson Welles refused to let us leave. He opened another magnum.

"The sun washes away your sins," he said. "Let's wait for the sun to come up."

At sunrise, I went back to my room with Annette. We were still making love when my assistant knocked on the door.

SIX months later, in Madrid, Annette, who was already pregnant, found the heat hard to bear. Brigitte told me that I was a monster of selfishness to make her stay with me. She talked some sense into the mother-to-be, who decided to go back to her parents in Copenhagen. Annette cried when we said goodbye at the airport.

Without love or a lover, Brigitte was depressed. We spent a few enjoyable evenings with the Gypsies and flamenco dancers, but most of the time she withdrew into her little entourage: Odette, her makeup artist, her hairdresser, her understudy and other admirers ready to cater to her slightest wish. I knew Brigitte's tendency to surround herself with yes-men and yes-women. "Yes, Bribri, you're so right" and "Let them talk, Bribri. They understand nothing" was what she wanted to hear.

Encouraged by success, she often lacked discipline or intellectual courage in her choice of films. But, as I have already said, she didn't really like the cinema. She was not capricious. During the shooting of *The Night Heaven Fell*, her conduct was exemplary, despite especially trying working conditions.

After Annette left, we moved from Madrid to Torremolinos, a small Andalusian village which was to become a kind of Spanish Saint-Tropez a few years later.

A small donkey had an important role in the film. Brigitte, who had named it Romeo, couldn't bear the idea of returning it to its owner; she bought Romeo, but the hotel wouldn't let it sleep in the garage. So Brigitte kept it in her room.

One morning she sent for me. I found her in bed, the donkey stretched out beside her on the covers.

"Vadim," she said to me, "I can't take any more. I'm going back to Paris. I'm counting on you to look after Romeo."

She left the next day.

She was completely exhausted and couldn't have finished the film without a few weeks' rest. I had several sequences to shoot without her. In any case, Raoul was covered by insurance.

I took charge of Romeo.

After the heat wave came the worst flood ever recorded for the south of Spain: six hundred dead in Valencia and two thousand drowned in Málaga and on the Andalusian coast. The floods in California that receive so much publicity on television and the front pages of newspapers every spring are nothing compared to the deluge that submerged a third of Spain that year.

Serge Marquand and I took refuge on the first floor of our house, watching the deluge with a sort of morbid fascination. We saw an old man sitting on a chair carried along by a stream of rushing water. He noticed us, and made wild gestures with one hand, holding onto the armrest with his other hand.

"We must help him," I said.

"No," said Serge. "He's just saying 'Hi.'"

Nevertheless, Serge was the first one to jump into the water. I followed him. We managed to catch the old man and his chair on top of a porch and raise him up to the window of the second floor. The house had been evacuated. While we were coughing up water and mud, the old man began insulting us.

"Son of a bitch! My chair. You've lost my chair."

Soaked and half drowned, he demanded that we pay him 125 pesetas, the tourist rates, for the chair.

"What d'you think?" asked Serge. "Do we throw him back in?"

The flood had been replaced by a fine, dull rain that never stopped. The film had been interrupted, of course. Raoul

Lévy talked to Lloyd's about the possibility of finishing it in a studio in Nice.

I had become ill. For three days I had a violent fever and hiccoughed incessantly. I was sure that I would succumb to infernal hiccoughing, like Pius XII. Raoul sent for Dr. Louis Schwartz, my doctor in Paris, He diagnosed a pancreas infection caused by some bizarre virus that normally attacks bovine animals, especially donkeys. I was too weak to get even with Romeo, but I enjoyed thinking up cruel tortures for him when I got well. After prescribing antibiotic injections that had to be administered intravenously, Dr. Schwartz went back to Paris. The Spanish nurse was a Carmelite nun who didn't believe in injections, and she made me swallow the vial with orange juice. She said El Caudillo Franco stayed young because he refused injections. "God created seven orifices in man: the ears, the nose, the mouth, the penis, and the anus; and two more for women—the breasts." She added: "I'm not going to pierce another hole and let the devil enter you. You seem like a nice young man and deserve to die a Christian."

Thanks to the nurse's principles, my fever didn't go down.

I was living in a small house about three hundred meters from the hotel in which the telephone was located. One night I woke up sweating profusely and obsessed with the thought that I must call Brigitte. I got up despite a fever of more than 103°F. After ten days in bed, I could hardly stand. I walked through the rain, along the beach, and kept thinking, I must call Brigitte. At the hotel I went into the office and sat in the chair by the switchboard; the operator had gone to bed long ago. I pushed in the plugs on the prewar board and got through to the exchange at Málaga, then Madrid, and finally, by some miracle, Brigitte's number in her apartment on Avenue Paul Doumer. No reply. I called her parents, and by another miracle (sometimes you had to wait two days for the call between Spain and Paris) got her father on the end of the line.

"Am I waking you?" I asked.

"No," said Pilou. "I was playing the musical saw."

Of all the musical instruments, the musical saw is the most archaic. It consists of a carpenter's saw which one bends and unbends while rubbing it with a sort of bow.

"Pilou," I said, "go over to Brigitte's place."

"Why? She just had dinner with us. She seemed to be in a very good mood."

"Please. Call her. If she doesn't answer, go and see her."

He didn't understand the reasons for my sudden anxiety. But he promised he would do what I asked.

When he telephoned Brigitte he was surprised that there was no answer. On leaving him, Brigitte had said she was going home to sleep.

He walked the hundred meters from the rue de la Pompe to Brigitte's building. On the eighth floor, he rang and knocked on the door, but there was still no answer. He was about to leave when he smelled gas. He broke down the door to the apartment and found Brigitte lying in the bathroom. The taps of the heating system had been opened all the way. It wasn't the gas, but Veronal pills that had rendered her unconscious. Pilou opened the windows and called for a doctor. Brigitte didn't have to be taken to a hospital. Her father had arrived in time.

Three days after this incident, my fever having broken, I returned to Paris. Like a good Christian, I had forgiven Romeo my pancreas infection, and he made the trip in a truck that was transporting props to the Victorine studios. I went to see Brigitte, who seemed in a better state than when she left Torremolinos.

"Almost as soon as I got back to Paris, I saw X again," she said. "He told me how much he loved me, with beautiful words. But he hid me in his dressing room at the theater, out of the sight of journalists. He was afraid to be seen with me in a restaurant; suddenly we were just eating sandwiches from a delicatessen. One day he took me home with him. Just as we were making love, a friend came back.

There I was running around picking up my clothes scattered about the room and rushing to the bathroom. It was like a Feydeau comedy. He left with his friend without a word. He could have excused himself with something like 'I forgot my keys' and come back and said to me 'I'm sorry, I must leave. I'll call you this evening.' But he didn't even do that. I sat there saying to myself, 'I'm nothing, nothing.' It's not that being nothing is all that difficult. It was the pretense that killed me. He's a poet who is brilliant when he talks and sings about love, and there I was, the star, the impossible dream of married men, as journalists call me, the French Marilyn Monroe, the sex symbol, sitting on a bathtub. What a symbol! I wished that my admirers and the women who were afraid that I would steal their husbands could have seen me! I was sad and furious, but I couldn't help laughing when I suddenly saw myself in the mirror. I thought of X who would be singing 'My hands like a cross. . . .' Men are something. Tender, madly in love, etcetera. Just words. When things go wrong, they take to their heels. I was humiliated, disappointed, unhappy. I wanted to die. And then, when I got home, I did something foolish. Not really because of X, but because of everything. Perhaps because it's hard to be a woman, or simply a human being. I love life too much to endure its betrayals.''

W E finished filming *The Night Heaven Fell* a month later in Nice.

Annette came back from Copenhagen, eight months pregnant and more beautiful than ever.

On the seventh of December 1957, which was also her birthday, she gave birth to a seven-and-a-half-pound little girl at the American Hospital in Neuilly. I registered her at the city hall as Nathalie Plemiannikov.

☆ 15 ☆

*A*S far as my career was concerned, the year 1958 was noteworthy for one thing: bad luck. I had barely returned from the United States when I learned that Brigitte refused to go to Hollywood to shoot *Paris by Night*. Raoul, who was rarely at a loss for ideas, suggested replacing the musical with a rather amusing story based on a young, naive but resourceful girl who becomes involved, reluctantly, with the Resistance. Brigitte was terrified at the idea of making a parachute jump, but she accepted the leading role in *Babette Goes to War* with the assurance that a stuntwoman would take her place when necessary.

Raoul set me to work on the subject with an American screenwriter.

A few days later *The Night Heaven Fell* was released. As I'd feared, it was not a success.

I had been working on the screenplay of *Babette* for over a month when I learned from the papers that Raoul Lévy had signed up another director, Christian Jacques, to direct the film. That Raoul, disappointed by the failure of our latest film, became frightened and decided to replace me, I

might have accepted; even the fact that he wasn't courageous enough to tell me himself. But Brigitte's attitude
surprised me. She could at least have picked up the phone
and told me that she found Christian Jacques a more suitable
director for this type of film. I was upset and sad. But I
stopped feeling sorry for myself very quickly and decided
not to ask for any explanations from my two friends.

During the summer I stayed with Annette and the baby in
a farm surrounded by vines and eucalyptus trees that I had
rented near Saint-Tropez. Fortunately I am able to forget
bad luck when I know I can't do anything about it. I
banished *The Night Heaven Fell, Paris by Night* and *Babette*
from my mind. Happiness was Annette and Nathalie. I
discovered that I had a gift for raising children. I adored
Nathalie and watched the stirrings of her little mind with
great excitement. I was able to feed her, change her and tell
by the way she cried whether she had a tummyache or just
wanted attention. I invented hundreds of games for her and
spoke to her like a human being, avoiding the stupid baby
talk that some parents use to address their children. We
didn't have a nanny. A neighbor, who also had children,
looked after the baby when we went out at night. In the
daytime we took Nathalie everywhere.

Claude Bourillot, a friend who was a racing-car driver,
had introduced me to the old Commendatore Enrico Ferrari.
His factory was launching a new model of sports car. Real
monsters, considering the times: 320 horsepower, 12 cylin-
ders and a maximum speed of 180 miles per hour. I had
agreed to participate in several races and rallies, including
the Tour de France, in exchange for which the commendatore
had sold me his latest model for the price of an assembly-
line Ford. It was the only Ferrari in Saint-Tropez that year.
Françoise Sagan drove an Aston-Martin and Gunter Sachs
(Brigitte's future husband) a Mercedes 300 SL.

There had been a great change in the shy tourist I had met
two summers before at the Esquinade. Sachs had inherited

the German Opel factories and now controlled an enormous fortune. He was fun-loving and spent his money like a king.

Our "gang" had a terrible reputation. The public, ill-informed by certain publications of true or false scandals, pictured us as debauched bons vivants. We were, in fact, overgrown college students, a little too exuberant for our age, and harmlessly anarchistic. We organized water jousting between Rivas. Our weapons were fire extinguishers that covered our adversaries with cold chemical foam. We went waterskiing on the wet sand, along the Pampelonne bay, shocking vacationers. At the Epi-Plage, a private restaurant and club where celebrities and stars of the moment congregated, our epic custard-pie fights would have made Laurel and Hardy and Mack Sennett green with envy. Nothing really nasty, as anyone can see.

What made Saint-Tropez special was the happy mixture of old and young, wealth and class. A person with no money could live like a millionaire and a millionaire could have fun living like a bohemian.

It is strange to think that such a liberated era remained officially puritanical. Policemen harried nudists even if they were out of sight behind bushes.

*T*HERE was a bend in the road three hundred yards from Tahiti beach. In the middle of the bend was a huge parasol pine. The road forked right and left of this tree.

One evening, the sound of a Ferrari drowned out the crickets. The roar of a Mercedes 300 SL replied to the Ferrari.

It was a duel.

The standing start was 150 yards from the parasol pine. At the signal (a whistle) the two racing cars took off. The two drivers couldn't see each other and each had to guess whether his adversary would take the right or the left fork.

If they found themselves on the same side of the tree, it would have been impossible to cross to the other turning—there would be a head-on collision unless one yielded by hurtling into the ditch. It was a sort of Russian roulette with cars, except that the loser had some chance of staying alive.

Gunter was at the wheel of the 300 SL. I was driving the Ferrari.

The judges were Françoise Sagan, Christian and Serge Marquand, Maurice Ronet and Marlon Brando.

There was a maximum of three rounds to the joust.

First round: The Ferrari went to the left; the Mercedes to the right.

Second round: The Mercedes and Ferrari came face to face on the left side of the tree. There was a split second to make a decision. Gunter lost his nerve and landed in the ditch. He wasn't hurt. The next day, a truck with a crane hauled the 300 SL from the ditch. It would cost Gunter a few thousand francs to repaint and repair the chassis—a pittance for him.

Gunter gave a big dinner at the Restaurant Tahiti to congratulate the winner and console the loser. There was an exotic orchestra and one hundred and fifty guests. In the middle of the feast, four Tahitian women brought out an enormous dish. At first we thought it was a giant salmon or a swordfish. But the fish was not edible: What was served was a naked Serge Marquand skillfully decorated with mayonnaise and small gherkins.

"*P*IPFUGL—will you give the baby a bath?" Annette cried from the kitchen where she was preparing a *fregadele,* a Danish national dish (meatballs with herbs).

"Not tonight. I'm on strike."

Before putting the *fregadele* into the oven, Annette wanted to wash and feed the baby. She picked up Nathalie, now nine months old, who was sitting on my knee chewing on the last pages of the Agatha Christie novel I was reading.

"You'll never know who killed the Marquise," said Annette, laughing.

She went off to the bathroom. Five minutes later I heard a scream. I waited, without moving. Annette ran out carrying Nathalie, naked, under her arm. She was holding out an air-mail letter which I had slipped into Nathalie's diapers. It read:

Nonotte [In private I often called her Nenette]:
   Are you free on Saturday, 27th August?
   I have to go to the town hall at La Londe-Les-Maures, and afterward lunch at La Reine Jeanne at Paul-Louis. Your presence would be greatly appreciated.
With love,
PIPFUGL

P.S. Our friend, the Count de Leusse, mayor of La Londe, will be waiting for me at the town hall to perform a marriage.

*A*NNETTE and I had talked about getting married. But she had never insisted on it. However, I knew through friends of hers that nothing in the world could please her more. Living with a man whose profession brought him in constant contact with many actresses, well-known and unknown, pestered by the press, which presented her as Roger Vadim's latest discovery, she didn't have a very secure self-image. Also, contrary to common belief, Danes were rather traditional about marriage. In Copenhagen an unwed mother was not exactly a symbol of female independence. Then there was the image of Bardot, to whom everyone compared her—a difficult legacy to accept. I had married Brigitte. "Why doesn't he marry you?" journalists would ask her. "Brigitte didn't even have a child with him."

I don't consider marriage either a proof of love or a social necessity. In fact, I have so little respect for the institution that I don't even have any prejudices against it. But if signing a document at a town hall can simplify your life, lower your taxes, protect your children at school from gossip or reassure your wife that you love her, why not? I married Brigitte because her parents wouldn't let us live together otherwise. If marriage would make Annette happy, it was a present I was able to give her.

To the despair of the lawyers, who couldn't use it for their own publicity, my divorce from Brigitte had been practically a formality. But the French law stipulated that one could not remarry until nine months after the separation had been ratified by the judge. That waiting period had just elapsed.

Our marriage was a real celebration, without protocol or tradition. I chose to get married in the small village of La Londe because its mayor, Count de Leusse, a former officer of the Foreign Legion, whom I had met in Morocco when I was a reporter, agreed to bend the law and not publish the marriage banns. (In France, the names of the future spouses must be posted on the door of the town hall three weeks before the marriage.) Thus we would be able to get married discreetly and avoid the press, which would have turned the ceremony into a circus.

Annette was more golden and radiant than ever. She wore a summer dress the same color as her eyes. I was wearing a cotton jacket and trousers, and no tie. Our friends were present. They had kept our marriage a secret, so there were no photos (except for the official town hall photo) and no television cameras.

After the ceremony they showered us with rice, and the whole wedding party, including the mayor, went to La Reine Jeanne, the villa that belonged to our friend Commander Paul-Louis Weiller. It had been built on a beach at the foot of the Bregançon fortress, where traditionally the President of France spends two weeks' vacation every year.

Paul-Louis Weiller was undoubtedly the last of the great patrons. He had sold Air France to the government; whenever a plane took off or landed he received a royalty. But this represented only a small part of his income.

The marriage luncheon at La Reine Jeanne was held at a large table set up in a natural grotto. We all wore bathing suits. The only people fully dressed were the Duke and Duchess of Windsor, who, as neighbors, came along for coffee.

F OR the next few days, Mr. and Mrs. Plemiannikov were invaded. Our farmhouse in the vineyards was besieged. The photographers had climbed up the eucalyptus trees, and even onto the roof. It was difficult to go out to a restaurant, and impossible to walk in the port. Strange how the signature at the bottom of a document could create such a commotion. I knew that just as a baby quickly tires of a new toy, the press would soon lose interest in us. It was the best solution to let them be.

At the beginning of September, Annette, Nathalie and I moved into the Hotel des Ambassadeurs de Hollande, which belonged to our friend Paul-Louis Weiller, at 72 rue Vieille du Temple. Pierre Feroz, Carlo Ponti's host and secretary, came to see me to propose making a film based on Choderlos de Laclos's erotic novel *Les Liaisons Dangereuses*. René Clément, Luchino Visconti, Alberto Lattuada and others had already shown an interest in making a film of this book but had abandoned the project. The novel, which had created a scandal in the eighteenth century when it was written but now was included in the curriculum of students of literature in many European universities, posed difficult problems for a director. However, I was very excited at the idea of showing that as far as morality was concerned, little had changed since the king of France banned publication of Laclos's novel in 1778. But for the public to understand this, the work would have to be transposed from the eighteenth to the twentieth century.

My response to Carlo Ponti was, "Okay, if I can set the film in Paris in 1959."

Sophia Loren's husband, a great producer, but not exactly an innovator, sold the idea to Edmond Tenoudji, president of Marceau Films. I worked on three different versions of the screenplay with three different screenwriters. I was almost finished but not completely satisfied. Then I thought of Roger Vailland, who had just won the Prix Goncourt (the equivalent of the Pulitzer). He agreed to write additional dialogue. Gérard Philipe and Jeanne Moreau were signed up for the two leading roles. I still had to find an actress capable of playing the model wife, of angelic beauty, whose sacrifice of faith and honor for her passion leads to her death.

With the same ingenuity she had shown when she wanted to get married, Annette let me know that she wanted to be an actress. Working together could only bring us closer. She worried about spending her life at home, waiting for the director to return, like Penelope waiting for Ulysses. Besides, she didn't know how to weave.

Annette was physically perfect for the role so I decided to do a screen test. She was far from being an actress, but her accent, charm and malleability convinced me that she could do the part—a difficult undertaking, because she would be playing opposite two of the greatest actors in French films.

*B*RIGITTE had made an excellent film, directed by Claude Autant-Lara, called *Love Is My Profession* (*En cas de Malheur*). Her co-star was Jean Gabin. The critics were already reveling in the idea of the pretty little doll being swallowed by the ogre. They were disappointed. Gabin's talent did not smother Brigitte's spontaneity. For the first time they spoke of Brigitte's qualities as an actress and not only of her charm.

While I was finishing *Les Liaisons Dangereuses*, Brigitte

was making *Babette Goes to War*. Her co-star was Jacques Charrier, a young actor who was beginning to make a name for himself. He was handsome in a traditional way, and he managed to look like a well-bred scoundrel.

She fell in love once again.

At the end of May she phoned. "Vadim, I must see you."

If she called me Vadim it was serious. "Shall we have dinner together?"

"No. Not in a restaurant. If Jacques finds out, he'll kill me."

"At your place?"

"Are you crazy?"

We decided to meet at the Porte de la Muette near the Bois de Boulogne.

"You'll recognize me," said Brigitte, "because I'll be holding a yellow rose."

I arrived in my Ferrari. It was raining. Brigitte was already there, waiting for me. I recall that she was warmly dressed. She sat next to me in the Ferrari.

"It's happened," she said.

"You're pregnant?"

"Yes. For a month."

We weren't far from her apartment on the Avenue Paul Doumer. She kept looking uneasily out the rear window of the car. I started the Ferrari, went into second gear and drove slowly towards the Bois.

"No one understands why I'm so scared of being a mother," she said. "Neither my parents nor my friends. You're the only one I can talk to."

"Do you want an address in Switzerland?"

"No. I'm trying to think of all the possibilities." She turned and stared at me. "Am I a monster?"

"Because you're frightened of having children?"

"Yes. I like dogs, cats, mice and doves, but I'm really afraid of children."

"Being afraid doesn't mean that you can't love."

"What you're saying isn't stupid. But it doesn't change the problem. Should I keep the child or get an abortion?"

For an instant I panicked. I love children, and my instinct told me to advise her against an abortion. But what if she hated the child after it was born? What if she died in childbirth? Was I going to cause nothing but unhappiness to human beings in the name of morality? No romanticism, I said to myself; subconsciously, she's already decided to keep the child. She just wants reassurance.

"Are you afraid that being pregnant will make you unattractive?"

"Yes. But that's not the real reason."

"Do you love yourself? Or rather, do you respect yourself?"

Silence.

Then: "But I think I'm a lot nicer than three quarters of humanity."

"Then you don't love men?"

"I like them too much, that's my problem."

I repressed a smile and added, "I mean man, mankind."

"I think they're cruel and cowardly . . . the greatest are usually the most wretched. I have never forgotten that Eisenhower, the savior of Europe, killed the Rosenbergs."

"But you loved the Rosenbergs?"

"Because they were victims. I didn't know them."

"Do you love Jacques?" I asked her.

"A good question. Yes. I think I love him. But, thinking you love someone isn't the same as loving them. He wants to marry me. Men are a pain in the neck. They want the looks, sighs and weaknesses that make up love, but they have to put it down on paper. 'Yes' in bed isn't enough for them. They need a contract. Well, if it makes Jacques happy, I'll say 'yes' to the mayor, too."

She looked at my dashboard. "How much did your Ferrari cost?"

"About twenty-five thousand dollars."

"Twenty-five thousand dollars! And you haven't even got a radio. You've been had."

"Actually, I only paid three thousand."

"Did you steal it?"

"No. Publicity. I'm going to do the Tour de France with Bourillot in eight days."

"Are you crazy? I forbid you to do anything like that again." She laughed and added, "Sorry. I forgot we're no longer married."

We were driving along the lake.

"Stop," said Brigitte.

She got out of the car and walked toward the lake, which was dotted with raindrops. She took some dry bread from the pockets of her raincoat and fed the ducks.

I waited for her in the car.

She came back and leaned against it. The window was open.

"We rented a chalet near Chamonix," she said. "Right in the mountains. No neighbors for miles around. It was terribly romantic. We made love all the time. But Jacques used to lock the bathroom door. He really wants to be a father. So here I am—pregnant."

"You must keep the child, Brigitte. If you don't, you'll spend your whole life asking yourself the same question."

"And what if I don't like the child? Or what if he doesn't like me?"

"He'll have a father."

"You're right."

On the eighteenth of June, Brigitte married Jacques Charrier at Louveciennes.

On the eleventh of January 1960, she gave birth to a boy, Nicolas.

☆ *16* ☆

*D*URING the late 1950s, President de Gaulle found himself leading a nation that was traumatized by two unpopular wars—Indochina, then Algeria. He had been elected to power with an overwhelming majority.

Imagine the United States, having suffered the war in Vietnam, facing yet another war, this time only forty-five minutes from its borders by air. The situation was even more painful for the French because two and a half million of them had lived in Algeria for over a century and considered the land in which they had been born part of France. Concern turned to anxiety and demonstrations to open revolt. A good part of the army supported the cause of these French Algerians, called Pieds Noirs. There was talk of an attack on Paris by paratroopers from Algeria. Army tanks blocked Orly and Le Bourget airports. The government had been in emergency meetings for the last three days.

On the Champs-Élysées, nine hundred people had gathered in front of the closed doors of the Colisée. It wasn't a barracks, but one of the most modern cinemas in Paris. In the crowd, among a dozen other celebrities, were Audrey

Hepburn and her husband, Mel Ferrer, who asked me if a revolution had broken out. They were holding an invitation to the film *Les Liaisons Dangereuses*.

"No, those people aren't dangerous agitators. They're my guests. The government decided to ban the showing of the film."

The censors had not become more lenient since the days of *And God Created Woman*. On the contrary. With General de Gaulle's Fifth Republic, straitlaced morality had become more than ever the order of the day.

The battle began with legal proceedings against me initiated by the Society of Authors. "You don't play around with France's cultural heritage," they said, referring to the Choderlos de Laclos book, which had been devoted precisely to shaking up the moralists and hypocrites of its time.

My lawyer was François Mitterrand, who is now President of France. During the trial he asked permission to call a witness.

"Has he registered with the clerk?" asked the President of the Court.

"No. He's dead. But he left a written statement," replied Mitterrand.

He read a few letters written by Choderlos de Laclos, who warned posterity against moralists who would wrap themselves in the artistic heritage of dead writers. François Mitterrand won the case, which set a precedent.

The film was submitted to the censors and banned.

Edmond Tenoudji, the producer, was understandably alarmed. But we did have a legal remedy. The Minister of Culture had discretionary power that permitted him to override the censorship commission's decision. I suggested that we present the film to André Malraux, de Gaulle's minister of culture. Malraux viewed the film and loved it, but because of the political climate of the times—explosive is not too strong a word—he refused to make a decision without the agreement of a certain number of his colleagues.

The opening had been set for a Wednesday. Invitations

had gone out to all of the top people in art, politics and journalism.

On Tuesday at noon we were told that the private screenings for the government would not take place until Thursday at nine in the morning. Tenoudji wanted to cancel the opening.

"How can you let nine hundred people know?" I asked.

"By telephone. Or radio."

"No. Don't bother. The guests will come back if the film is approved Thursday. Can you imagine better publicity?"

"And if there's a riot, they'll send the police. The minister of the interior doesn't want the film shown. They'll use disorder in the streets as an excuse to ban it forever."

The argument was valid but I still believed that we should take the risk.

I telephoned Maurice Papon, the Paris police chief, who agreed to meet at the bar of the Élysée-Matignon (in my archives I have a photo taken during our meeting). I told him that it was too late for us to cancel the opening. Given the edginess of Parisians at the time, the sight of armed policemen guarding the closed doors of the Colisée could provoke serious disturbances.

"I have to send over fifty policemen. It's orders from the minister," Papon said to me.

Maurice Papon was a man of culture, a humanist with qualities of intellectual honesty that one would not necessarily expect to find in a head of police. He promised me that there would be no uniformed police in front of the Colisée. He would send fifty plainclothesmen instead.

The next day, despite the huge crowd and the tense atmosphere, there were no incidents.

On Thursday morning, nine ministers viewed my film. It was a historic screening if one bears in mind that the government was sitting on a time bomb. This jury acquitted me by a vote of five to four. *Les Liaisons Dangereuses* could now be released.

It broke all box-office records during its exclusive engagement.

Annette also came out of the whole thing a winner. She had held her own in a remarkable cast. Some reviewers criticized me, but they all praised the actors. Annette was particularly applauded for being able to measure up to Gérard Philipe, Jeanne Moreau, Boris Vian and Jean-Louis Trintignant. Yes, I had given Trintignant another chance. He had returned from military service and was already replaced in Brigitte's affections by a new lover.

Annette had taken her new profession seriously.

We were still shooting at the Billancourt studios when a young man in a worn jacket and trousers impossible to describe came up to me at the studio bar. He was wearing dark glasses long before rock stars made them fashionable. He mumbled his name, which I didn't have the rudeness to ask him to repeat.

"I have a part for your wife," he said.

I have always been open to helping young people who want to make it in the jungle of the movie world. Even though I was pressured on the set, I took time to speak to him.

"Do you have a screenplay?"

"Yes," he said. He handed me a box of matches, which he opened.

I could make out a few words: "He's a hooligan. Obsessed by heroes of American films. She has an accent. She sells the *New York Herald Tribune*. It's not really love, it's the illusion of love. It ends badly. Well, no. Finally it ends well. Or it ends badly."

"Is that the screenplay?"

"Yes."

He added, "I've made documentaries. I'm a genius."

I have met hundreds of eccentrics, all future geniuses. But for some reason I believed this fellow.

He ordered coffee, took a cube of sugar from his coat

pocket and dropped it into his cup. "I steal sugar from cafés," he said.

In front of him was a dish full of sugar cubes. Apparently, stolen sugar tasted better.

"I'll speak to Annette," I told him.

He pointed to the matchbox. "Show her the screenplay."

I spoke to Annette about it on the set. "There's the guy who wants you to act in his film."

"Who is he?"

"I don't know. But he seems to know what he wants."

She had read somewhere that great actors and actresses never accept a role until they have read the final screenplay.

"Does he have a script?"

"Yes."

I showed her the matchbox. She burst out laughing.

"You should talk to him," I said.

"You are making fun of me."

I directed the next sequence and went back to the bar. The man with the dark sunglasses was still there.

"She wants a screenplay with dialogue," I told him.

"Oh, yes. That's normal."

He grabbed some sugar cubes from the dish, stood up, thanked me and left. My assistant, Jean-Michel Lacor, who had come to find me, asked, "Do you know him?"

"No."

"He's Jean-Luc Godard."

I regretted not having thanked him for his review of *No Sun in Venice*. The screenplay he had written on the matchbox was to become the film *À Bout de Souffle (Breathless)*, with Jean-Paul Belmondo and Jean Seberg, who played the part my wife had been offered.

For Annette's next film, I came up with the idea of having her play a female vampire. In a role of this type her beauty would conceal her lack of experience.

I should have gone to an analyst to find out why I was sacrificing my career to fulfill the desires of a Danish beauty who had suddenly imagined she was an actress. After the success of *Les Liaisons Dangereuses,* I received many offers and could have directed a major international production.

But I didn't see an analyst, and in the beginning of 1960, in Rome, I began shooting *Blood and Roses* with Annette Vadim, Elsa Martinelli and Mel Ferrer. It was a strange work, a little ahead of its time, but nevertheless well received by some because of its esthetic qualities.

I learned from the newspapers during the shooting that Brigitte had given birth to a son. I wondered how she was reacting to being a mother.

When we finished the film I decided to spend a few days skiing in Klosters, Switzerland, before going back to Paris to supervise the editing. I had reserved rooms at the Chesa Kiruna, a very romantic, comfortable hotel, and I couldn't understand why Annette showed so little enthusiasm for the trip.

A week after our arrival, it began to snow. With Serge Marquand, our writer friends Peter Viertel and the late Irwin Shaw, as well as a charming Italian woman, Countess H, we decided to ski anyway. At nine thousand feet of altitude, visibility was almost nil, and to make matters worse, I had forgotten my glasses. Thinking I was following Serge Marquand's tracks, I jumped over a cliff and found myself free-falling. I crashed thirty meters below in the deep snow. I was all right except for my right ankle, which was broken in more than ten places.

I shall skip the details of the rescue at the height of a storm, the return to the ski station and the visit to the doctor, who merely put the ankle in a plaster cast.

I have lived in mountains. For two winters, I was a member of the Espoirs de l'Équipe de France ski team, and I am very familiar with problems related to broken bones. If I wanted to save my ankle, there was only one way: consult a specialist immediately. All the flights to France were booked. Countess H called Milan and spoke to her friend Gianni Agnelli, owner of Fiat Motors, who sent his personal plane to Zurich. A few hours later I was in Professor Robert Judet's office in Paris.

"Two solutions," he said. "The traditional operation, which will give you back ten to twenty percent mobility in your ankle. Or I can try out a new method that may give you back almost complete mobility."

"There's only one choice," I said.

"So far, I have only experimented on monkeys," Judet added. "You'll be my first human guinea pig."

I decided to be his guinea pig.

The operation took more than four hours. When I woke up in the middle of the night, I was alone in my room. I called home. It wasn't Annette, but Mlle. Millet, Nathalie's nanny, who answered.

"Madame left, with our Puce." ("La Puce" was her nickname for our daughter.) "She took the Train Bleu. For Saint-Tropez, I think."

Was it the side effects of the Pentothal that opened the doors of my subconscious? I don't know, but the truth was suddenly obvious, clear as daylight. The exorbitant bill for telephone calls from Rome—production would pick it up so I hadn't paid much attention to it—Annette's changing moods, her lack of enthusiasm for the trip to Klosters, all led to one name: Sacha Distel. This young singer, much talked about in the last few months, had been seen often with Annette while I was away in the United States. On my return I had asked my wife if it was all innocent. (Like Hollywood and New York Paris is a village; there are no secrets.) Annette had burst out laughing. "You're crazy! Sacha is a good friend, that's all."

This "good friend" had already been noticed by the press because of his hardly discreet affair with Brigitte Bardot. Disappointed by her adventure with X, she had consoled herself in the arms of this physically attractive singer-crooner, then unknown but not without talent. The charming house that she had just bought at Saint-Tropez, on the bay of

Cannoubiers, made a cozy nest for this new great love affair.

The press immediately had Brigitte and her singer, who became "Mr. Bardot," engaged. Ed Sullivan proposed that he come to New York to sing on his show. But it wasn't the charming young French singer Sacha Distel whom Sullivan introduced to forty million television viewers; it was "the luckiest man in the world," the man who held Brigitte in his arms.

A surprise awaited Sacha when he returned to Paris. In his absence, Brigitte had met Jacques Charrier. But if Distel had lost a fiancée, he hadn't wasted time. His name would soon shine in neon lights on music-hall marquees.

Confined to my hospital bed, I turned these images over in my mind. Sacha seemed to display a marked penchant for my women. It was a tribute to my good taste that I would have willingly done without. I urged friends who had come to visit me to tell me the gossip. They confirmed that Annette had left Paris for the Côte d'Azur with Sacha Distel.

She could have chosen a better time, I thought.

"What'll you do?" asked Claude Brûlé. Claude, a journalist at *Paris-Presse,* was a good friend.

"I'm going to get a divorce," I replied.

The next day the news made the front pages.

The day after, Annette was back in Paris. She had got on the first plane after reading the news. She came into my room with Nathalie and began crying.

"Pipfugl, it's not possible. You can't abandon us."

I left the hospital on crutches ten days later, not knowing whether my ankle would respond to the operation as well as Dr. Judet's monkeys had. To limp or not to limp, that was the question.

I had just rented an apartment on the ninth floor of a

modern building on the Avenue Ingres. The windows looked out onto the Bois de Boulogne. Life with Annette and Nathalie returned to normal, as if nothing had happened. With guileless disregard for logic, she became fiercely jealous. Forgetting her recent fling with Sacha Distel, she would snatch the latest *Vogue* from my hands if I showed too much interest in the photos of a gorgeous model.

I N May, Brigitte began shooting *The Truth* with Henri-Georges Clouzot, the great master of suspense and the *film noir*; as director he is best known in the United States for *Diabolique*. Clouzot belonged to the race of directors who believe that the way to bring out the best in actors is to torture them. His cruelty was particularly reserved for actresses. With Brigitte, however, he had chosen the wrong victim. On the third day of shooting, in the middle of a take, he grabbed her by the shoulders and shook her violently, screaming, "I don't need amateurs in my films. I want an actress."

Brigitte would never put up with any kind of physical aggression. The fact that the aggressor was a genius didn't impress her in the least. She slapped the director on both cheeks in full view of the petrified crew. "And *I* need a director. Not a psychopath."

With that, she left the set.

Like many sadists, Clouzot couldn't resist the pleasures of masochism. A few years before he died, he admitted to me, "It was the first time a woman slapped me in public. I loved it!"

The shooting continued without any more physical confrontations. But it was hard going and demanding. Brigitte, who was still not accustomed to Clouzot's tyranny, suffered a great deal.

Her emotional life was lived in its usual vacillating style. During the shooting of *And God Created Woman* she fell in love with Trintignant. During *Babette Goes to War* she fell in love with Charrier. And then, with *The Truth,* she fell in love with her young co-star.

Sami Frey had what it takes to be seductive: piercing eyes, a shy, devastating smile, the charm of the devil. Was he a dangerous terrorist or a poet lost in a cruel world? It was up to women to decide. He lacked humor, perhaps, but not mystery. And Brigitte fell for him. She had been married less than a year, and a mother for only four months, but her heart again played a dirty trick on her. As usual, she panicked because she had to make a choice.

She asked me to come over to the studio to see her. Something must be going wrong, I thought; Brigitte never called just to keep in touch or to tell me good news.

I found her in her dressing room, her feet propped up on her makeup table. She was wearing a dressing gown and was eating an egg and lettuce sandwich with a glass of red wine.

"Vava. It's nice of you to come to see me."

I kissed her.

"So, they didn't cut your leg off after all."

I was still walking with a cane.

"I've ordered your vodka and caviar."

I noticed one hundred and twenty-five grams of gray Beluga from Petrossian and a small bottle of vodka on her makeup table.

"The guy's driving me insane."

I gathered that she was referring to Clouzot.

"You don't have to drive people crazy to be a good director," she said. "Oh, and how old is your daughter?"

"Two and a half. Tell me, what's it like to be a mother?"

"Believe it or not, I don't feel any different. Not for the moment anyway. I'm waiting for him to grow up to see how we get along."

After my third spoonful of caviar, she began talking about her real problem. She was in love with Sami Frey, but couldn't bear the thought of leaving Charrier.

"Even so, I'm not going to hop from one lover to the next until I'm old. If only men were like the sun. I could spend the rest of my life stretched out sunbathing in peace. But with men I have to keep moving on."

She stood up, and her dressing gown partly opened on her perfect body that motherhood had not altered in the least. Her figure still defied the laws of gravity; her soft stomach was neither flat or too round, her thighs were firm and long. She pressed herself against me. "Vadim, I'm so unhappy." The star had not yet eclipsed the little girl in Brigitte.

Odette, her makeup artist and confidante, came into the dressing room and began fussing over the mascara that had run down her cheeks. It took ten minutes to repair the damage.

I couldn't help Brigitte. Besides, she didn't want advice. She really just wanted to complain and be comforted without being criticized. That's why she remained attached to me. I accepted her as she was. I didn't judge her.

My beautiful Danish wife still hadn't forgotten Sacha Distel. She made laudable attempts, but her willpower was as light as a feather in the wind. She was a walking manual of good intentions, which she rarely put into practice.

I had dazzled this girl despite the fact that many men chased her. I had introduced her to a world she thought she understood, but which was beyond her. I had made her a star, and she confused talent with her photos in magazines. She proved to be vulnerable to the advice of false people who were expert at destroying a married couple's always delicate balance. "You're living in the shadow of a famous director," they told her. "You must take your life in your own hands." With Sacha Distel she thought she was asserting her independence, and she became intoxicated with power. Annette was going through the first stages of the famous "identity crisis" that was the slogan of women in the sixties. She hated being always associated with the image of Brigitte, and I understood that. People thought of her as my creation; she wanted to be a goddess in her own right. But, like other professions, that of goddess must be learned and deserved. She forgot, or rather, didn't understand, that.

Hoping that time would endow her with a more sober image of herself and of the world, I suggested that she accompany me to Tahiti, where I had to scout for locations for a Paramount project.

They were going to do a film based on Sterstevens' novel *Satan*. The trip was a wonderful adventure. Tahitians and their islands had not yet been polluted by the French atomic bomb and Marlon Brando's film *Mutiny on the Bounty*. For three weeks a large sailboat took Annette and me from one paradise to another, from Papeete to Huahine, from Huahine to Moorea, from Moorea to the Tuamotu archipelago.

But Annette didn't forget her singer-crooner.

In our hut in Papeete, on the eve of our departure for Paris, I felt that she was somewhere else; her blue eyes were clouded.

"Are you happy?" I asked.

"No."

"If you don't love me any more, tell me. It's not a sin."

"I do love you," said Annette. "You're my life. You're my family."

A family on the edge of a precipice, I thought. But I kept this to myself.

O N September 28, *Blood and Roses* was shown in Paris. After the rather well-received screening, the guests were invited to a party at Maxim's. It was an unusually brilliant evening. The cream of Paris thought that having supper with a female vampire was great fun.

"I loved your cannibal with such pink skin," said Salvador Dali. "Does she strike the hour?"

He turned to André Malraux, to discuss the "skin" of stones. "Imagine Notre-Dame completely white," said Dali.

I don't know whether or not he was inspired by Dali that

evening, but the following year Malraux ordered the monuments of the capital cleaned and sanded, and Paris became several centuries younger.

Annette had gone to the ladies room. I learned later that she had called Sacha Distel. Annoyed at not having been invited to the party, her ex-lover said to her, "If you don't come over immediately, I'll never see you again." As usual, Annette left without a word to me.

I am not a sexist. Nevertheless it seemed to me that being a woman was no excuse for this type of behavior. It's hard for me to admit it, but I was hurt.

At that very moment, Brigitte again was suicidal. The curious crowds that never left her alone and the intrusion of the press into her private life became an increasingly unbearable price to pay for fame. She loved her husband and didn't love him; she loved Frey but didn't know if she *really* loved him. Filming *The Truth*, under Clouzot's direction, had exhausted her. And December 28 was always an ordeal. Her birthday depressed her. She celebrated her twenty-sixth birthday in a villa near Nice. Even though she was surrounded by friends, the large house seemed deserted. Neither Sami nor Jacques was there. After swallowing a heavy dose of sleeping pills, she slashed her wrists and ran out into the night. She didn't want to be rescued.

While Brigitte, blood running from her wrists, stumbled around the grounds and collapsed on the coping of a well, I went home alone to my apartment on Avenue Ingres.

A little drunk, I dropped on the sofa and fell asleep, putting off thinking about my problem until the next day. I had no premonition at all that my little Sophie was near death.

Before dawn, a thirteen-year-old boy who had hidden on the grounds to watch the festivities from a distance and had fallen asleep, suddenly woke up, terrified at the thought of the punishment he was going to receive from his father. It was he who discovered Brigitte, unconscious on the coping of the well.

Brigitte's suicide attempt could not be kept secret this time.

Photographers tried to force open the doors of the ambulance taking her to the hospital. Her life was in real danger. Each second counted, but an exclusive photo was worth two thousand dollars, and three times that, if she died. A journalist from *France-Dimanche* (the French equivalent of the *National Enquirer*) blocked the road with his car. He managed to leap into the ambulance.

"She can't talk," said the nurse. "She's in a coma."

At that moment, a strange sound came from Brigitte's lips . . . *"Vrrche."*

It was a moan, but the journalist cried, "She said Charrier."

She arrived at the hospital just in time.

The next day the headlines read: "DYING BRIGITTE MURMURS NAME OF HUSBAND."

The collapse of the Eiffel Tower couldn't have created a greater stir in newsrooms.

"CHARRIER: I SHOULD HAVE KNOWN SHE HAD ALREADY DECIDED TO DIE."

"PEOPLE BEHIND BRIGITTE'S SUICIDE ATTEMPT."

"CLOUZOT FORCES HER TO KILL AND TO DIE."

I have quoted some of the headlines in the French press, but the foreign press was not to be outdone.

In the United States, John F. Kennedy was campaigning against Richard Nixon; the UN was in an uproar over France's first atomic bomb; but for more than a week, Brigitte's suicide attempt was front-page news.

The reasons behind her failed suicide attempt were exploited, explained, and sometimes analyzed intelligently. But not a single journalist or psychologist knew the truth. They couldn't know that at the age of sixteen, before success turned her life upside down, before the failure of her marriages, before her successive splits with lovers, and before the stress of sometimes painful filming, Brigitte had already wanted to die. Neither films, fame nor having to choose between two lovers were the sole causes of her attempt. When a poet kills himself, one often speaks of his "world-weariness." Brigitte also suffered from "world-weariness."

TWO

D•E•N•E•U•V•E

☆ 17 ☆

*T*WO young girls were dancing together.
    One was Françoise Dorléac, an already
    established young actress whom critics compared to Katharine Hepburn. The other, not quite two years younger, with shoulder-length brown hair, was Catherine Deneuve. It was Catherine who interested me.

The Epi-Club, where we were spending the evening, was the "in" place. On the ground floor you could buy fruit and vegetables. A staircase led to the disco in the basement. Without dethroning Saint-Germain, Montparnasse was becoming fashionable again. The Epi-Club was a few doors from La Coupole, where Hemingway and his friends had met in the thirties.

When the two sisters left the dance floor, a curious phenomenon occurred. Françoise's attitude didn't change at all. She remained self-confident, elegant and friendly to the people who rose from their tables to speak to her. But Catherine reminded me of a hermit crab that had suddenly withdrawn into its shell. Wild only a few seconds earlier, she had now become transparent. The looks directed at her sister went through her like light through a window. I was fascinated by Catherine's metamorphosis.

I was the only one who found her more beautiful than her sister. Ten years later, the press would refer to her as "the most beautiful woman in the world." I didn't need the silver screen and the photos that would one day be distributed all over the world by Chanel to realize that her delicate nose, her intense but slightly cold expression, her mouth with the finely drawn lips, so classically perfect that they concealed deep sexuality, were the very image of romantic beauty.

Françoise Dorléac's charm and fame and intelligent personality rather overshadowed this budding sensation. Catherine herself was convinced that she was just a pale reflection of her older sister, whom she admired, adored and respected without being jealous. For brief moments, however, her dynamism exploded. I had just seen an example of it on the dance floor.

My assistant, Jean-Michel Lacor, who had become a friend, knew the two sisters very well. They came to sit at our table. I spoke with Françoise, who was working the next morning, until she got up to leave. I realized that banter or false humor would be out of place with Catherine. So I said quite simply, "I would very much like to see you again."

"I'll be at the Billancourt studios tomorrow afternoon. On the set where my sister's shooting," she replied.

We shook hands politely and she left.

Often it takes time after an accident to realize that you've been hurt. And this is also true of certain incidents that change your life. It was only two hours later, at home, that I realized what an impression Catherine's face had made on me. But I finally went to sleep.

Around eight o'clock the next morning Nathalie slipped into my bed. She had an excellent vocabulary for a little girl three years old.

"You mustn't wake up," she said.

She put a finger in my ear.

"It's funny that we listen through a hole," she said.

Silence.

"Don't wake up," she said again.

Silence.

"It's a pity you're asleep."

"Why?" I asked her.

"Because I did a drawing."

She put a sheet of paper on my face.

The day began too early for my taste. I had drunk a little too much and had only slept for three hours.

*E*IGHT hours after the famous evening at Maxim's, Annette had come home, already disappointed in her lover. Certain that he had the situation under control, Sacha Distel showed himself in a different light. He should have been wiser and waited before proclaiming victory.

When Annette returned to Avenue Ingres, suitcases in her hand, claiming that she was overcome by remorse and more in love with me than ever, I neither reproached nor questioned her, and she took that as uncaring. I knew that she would go off again one day or another, and I refused to satisfy her ego by playing the passionate, jealous husband.

As I had expected, she packed her bags only two weeks later and went to Rome, where she had been offered a role in a film. My understanding of and tolerance towards Annette—an attitude that my friends considered neglectful and cowardly—were rewarded when she decided to leave Nathalie with me.

"You love her too much," she said. "I've hurt you enough. I can't take her away from you."

Many people thought that she was a bad mother and a bad wife, but nothing could be further from the truth. She really loved her little girl. But she sincerely believed that Nathalie would be happier with me. Annette's future was too uncertain. I can't help thinking of Meryl Streep in the film *Kramer vs. Kramer.* She leaves her son with her husband because she is afraid that she will be unable to take on the dual responsibilities of her own independent life and of her life as a mother. And yet, she adores her son.

"You're as much a mother as a father," Annette often said to me.

In Rome she was treated like a queen. The few months she spent there were undoubtedly the most glorious of her existence as an independent woman.

I had lived the most joyous and carefree years of my life with Annette. She was lively and amusing, a woman who liked her home but who opened her house to friends at any time of the day or night. And my friends adored her. She was sensual, but had no sense of mystery or naughtiness in bed. I don't think I loved her as deeply as I loved Brigitte. That is why, when she left me, I was surprised to find that I suffered more from our separation than from my divorce from Brigitte. Was it the repetition of failure? A wound opening for the second time?

Two months after Annette left for Rome, I knew that the pleasure I experienced at the thought of seeing the little brunette of the Epi-Club again was a sign—I was coming out of convalescence.

I saw Catherine in a dimly lit corridor, behind set C. She was dressed in a white blouse and a wraparound skirt. When she saw me, she raised her head without changing her expression and continued walking right toward me.

A nightclub setting and the optimism encouraged by a few glasses of alcohol often glamorize women with ephemeral beauty. But Catherine's physical beauty was not at the mercy of variations in lighting or a change in decor. She seemed very young and rather feline, despite her rather jerky manner of walking.

"Oh, hello," she said. As we walked toward the bar, she added, "I was hoping that you would come."

We spent over two hours talking at the studio cafeteria. Catherine was wary of me, or rather, of my reputation. She was expecting to find a superficial, cynical and, no doubt, intelligent man. She discovered that I was rather tender and a good listener. I realized that she had both a sense of humor and of the absurd—more an Anglo-Saxon than a Latin trait, and rare in a girl of seventeen. I drank a glass of Perrier, a tomato juice and a Campari and soda. Catherine drank two vodka-and-tonics.

At the end of the day's shooting, Françoise Dorléac made an entrance into the bar, rushed to her sister, hugged her, barely said hello to me and left with her friend, Jean-Pierre Cassel.

I didn't have any idea what we'd do that evening when Catherine and I left the studio and got into my car. I began searching for the car keys in my pockets but couldn't find them. After three minutes of discreet fumbling in my pockets and under the seat, I gave up. Catherine burst out laughing.

"A Ferrari without a key isn't much good," she said.

"I must have dropped them at the bar," I said.

The studio bar was closed.

"Let's call a taxi," said Catherine.

"I don't have a cent," I said. "I forgot to bring my wallet."

"I can pay," said Catherine.

We got into a taxi.

"Where to, sir?" asked the driver, waiting for an address.

I didn't want to take Catherine home with me. I could have taken a prostitute to the bed I had shared with Annette, but not a woman with whom I thought I was in love. I remembered that Christian Marquand was out of town and I knew where he kept the key to his studio.

"Fifteen rue de Bassano," I said to the driver.

Catherine paid for the taxi. We passed by Mlle. Marie's window. She had taken to drink to drown her nostalgia for the good old times she'd had under the Nazi occupation. We went up the stairs. I found the key and we went into the bedroom where Jean Genet's lampshade, a little faded and tilted toward the floor, reminded me that I had made love with Brigitte for the first time on the same bed in this room ten years ago. I kept that thought to myself.

Society passes severe judgment on women who sleep with a man less than twenty-four hours after meeting him. I, on the contrary, respected Catherine for her attitude, which I considered a sign of trust in me. Catherine was attracted to me. She knew the attraction was mutual and sincere. She yielded to the desire we felt for one another without pretense.

Her body was very white, rather fragile, and as delicate as the features on her face. I remember thinking I'd never seen such beautiful breasts.

Being in love with a woman often makes your first sexual experience with her a little strange—sometimes, even a little sad. Like the mind, sexuality unfolds gradually.

Catherine was seventeen and I was thirty-two. But age didn't make a difference. Neither did experience, for women know many things without needing to learn them. She dressed silently. I couldn't guess what she was thinking.

"We could go back to my place," I said. "I'll get my wallet and take you out for dinner."

"No. I must go home. I'll drop you off on the way."

In the taxi, she cuddled up against me without talking. We kissed on the lips before parting.

It was still early, barely ten o'clock. Nathalie had just suffered one of her coughing fits. As a child, I had been tortured by the same condition. Doctors' prescriptions had been useless; only hot milk and honey had occasionally helped me. I gave Nathalie a bowl of milk and honey and recited her favorite story: Melchior, the sad dolphin who had learned to read and write, wanted to convince the President of the Republic to accept little dolphins at the local public school. (Later, I suffered the consequences of this educational tale: Nathalie refused to go to nursery school because there were no dolphins as pupils.) About three in the morning, Nathalie finally fell asleep.

At eight o'clock, she slipped into my bed. "Above all, Daddy, don't wake up."

At eight-fifteen, we had breakfast in the kitchen with Mlle. Millet.

At nine, I called Jean-Michel Lacor, who gave me Catherine's phone number.

Madame Dorléac answered the phone and grudgingly called her daughter.

"When can I see you again?" I asked Catherine.

"Right now."

☆ 18 ☆

CREATED over three hundred years ago by Louis XIV, the Comédie Française is to the theater what the Louvre is to painting and sculpture. Until the Second World War, the actors of this national theater, who enjoy great prestige, were idolized as stars. Aimé Clarion, a *societaire* (member for life) of the Comédie Française, who was also known for his work in films (particularly Jean Renoir's *Le Carrosse d'Or*) had a young mistress named Renée Deneuve who became pregnant with his child. He had talked of marrying the actress but didn't seem too anxious to keep his promise. Unwed mothers were treated cruelly in those days, and so Renée agreed to marry Maurice Dorléac, an actor less well known than Aimé Clarion, but undoubtedly more sincere in his feelings toward her.

Renée abandoned her career in order to devote herself to being a wife. Three more girls—Françoise, Catherine and Sylvia—were born from her marriage to Dorléac. The acting profession is one of the hardest things in the world if one isn't a real success. Repeated unemployment, uncertainty and anxiety about the future are daily concerns. After the war, in order to give his family some kind of security, Maurice Dorléac became a specialist in dubbing foreign films. In 1960 he was director of the Paramount auditorium in Paris.

Their apartment on the Boulevard Murat near the Porte de Saint-Cloud was small for a family of six, but comfortable. A typically Parisian elevator (so tiny that two people couldn't fit into it after a full meal) rose in a clamor of rattling metal to the fifth floor. The front door opened onto a corridor where coats were hung. A friendly living room, a kitchen, one bathroom and three bedrooms sheltered this very close and happy family.

Françoise and Catherine slept on bunk beds. I never thought to ask who slept on top and who slept underneath.

Françoise had decided to become an actress. She had been given the talent and luck necessary for success. At not yet twenty she was already famous. Every evening, after being applauded at the theater or filming at a studio, and sometimes after an evening at the Epi-Club, the Éléphant Blanc or Maxim's, she went home to her little wooden bed. She never left the family nest except for a film on location, outside Paris, or a brief vacation.

At this time Catherine was still going to school. There was a year and a half between the two sisters, but they loved each other like twins.

One day, Jacques Villa, a young director, had asked Catherine if she would like a role in his film *Les Petits Chats*. She was only fifteen at the time and hadn't thought of becoming an actress. Devotion and admiration for her sister had prevented her harboring any personal ambitions in that area. But her father advised her to accept.

"Two weeks of shooting won't interfere with your school-work," he said. "And you'll see whether you like acting or not."

It was then that Catherine decided to take the pseudonym Deneuve, her mother's maiden name, so that her sister could be the only Dorléac of her generation.

The experience was neither positive nor negative. *Les*

Petits Chats was never released. A year later, for fun, Catherine accepted a cameo role in one of Françoise's films, *Les Portes Claquent*.

When I met her she was just finishing the equivalent of the sophomore year in the United States at the lycée, and had no precise idea about what she would do in the future.

Many people thought that even if Catherine was sincerely in love, she also hoped that a relationship with a well-known director would advance her career. Nothing could be further from the truth. Even if she had thought of a film career at the time, Catherine was not the type to use sentiment for professional ends. She is an ambitious woman, but she was never an *arriviste*.

The second time we met, I forgot my lofty principles and invited her to Avenue Ingres. We had gone from the living room to the bedroom, and she was casting a critical eye at the Danish modern decorations when the telephone rang. It was Brigitte.

"Vadim. You've got to save my life."

"Can I call you back tomorrow?" I asked. "I'm busy."

"No. I'm putting Francis on the phone."

Francis Cosne was an important producer and a friend. He had known me when I was an apprentice screenwriter, but I had never worked with him.

"We're in real trouble," he said. "Aurel has cracked up."

One of Brigitte's traits was her capacity to go from deep depression to lightheartedness and joie de vivre almost without transition.

After her famous suicide attempt, she had decided to try singing to take her mind off things. Some of her creations, like "La Madrague," were charming, funny and poetic. Brigitte was neither Piaf nor Judy Garland, but she was a decent success in this new area.

After *The Truth, (La Verité)* she decided to make a comedy, *Please Not Now!* She had had her fill of masterpieces directed by geniuses. Jean Aurel belonged to that new generation of directors which had spontaneously burst forth in the New Wave. It was the time when producers hired directors only if they had never made a film before and were, preferably, callow young men.

Aurel, who had directed a number of short features, was overwhelmed by the financial and technical responsibilities of a big-budget film and a star who was not always easy to handle. On the third day of shooting there was chaos on the set. No one knew what the director wanted, and he knew least of all. Aurel realized that his career would be over before it had begun if he was responsible for a resounding failure. So he agreed, with Brigitte and Francis Cosne, that I should be called in to help.

I had no wish to take on a film begun so badly, and with a screenplay that would have to be completely redone. Nevertheless I promised to be at the studio the next morning.

Two hours later, I drove Catherine home. I suddenly found myself plunged back to the time ten years ago when I had driven home the young Brigitte, who, like Cinderella, had to be in before the final stroke of midnight.

Although Mr. and Mrs. Dorléac had been actors, they were rather strict with their children. Catherine was allowed to stay out until midnight twice a week. She was allowed to stay out later when she was with her sister. Several times, when Françoise was out, Dr. Dorléac locked Catherine in her room for fear that she would leave the apartment in the middle of the night to meet me. My reputation as a Don Juan and a director of shocking films had frightened him.

I arrived at the Billancourt studios early in the morning, as I had promised. Consternation was rife; technicians, actors and producers were afraid that filming would have to be suspended indefinitely. I didn't want to take on this perilous salvaging operation, but after two hours of discussion, I gave in to Brigitte's and Francis's pleas and arguments. Jean Aurel himself had come to see me; pale and nervously biting his lips, he seemed about to burst into tears. He pleaded with me to "get him out of this mess."

After reading the screenplay, I asked for forty-eight hours

to make the most urgent revisions. I went with Brigitte to her apartment on Avenue Paul Doumer to discuss her character and the screenplay. She had already separated from Jacques Charrier and was, apparently, living alone.

"Where's Nicolas?" I asked.

"With his father's parents," she said.

I had only seen Brigitte once with her son. Nicolas was six months old at the time. He was a very handsome baby bursting with health. Brigitte was going out, and she had put on a broad-brimmed hat with artificial flowers. It was not her usual style. When she leaned over Nicolas's cradle to kiss him, he began howling.

"You see, he hates me," she had said.

"No. It's your hat that frightens him."

Brigitte had just stated in an interview, "I wanted that child. I wanted him when I was very young and I wanted him to be a boy."

Of the journalists who had hounded her, she added, "When Nicolas was born, it wasn't my fault that I had to fight off a siege of photographers; I never called them. They were everywhere: at the door, in stairways, in rooms, even on rooftops with their zoom lenses. . . . There was even one who tried to get onto my terrace. His rope broke and he almost landed on the maid, who was watering the flowers. She almost had a heart attack. . . . Nicolas is mine, and I don't want anyone to touch him. No one's going to take him away from me."

W ITH Claude Brûlé's help, I worked day and night for forty-eight hours on the revisions of *Please Not Now! (La Bride sur le Cou)*. We began shooting again on the Billancourt set. Nevertheless, I found time—how I managed it I really don't know—to see Catherine.

The Dorléac clan tried in vain to persuade her to stop seeing me. But Catherine was in love and not the kind of woman to let herself be influenced by others—even by her family, whom she adored.

In January I had to shoot some exteriors in Villar de Lens, a winter sports resort, and I asked Catherine to come with me. It was a decisive step in our relationship, and she didn't hesitate to take it. She told her father that she was going with me, with or without his permission. She would be an adult legally in only ten months. Her father knew that and gave his permission, knowing that she would go with or without it.

Although many journalists came on location, I was able to pull off a tour de force. Not one photo or article on Catherine and our affair appeared in the press.

There were a number of reasons for this miracle. Brigitte didn't have an official lover, and that created speculation about a rekindling of the flame between us. *Jours de France,* for example, did a five-page spread entitled BB REDISCOVERS HER MASTER: VADIM, suggesting that remarriage was a possibility.

Having been a journalist, I knew the tricks of the trade. I shuffled my cards so well that no one guessed the truth. Above all, the reporters couldn't imagine that the taciturn, shy little brunette they often saw me with had the slightest chance of succeeding my two glamorous ex-wives. If a reporter raised the question, his colleagues always answered, "She's not at all his type."

Nevertheless, Catherine already had the qualities which everyone would recognize in her later. She was intelligent, she was capable of scathing humor, which I found particularly attractive, and she was very passionate under her rather cold exterior. Being both sensual and intellectual, she showed a great deal of imagination in what are discreetly called intimate moments. It is not by chance that the two films that stand out in her career are Jacques Demy's tender and romantic *Umbrellas of Cherbourg (Les Parapluies de Cherbourg)* and Luis Buñuel's *Belle de Jour,* which illustrates brilliantly the erotic fantasies of a slightly masochistic middle-class woman.

She sometimes showed surprising strength of character. One day we were walking on a toboggan path high in the mountains. Nightfall took us by surprise, and I suggested cutting across fields of snow to reach the valley. The rain of the day before had turned to ice overnight. It wasn't a problem for me, an experienced mountaineer, but Catherine, who was wearing leather-soled boots, couldn't stand up straight. Every time she fell, she would slide about ten meters. Farther down, there was a ravine jutting out over a freezing, bubbling torrent of water, I wanted to take her back to the toboggan path, but she refused. "I'll manage," she insisted. "Let's keep going."

She was wearing black ski trousers and a black parka. When she slipped and fell on her stomach, she looked just like a little seal slipping on an ice field. Twice I caught her at the edge of the ravine. By the time we got back to the hotel, she was black and blue, frozen to the bone and on the verge of complete exhaustion. But she had not collapsed.

That evening she called Françoise and her parents and chatted with them for a long time. I called Nathalie at my mother's home in Toulon. My daughter was still coughing a great deal and the doctor had advised me to send her south, where the winter was much milder than in Paris.

I have tender memories of our rustic bedroom with its pine walls. I taught Catherine how to play chess. We also played poker. Usually she won. She bluffed with the innocence of an angel and the nerve of a professional.

One Saturday evening, after the day's shooting, production gave a dinner for the crew in a hotel restaurant on top of a mountain, which we reached by cable car. We were supposed to go down again around midnight, but a sudden snowstorm which had defied the meteorological station's radar kept us prisoner until the following afternoon.

The few spare rooms were given to the actors. The crew slept in armchairs in the lounges, and I requisitioned the billiard room for Catherine and me.

The wind was blowing so hard that Brigitte drew up her will, fearing that the hotel would be blown away like Dorothy's house in *The Wizard of Oz*.

Brigitte—a 15-year-old at the time I met her

Brigitte—at 17

This photo was taken the day the family officially announced our marriage.

4

The wedding
at the church

Brigitte, me and Clown in Saint-Tropez

5

Brigitte drew this portrait of me.

Together after our marriage

8

In our apartment

In a little French bistro

9

On the set of
Please Mr. Balzac

10

11

The breakthrough:
*And God
Created Woman*

12

13

Brigitte, Trintignant,
Christian, Marquand,
Poujouli

14

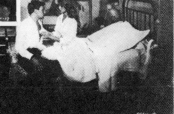

Trintignant and Brigitte

During the shooting of *Please Not Now*, we were already divorced.

Love on a Pillow.
We had been divorced
six years.

With Jacques Charrier
and Nicolas

Brigitte and Vanessa celebrating
their birthdays with me—
both born on September 28.

Brigitte today

With Françoise Dorléac—her sister

2   With friends in Saint-Tropez

With Brigitte in background
during the shooting of
Please Not Now. We were
trapped with the crew
in a hotel at the top of a
mountain during a
snowstorm. Serge Marquand
is standing near Catherine.

In Saint-Tropez

5

Working together

6

During the shooting of the
first movie I did with
Catherine, *Vice and Virtue*

7

Catherine with
Annie Girardot

Our life together kept
touching my past. (8) Here
I am in 1959 with
Nathalie.

At a screening
sitting next to
Brigitte and
Sami Frey

Catherine was as beautiful in public (12) at a premiere as in private (13) in the hospital having Christian.

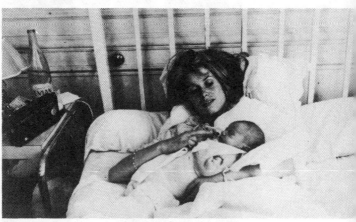

She also evolved into a wonderful actress from
The Umbrellas of Cherbourg to *Belle de Jour.*

Today

Jane was so young when we met.   1

In Megève, France   2

In Arcachon, France

3

This photo was taken on our farm near Paris.

4

5

When we worked together
it was just us.

6

We got married twice—in Las Vegas, then in Paris. Absentminded, as usual, I had forgotten to register the marriage in Las Vegas at the French consulate. Because it was too difficult to go through the legal procedure retroactively I thought it would be easier to get married again in France.

9

Our working association
was equally successful.
Here we are making
Barbarella and Jane's only
costume film: *Spirits of
the Dead*

12

As a star and a mother—
with our daughter, Vanessa

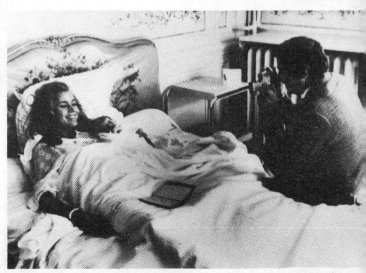

13

On the beach in Saint-Tropez with Vanessa   14

This is the last picture I took of Jane before our separation.

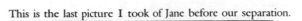

15

Facing the future, at our farm near Paris (16) and grasping it (17)

I played strip billiards with Catherine. I'm better at that than at poker. I had only lost my pullover and shoes. My opponent was in her pants and wool socks when Brigitte walked in.

"I can see you're not bored in here," she said.

"We're playing strip billiards," I told her.

Brigitte suggested that we celebrate the end of the world. We organized a raid on the bar to steal a few bottles of red wine and vodka. The end of the world was celebrated with much drinking. It wasn't our fault that the world was still turning the next day.

Before leaving to go to bed, Brigitte, referring to Catherine, whispered to me, "She's stronger than you. Don't come crying on my shoulder when you're unhappy."

FORTUNATELY there were no press photographers with us during the storm. Many stars—and not only film stars—complain about the tension caused by the intrusion of the press into one's private life. Often these complaints are mere hypocrisy, for the day the media stops following them, they do all they can to attract attention. But Brigitte truly suffered from their attentions. She often expressed her confusion in shattering terms. I quote a few typical remarks from old interviews.

"I don't go out any more. I don't go anywhere. Not to restaurants or theaters or cinemas. . . . And, believe me, it's enough to drive me crazy! Sometimes in the evening, at home, I think about all that. I start screaming and crying all alone because I'm so fed up with this life and all the nastiness. . . . You can't imagine what it's like! I've even been so shattered after reading an article that I've shut myself in for three days. It is the unfairness that I can't bear. If I deserved it, I wouldn't care. But people judge me without even knowing me."

It is true that certain journalists are sometimes even more

cynical than the most hardened politicians and lacking in any charity toward their victims. But then, why this masochistic persistence in reading everything written about you? For more than thirty years I have resolutely *never* read an article about myself unless I have been told that it is objective and interesting. And even then . . . I avoid useless, unproductive anger. Brigitte never practiced this very logical form of self-defense.

"I can't stand it any more! I just can't take any more!" she would repeat. "I wish people would forget all about me. That's the only way I'll be able to begin living. . . ."

But to be fair to her, it wasn't only journalists that she feared. It was, above all, the public.

"If I appear at a gala, people say, 'When will she stop showing off her millions!' But if I'm seen without makeup and dressed any old way because I like it and want to feel relaxed, then they say, 'Is that BB? She calls herself a star. But she's really rather ugly.' "

Sometimes she was physically attacked. She told me that one day, after visiting a friend in the hospital, she found herself alone in the elevator with a nurse who attacked her and scratched her face, screaming, "You're nothing but a whore!"

A misadventure at Villar de Lens shows how normally harmless people can abandon themselves to unforgivable behavior toward actors whose photos they see every day in the papers. Brigitte asked me to go for a walk with her so that she could avoid ten or so boys and girls who were waiting for her in the hall of the hotel. We left by the service door. About a kilometer out on the highway they caught up with us. Brigitte was annoyed and refused to talk to them or sign autographs. When they insisted, she screamed, "I want peace. Is that too much to ask?"

They became openly aggressive. One boy caught hold of her blouse, and I had to push him away. Others threw snowballs in her face. She began crying and running. They ran after her.

On the side of the road there was a road-repair cabin with a padlock that hadn't been fastened. Brigitte ran into the cabin. I joined her and managed to block the door. Hoping that they had left, I went to open the door. But it had been locked from the outside with the padlock. Suddenly thick smoke poured into the cabin. They had found some twigs and had set fire to the wooden cabin. In seconds the flames rose to the roof. We could hardly breathe and the heat was becoming unbearable. I heard a girl scream, "Open the door! Open the door!" And a boy shouted, "We don't have the key." They had closed the padlock without thinking that they wouldn't be able to open it.

With a pick ax I found among other tools, it wasn't difficult to break down the door. We rushed out into the fresh air, coughing, our eyes and throat burning.

A few seconds later the cabin went up in flames. The youths ran off in a panic, realizing rather belatedly the seriousness of what they had done.

☆ *19* ☆

*C*ATHERINE didn't go home after our holiday in Villar de Lens. She came to live with me at the Avenue Ingres.

My apartment, on the ninth floor of a luxury building, was spacious and sunny. From the large balcony which Annette had decorated with flowers the view of the Bois de Boulogne and Paris was superb. The furniture was modern and spare but comfortable: thick carpeting, deep sofas and a long table where we ate our meals. There was no dining room; I've always hated dining rooms. There were three bedrooms: ours, Nathalie's and Mlle. Millet's.

Catherine adapted to her new role as mistress of the house without any apparent effort. Many of our friends came to visit, often without warning, but she was a good hostess and a joyful companion. When her trust had been won, she was amusing and dynamic. Our evenings at home were never dull. However, in public, or with people she didn't know, she was reserved and a little on the defensive.

Irving Lazar never forgot his first evening at the Avenue Ingres. I had gone to meet him at Orly Airport, and had invited him to have dinner with us at home. He observed the charming little brunette who was preparing scrambled eggs in the kitchen—it was the maid's day off—and he didn't know what to think. He had known me with Brigitte and then with Annette, and he was surprised at my sudden change of taste in women. Years later, when he again saw Catherine, who was now blond, radiant and sure of herself, he admitted to me, "I'd never before witnessed such a metamorphosis in a person."

One evening, coming home from the studio where I was supervising the editing of *Please Not Now!* I found Catherine reading in the living room. She gave me a nice kiss, but she had a strange look.

"Are you all right?" I asked.

"Yes. All right."

I helped myself to a whiskey. "Nothing special happened today?"

"Your mother called from Toulon. Nathalie's doing fine."

She took my glass and drank a huge gulp of whiskey.

"Oh, by the way," she said, "there's a beautiful blonde sleeping in our bed."

I quickly shut the door. "It's Annette," I said.

"I know it's Annette."

"So, what are we going to do?"

It was a stupid question. I'd been taken unaware and was playing for time.

"Usually," said Catherine, "it's the wife who surprises the husband's mistress in the marital bed. When it's the mistress who discovers the legitimate wife in her bed, what is she supposed to do?"

Annette joined us and spared me the difficulties of replying to Catherine's pertinent question.

"My Pipfugl . . . !"

She kissed me. "You've gotten thin. It's time for me to take care of you."

Catherine, who had helped herself to a glass of vodka,

began coughing. I patted her on the back until she got her breath back.

We sat down, and I let Annette talk.

She was disappointed with the Italians and with her last film with Vittorio Gassman. I knew from the papers that she was having a passionate affair with the famous actor.

"He lives with his mother, and he put me up at a hotel," said Annette. "She doesn't want any of his women in the house. I've given Vittorio twenty-four hours to decide between his mother and me. He can't decide. I've thought things over, and I've realized that I was crazy to leave you."

"It's never too late to do the right thing," said Catherine amiably.

Annette did not pick up on the sarcasm.

"How's our little girl?" asked Annette.

I get it, I said to myself; she's taking out her secret weapon. If I throw her out, she'll use the child to blackmail me. No doubt I was being unfair to Annette, but I lived in constant fear that one day she would come back for her daughter.

"Nathalie's much better," said Catherine. "The sun in the south is doing her a lot of good."

"We're having dinner this evening with Marc Allégret," I announced.

"I'm too exhausted to go out," replied Annette. "I'll have a bath and get some sleep. Kiss Marc for me."

As she made her way to the bathroom, Catherine said, "You have to give her credit for one thing: She certainly has nerve."

It was an understatement. Annette was behaving with incredible gall, and no sense at all of reality. She was convinced that all she had to do was to show up, and I would take her back. This astounding attitude lasted for years. I must admit that I never did anything to convince her of the contrary, because I thought it was the price I had to pay to keep Nathalie. Beyond the fact that the little girl was very attached to me, I knew that Annette's unpredictable and chaotic life would not provide the security and attention that a child needs so much in the early years of life. With me she had a home base; I had always been there for her. Actually, I spent a lot of time with her. And the future would show that, despite the emotional trauma of divorce and the presence of different stepmothers, Nathalie never knew the sort of dramatic crisis that destroys so many adolescents. I know she sometimes suffered, but she never became rebellious, bluemic, asthenic, drug-addicted, or disappointed with life. Now, twenty-seven years old and living in New York, she is brilliantly managing her career as an assistant director. She lives with an intelligent man whom she loves and who loves her, and we have the best and most tender relationship in the world.

Catherine, despite her youth, understood the reasons behind my rather surprising attitude toward Annette. I was full of admiration for the calm and composure she displayed on such an unpleasant occasion.

"Give me twenty-four hours," I told her. "I know Annette."

*D*INNER at Marc Allégret's was enjoyable. Catherine made us laugh by recounting her own way the beautiful Danish woman's surprise visit.

We spent the night at the Hotel Bellman. The state of the bed the next morning was witness to the fact that our feelings for each other had not been affected by this event that bruised Catherine's pride. I even suspect that she found a perverse pleasure in making love that night.

I went home alone to the Avenue Ingres and found Annette packing her bags.

"Pipfugl!" she said, throwing herself in my arms. "I'm sorry. Vittorio called. He's waiting for me at his place. He can't live without me. He wants me to marry him."

Before getting into the taxi, she asked me, "Can you take care of the divorce?"

"Of course," I replied. "Don't you worry about such details."

ADMIRAL Philippe de Gaulle, the son of the president of France, lived on the floor below us. Because of the existence of the OAS*, the security in our building was very strict. Visitors' handbags and parcels were carefully inspected at the door. These precautions were not superfluous. We knew the admiral's bodyguards. They kept us up to date on state secrets in exchange for gossip about the affairs of Belmondo, Jeanne Moreau and Brigitte Bardot.

One evening I forgot to turn off the tap in the bathtub. Water flooded the bathroom and dripped through the ceiling, flooding Philippe de Gaulle's bedroom. Awakened by drops of water on his nose, the admiral must have thought his ship was sinking. When he recovered from the shock, he put on a bathrobe, walked up to our floor and rang the doorbell. Catherine and I spent the rest of the night on our hands and knees, along with the admiral, drying off our bathroom floor and the carpet in his bedroom.

This incident did not endear us to Madame Philippe de Gaulle, who complained some time later that they couldn't sleep because of Nathalie's crying at night. My daughter was going through a difficult time. She had nightmares and would wake up howling. Mlle. Millet, Catherine and I took turns at her bedside, trying to calm her.

The concierge had warned us that we had to stop the child from crying after ten o'clock in the evening. Catherine went to the president's daughter-in-law and very politely asked her to sign a letter authorizing us to give Nathalie red wine before she went to bed, since tranquilizers prescribed by the

---

*OAS: A secret pro-Algerian movement responsible for many terrorist attacks.

doctor had no effect. We never heard another word from our famous neighbor. Two weeks later, without the help of pills or red wine, Nathalie stopped having nightmares.

*I*N August 1962 I drove my Ferrari in a race at Dijon which was among the events of the French racing championship. I had some tough competition: Schlesser (who died in a race some years later), Jean Guichet (then the French champion) and Claude Bourillot—but I won the event.

Catherine and I were on our way back to Paris with the winner's trophy on the back seat when we were forced to slow down by a convoy of official cars, moving at ninety miles an hour. French law forbids overtaking military escorts, but not civilian ones, regardless of whether they are accompanying ministers, presidents or visiting royalty.

Despite the vehement gesticulations of the motorcycle escorts surrounding the convoy, I decided to pass. I took off on the left side of the road at a hundred and twenty-five miles an hour. Catherine was always game for this kind of extravagance. With the Ferrari's roof down, I had an excellent view of the cars I was overtaking, and I noticed with uneasiness an unusual number of revolvers and machine guns pointed at us. Then I recognized a familiar face in one of the black Citroens.

"Shit," I said to Catherine, "it's de Gaulle."

Having gone this far, we had no choice but to keep going. A hundred meters farther on, we found ourselves on open road. I was unaware that de Gaulle had just miraculously escaped an assassination attempt near Petit Clamart. After a bomb had exploded only a few meters from his car, killing several policemen in his entourage, an attempt had been made to machine-gun him down. The official convoy had turned off its scheduled route and was returning at full speed to Paris on highway 3.

The next morning, one of the bodyguards on duty at the

Avenue Ingres told us that we had a narrow escape. He was in the president's car when I had passed it.

"You're lucky that I recognized you, buddy. For the guys were going to take pot shots at you." He'd been very amused by the adventure. I invited him to have a drink when he came off duty. He gave me a few more details.

As the Ferrari went by, de Gaulle had asked, "Who's that blonde?"

"The actress Catherine Deneuve, *mon Général*."

"If she's always in such a hurry, she'll be a star very soon," was Charles de Gaulle's comment.

RAOUL Lévy had fallen madly in love with Jeanne Moreau. This remarkable woman (who was born on exactly the same day and year as I) had a brief infatuation for him and then ended the affair. Raoul took sleeping pills, slashed his wrists, turned on the gas, took his revolver out of a drawer—and then phoned several friends. Philippe Grumbach, editor in chief of *L'Express*, was the first to arrive at Raoul's place. Raoul was taken in a terribly agitated state to a clinic on the outskirts of Paris where they treated disturbed people and manic depressives. At his request, relayed by Philippe, I went to see him.

They had put him in a room on the top floor of the clinic. The walls were covered with mattresses, and the window had steel bars. A sane person would surely go mad in such a place. He was legally a prisoner, for weeks, months or perhaps even years.

"You're going to get me out of here," he said to me.

We worked out a plan of escape. The door of his room was locked from the outside with a bolt. We were lucky; we wouldn't have to steal the key. The problem was how to get into the clinic and leave without alerting the nurses on guard.

I bought two white uniforms and repeater firecrackers, and around ten o'clock in the evening I returned to the clinic. An intern was dozing in the entranceway. I lit the firecrackers and threw them into the half-open door. At the third detonation, the intern ran off to call for help.

I used that moment to cross the hall and walk up to the fourth floor. I opened Raoul's door, helped him to put on one of the white uniforms, dressed myself in the other and propelled him toward the stairway. Thanks to the chaos created by the firecrackers, we left the clinic without any trouble.

I drove Raoul to the Avenue Ingres. It was spring. Nathalie had left with Mlle. Millet for La Bourboule, a health resort that would cure her forever of her coughing fits.

Catherine accepted this disturbing intrusion in our lives. We gave Raoul our bed, and we slept in Mlle. Millet's room. The bed was narrow, and we fell onto the floor in turn, several times a night. But the rest of the night we slept tenderly entwined in each other's arms, much like mountain climbers clutching at a projecting ledge in the middle of a slippery rock face.

The doctor had prescribed sleep, but Raoul didn't respond to injections. His dynamism and energy were unbelievable. The doctor tripled the doses, without effect. Raoul woke up every three hours. Half asleep, he would smoke cigars, stumble into the kitchen and then into the living room to listen to music. In less than a week the apartment was completely destroyed. A horde of Huns could not have done a better job.

Before dropping off to sleep again, Raoul would confide the strangest things to me: his jealousies, his betrayals, even how he had declared the expenses of my trip to the United States as salary to the tax authorities.

Back in shape after ten days, he kissed me and said that I was his brother, his only friend, and that he would never, never forget what I had done for him. Then he left us.

Catherine looked at the burned carpet, torn curtains, shattered vases, broken chairs, the bedspread with a hole in it, and what was left of the china.

"Do your friends often commit suicide?" she asked.

A week later, I got a hysterical call from Robert Hossein. Robert, with whom I had made *No Sun in Venice*, was one of my closest friends. When I was eighteen years old, he stole my only suit in order to go to a concert given by his father. In his enthusiasm he had torn the jacket. When I complained, he became indignant: ''Don't you have any family feeling?'' he asked.

Hossein was to play the part of a genial anarchist in my next film, *Love on a Pillow,* which would star Brigitte Bardot. It was an adaptation of Christiane de Rochefort's best-selling book, produced by Francis Cosne. (*Please Not Now!* had been a box-office success.)

By chance Hossein had just had dinner in Madrid with Raoul Lévy. Later in the evening, Raoul had told him, ''The Vadim-Bardot team is no longer worth anything at the box office. Francis Cosne needs money from Columbia, but the Americans will never give a cent for Vadim's name. The film will never be made.''

Obviously, Raoul was not yet in form. I should have let him stay in his padded room at the clinic a few weeks longer. His story was so farfetched that I was unable to bear him a grudge. But I smelled something rotten in filmdom.

In Hollywood, there is a saying that success is not enough to make you happy, your best friend had to have a flop.

I reassured Robert Hossein over the phone. ''We'll be shooting *Love on a Pillow* in three months, on the scheduled date.''

It was at this time that Catherine decided to act in films. She had reacted with courage and common sense when confronted with BB's fame and Annette's legendary beauty. Instead of accepting the comfortable and flattering (but unfulfilling) role of Roger Vadim's mistress, she took up the challenge.

When she made her decision, she aimed high: She would be a star. I believed that she was made to be an actress. Her relationship with me hastened the process. I merely acted as a catalyst.

She had just been offered an uninteresting role in a mediocre film that was considered to be part of the New Wave. There were a few good actors in the cast, but

Catherine had no illusions. She wanted to work and was not looking for fame before having acquired experience. The producers and director phoned the next day to suggest a deal.

"We'll give the part to Miss Deneuve if you agree to be the artistic supervisor of the film."

I was about to start shooting *Love on a Pillow,* and I couldn't imagine how I would manage to supervise *Satan conduit le Bal* (the title of the film) at the same time.

"Give us one day," they said. "You'll direct a scene with Catherine. That's all we want." But they forgot to offer me a salary for my name and modest contribution. Finally I accepted, for Catherine's sake.

It was then that she dyed her hair blond and let it cascade down her shoulders. Some journalists wrote that she resembled Brigitte Bardot; others said that I had forced her to make herself over in the image of my first wife.

The truth is that I felt a lump in my throat when I saw her blond hair. What had become of the little Catherine that I was in love with?

She left to shoot *Satan conduit le Bal* in the south of France, near Perpignan. I took off for Florence with Brigitte Bardot, Robert Hossein and Francis Cosne.

We settled into the Villa San Michele in Fiesole, a splendid fifteenth-century residence that had been converted to a hotel. It was a paradise for young lovers, but we were all celibate for the moment.

Brigitte had just made *A Very Private Affair (Vie Privée),* a film based on her own character and directed by Louis Malle. Actually, the film dealt more with a superficial form of neurosis than with deep anxieties. Thanks to her few suicide attempts, Brigitte was made out to be a victim of love, a martyr to success. This was partly true, but Brigitte also had a tendency to devour those she loved. It was when she was devouring that she was most beautiful. Besides, to be devoured by Brigitte was to be the subject of a unique culinary experience.

A Very Private Affair was a very good film, which got the

success it deserved. Brigitte's co-star was Marcello Mastroianni. But the romance between the two stars, which the press had hoped for, never occurred. It was not surprising: Brigitte was attracted to unknowns. She had loved Trintignant, Charrier and Sacha Distel when they were starting out in their careers. One exception was Mr. X, with whom she had a brief affair. There were many famous and very attractive men in her professional life—Gérard Philipe, Daniel Gélin, Kirk Douglas, Louis Jourdan, Alain Delon, Sean Connery, among others—but she never fell in love with any of them.

While she was making the film with Mastroianni, her lover was a bartender-master of ceremonies named François Giulietti. At Saint-Tropez and then at Megève, he had launched the most fashionable nightclub of the day, L'Esquinade. He couldn't compare to a Brando or a Julio Iglesias, but he was one of the most amusing men I have ever met. And that was a period of her life when Brigitte needed to laugh. Her ex-husband Charrier's insane jealousy and Sami Frey's intensity had pushed her to the edge of depression. But François didn't remain in her life for very long (except as a great friend), and she was alone when we began shooting the exterior sequences of *Love on a Pillow.*

Brigitte complained that the crows had made their nest on the rooftop above her bedroom and that they prevented her from sleeping. We found an old blanket, a book of poems and beer bottles on the roof. It suggested a new and rapid mutation among these birds, known for their intelligence. A few days later, a tramp entered Brigitte's bedroom through the window. He had a crossbow in his hand.

She thought he was going to rape her, but instead he held out a notebook and asked her to read a poem that he had written for her. Brigitte had difficulty reading his handwriting, and the poet of the rooftops became angry. He screamed that he was going to cut his throat "and spill my blood on your flaming locks" if she did not recite his poem correctly "and with suitable passion."

"Can I call my speech teacher?" she asked, and then

called me from the phone in the next room. "I've got a madman sitting on my bed. He's holding a crossbow. He says he'll slit his throat or mine, I don't quite know which one, if I don't read his poem correctly. And I'm in a real mess because his handwriting is incomprehensible."

I alerted Francis Cosne, and told him to call the police. Then I ran to Brigitte's bedroom. I had scarcely opened the door when the tip of an arrow touched my Adam's apple. The poet with the arrow and crossbow let me enter the room and bolted the door behind me.

"We're in a jam," said Brigitte.

I was ready to play the hero, but the poet didn't give me time. He collapsed on a chair and began to cry.

He was a man about sixty with an emaciated face and practically no teeth. Long wisps of white hair fell over his shoulders and his beard was as magnificent as Leonardo da Vinci's. He must have been wearing the same jacket and the same trousers for at least a decade. In his very clear blue haggard eyes there was something tender and desperate. We felt sorry for him and we tried unsuccessfully to console him.

A minute later the door was broken open.

The policeman who took Brigitte's statement kept eying her transparent nightgown; his hand was trembling so much that he could hardly write.

Two days later, Brigitte and I visited the unhappy poet, who had been locked up in the hospital. He kissed her hands effusively.

The Florentine police kept the notebook of poems and filed this incriminating evidence among their dossiers on the whores of the Ponto Nuovo. We'll never know whether or not it was an immortal work.

*T*HE Marquis Simone de San Clemente, whom I met in Rome in 1955, was one of those Italian noblemen who love to give great parties and who enjoy the company of stars. He owned a castle near Florence, the dining room of which was decorated with a fresco attributed to Botticelli. His stables bore the stamp of one of the Medicis' architects.

Simone had organized a party in honor of Brigitte. She left after coffee, perhaps because she was tired, perhaps because she couldn't find anyone she liked at the party.

"It's probably for the better," said Simone. "I'm not sure she would have appreciated the surprise."

The "surprise" was in the style of the Italian festivities of the day. The master of the house had rented the services of twenty of the most beautiful Roman call girls. It must have cost a fortune, which he could have used to renovate a wing of his castle.

At midnight they were let loose in the park, completely naked (it was the beginning of summer). Simone gave the signal for the hunt to begin. If you managed to touch a girl, she belonged to you for the night.

At the beginning, the old Marquis S. de Savoia, who was well over eighty and who got about in a motor-driven wheelchair and seemed at a disadvantage in this very special treasure hunt, was the first to arrive on the grounds. But he had a secret weapon. A Social Democratic deputy in the chamber, where he had great political influence, he was always accompanied by four bodyguards.

The hunt was an amusing game, but the Marquis S. de Savoia took it seriously. Thanks to his henchmen (two of them worked for the secret service), he returned to the living room with twelve of the twenty girls who had dispersed in the park.

I was one of the guests who came back empty-handed.

"*Marchese,* you're surely not going to keep all these beauties for yourself?"

"Yes, I am."

"It's dangerous for your health, *Marchese.*"

"No."

"*Marchese,* dear friend, give us the big blonde."

"No."

"*Marchese*, keep them for an hour and let them go."

"No."

The twelve nymphs followed the old marquis in his wheelchair and disappeared into his bedroom, where they remained until the morning.

Two of the girls had not been found. Serge Marquand, Baron Renzo Avenzo and I decided to return to the woods to track down the two crafty wenches. Renzo (Renzino to his friends) was quintessentially Italian, with a Florentine face, a huge nose and forehead, and facial lines that indicated intelligence rather than age. Thin and agile, he was or had been the lover of all the stars exiled in Rome. Broke, like many Italian aristocrats after the war, he earned his living in films, serving as artistic director of the Technicolor studios in Italy.

The sun was rising. We hadn't found the two ladies and we had stopped looking for them. Renzino had taken off his clothes, placed a vine leaf over his genitals, a crown of laurel leaves on his head and, with a reed in his mouth, was pretending to play it, leaping from bush to bush like a real faun.

At that very moment all the villagers, a mixture of Christians and Communists, having just left six o'clock Mass, were marching on the Marquis de San Clemente's castle to complain about some social injustice. One villager carried a cross, another a red flag.

Renzino emerged from the woods and leaped onto the road a few feet from the procession. The Communist mayor, the Catholic priest and the villagers dressed in their Sunday best with ties and ironed shirts saw a faun from a mythological past staring at them in terror.

The Baron Avenzo quickly collected himself. Instead of trying to run to the other side of the road and disappear, he placed himself at the head of the procession. Bare-assed and whistling the Internationale on his reed, he led the way to the gates of the castle.

Awakened, the Marquis de San Clemente spoke with the

Communist mayor and the priest, sounded off, cried poverty and finally worked out an honorable agreement.

Meanwhile Renzo had escaped. He opened the Marquis-Deputy S. de Savoia's bedroom door, liberated the twelve beautiful girls and shepherded them to the kitchen for morning coffee.

We were joined by Mayor Mario Panazo, Father Enio Farzi and Simone. The mayor explained to the ladies that in a true socialist society they would never have to sell their favors. The priest told them that the mayor was right, but religion could replace money. Simone de San Clemente remarked that people with money were often necessary to those who had none. And everyone agreed.

The mayor remained a Communist; the priest a Catholic; San Clemente, a marquis; and the call girls, call girls.

We had an excellent breakfast.

*H*AVING a few days' break between shooting the exteriors in Tuscany and my return date to the studio in Paris, I went to see Catherine on the set of *Satan conduit le Bal*. She had changed in subtle ways, and the change was not due to the color of her dyed hair. At first I thought she had taken a lover, but I realized quickly that something much more important had occurred. She was now an actress.

I directed, as promised, a ridiculous neo-erotic scene. It made me feel vaguely uncomfortable. That very night Catherine cried after making love. She often did this.

Then she told me that she couldn't have children.

"You're eighteen. How can you be so sure?"

"I've never taken precautions when making love. I've seen several gynecologists. They all told me I was sterile."

"Without suggesting a treatment?"

"Believe me, I've tried everything."

"Why didn't you ever tell me about it?"

"I don't know."

I felt that her tears after lovemaking were a sign that her problem was psychological. Why this intense desire to have a child in one so young? She was beginning a difficult career, and a pregnancy at this stage of her life did not seem indispensable. But she wanted a baby—she wanted it desperately.

I gave Catherine the name of a famous endocrinologist. Eight months later, Catherine told me, "I'm going to have a baby."

From that day on, she never cried in my arms after making love.

I admit, blushing, that I missed it.

☆ 20 ☆

*A*FTER filming *Satan conduit le Bal*, Catherine joined me in Paris.

She was devoting more time to her wardrobe now. Chanel-style suits replaced the shirts and little blouses, and she developed an obsession for shoes. Without spending all her money at the major couture houses (we couldn't afford it), she created her own style.

She spent a lot of time doing her hair and making up before going out. At home, or among friends, she remained completely relaxed.

She took good care of Nathalie, kept a steady hand on our purse strings and was rather strict with the domestics and the governess. She sometimes cooked but was no cordon bleu.

To outsiders she appeared to be balanced and self-controlled in all circumstances. Nevertheless she did have moments of extreme irritability, and she gave in to sudden fits of jealousy, which were rarely justified.

The French expression *avoir une araignée au plafond*, which means literally "to have a spider on the ceiling," is an amusing way of saying that someone is a little unhinged. I named Catherine's "spider" "Aglaée."

In her moments of melancholy or depression she would say "Aglaée has come back again." But most of the time Aglaée slept quietly in her attic.

Catherine saw her sister, Françoise, and her parents quite regularly. Her life had all the ingredients for perfect happiness. Nevertheless it seemed to me that something was lacking. Was it that most human beings, even if they have everything, can never be completely satisfied? Or, as an Irish poet (whose name I forget) wrote, "Happiness, that thing which does not exist, but which, nevertheless, one day, ceases to be."

Did she feel that I didn't love her enough? It was a possibility. She often criticized me as someone who could never be pinned down. Women, even though they sometimes claim the opposite, need to be constantly reassured.

Not long ago I saw again an amateur 16-millimeter film I made one summer in Saint-Tropez. Catherine looked happy, but just for a second the expression in her eyes dimmed with something like anxiety. One scene shows her teaching Nathalie how to make herself up as a clown; another, at La Madrague with Brigitte, who is giving her a guitar lesson.

I hoped that Catherine would be able to pursue her career without having to make a film with me. I didn't want people to say the same thing about her that they had said about Annette: "It's Roger Vadim who made her. Without him..." etc. I was convinced that she would be happy to prove that she could make it without my help.

But *Satan conduit le Bal* had not opened studio doors for her. Since she had no project in sight, I decided to give her a role in *Vice and Virtue*. The stars already signed were Annie Girardot and Robert Hossein, so Catherine would not be responsible for making the film work. She would, nonetheless, have the experience of playing an important role, with the support of a man who was used to directing beginning actors.

The story was based on a theme vaguely inspired by the Marquis de Sade: the adventures of two sisters, one of whom symbolized vice and the other virtue. Vice led a life of glory and pleasure. Virtue suffered every imaginable abuse and torment. At the end of the film, vice died and virture was finally rewarded. The action took place in Europe during the Nazi occupation. The film wasn't realistic but wildly baroque in style.

During this shooting I discovered another aspect of Catherine's personality. On the set she was professional but unexpectedly demanding with technicians, the makeup artist, the hairdresser and the assistants. Rather unfairly, people said, "She already thinks she's a star." With me, she was docile. But I did notice that she wasted no time in getting her own way. In principle, I think this is one of Catherine's qualities, but she expressed it too soon, and too impetuously, for my liking.

The filming of exteriors at Souillac, in the heart of Périgord, the land of truffles and foie gras, was exceptionally pleasant—and eventful. Many of my friends were there: Jean-Michel Lacor, Serge Marquand, Paul Gegauff* (who played a sadistic SS officer stabbed to death by one of his victims) and Robert Hossein. Twelve young actresses, each one more beautiful than the next, caused interminable give-and-take, which added to the festive atmosphere. Despite the temptations, I remained faithful to Catherine.

She went to bed early and rarely joined in our festivities. I was surprised because she usually liked to have fun. But she took her profession very seriously.

One night I dreamed that my friend Claude Bourillot had been in a train accident and was crushed to death in a

---

*Paul Gegauff, the most talented screenwriter of the New Wave, wrote the best films of Chabrol and Jean-Luc Godard, among other works. He was stabbed to death by his wife in 1983.

tunnel. Catherine didn't believe in premonitions (or perhaps she was afraid of them), and she told me that the dream contained quite simple Freudian symbolism.

The next day I received a telegram from Claude Bourillot: ARRIVING SATURDAY. KEEP THE TRUFFLES WARM. BEST WISHES. I phoned him and asked him not to take the train.

"I've already reserved a seat," he said.

Bourillot flew a Cessna. "Take your plane," I told him.

"The weather forecast is bad. It's a bit risky."

I couldn't tell him about my dream. He would have burst out laughing.

"I need a Cessna for the film and the producer has refused to pay for a pilot," I said.

Like the good friend he was, Claude made the journey by plane. It was two hours after he landed that we heard about the derailment over the radio. The front car, in which he would have been sitting, was now just a pile of scrap iron. It was one of the most serious railway disasters of the time.

When Claude told Catherine I had saved his life, she replied, "Vadim can see into the future, but he's incapable of guessing the color roses that I prefer."

*M*ARC Allégret was about to direct one of the sketches for a film called *Les Parisiennes*. Four stories would illustrate the faults, qualities and charm of Parisian women of different ages and social milieus. He asked me to write the sketch for which Catherine had been signed.

We were still searching for the actor who would co-star with her. I suggested Johnny Halliday, the singer, who had irritated the conservative public and been crucified by critics for importing Elvis Presley's style into France. His talent was finally beginning to be recognized, and the idea of the Deneuve-Halliday couple was accepted by Marc Allégret and the producer.

I must have suffered a serious blackout in suggesting that

Catherine and a singer-guitarist be thrown together. Apparently I had learned nothing from the past.

Hundreds of details made me wonder if their romance in front of the cameras was being continued off the set. Perhaps it was just an innocent flirtation. I never learned whether or not Catherine was Johnny's mistress during the making of the film. Lies or half-truths are harder for me to live with than the certainty of infidelity. Unlike most men and women, I prefer to know. After the first shock, I can forget. I easily become more trusting. It's doubt that poisons a couple's relationship.

I remember joining Catherine and Halliday in the studio restaurant and sitting down at the table where they were having a drink.

"Do you know the story about the guy who never finds out whether or not his wife is cheating on him?" I asked.

"No."

I told them the story, which ends as follows: "They went directly to the bedroom, said the P.I. who was shadowing the wife. He undressed her completely and then took off all his clothes. He pushed her on the bed and lay down next to her. He took her in his arms. . . ."

"And then?"

"Oh, then, I don't know," said the detective. "She turned off the light."

"Oh, the uncertainty," cried the husband. "Always this uncertainty."

All three of us had the good taste to laugh.

Another day I asked Johnny, "Are you in love with her?"

"Yes," he answered.

Later, at home, I asked Catherine, "Are you in love with him?"

"Don't be ridiculous," she replied. "He's a good friend, nothing more."

That sort of reply always leaves me suspicious.

When Catherine was jealous, it was never because of any particular woman or my habit of always being late—I was incorrigible in the latter area. I would arrive home at eleven o'clock at night with my friends. It was my attitude and the way I behaved with women in general that made her unhappy.

She showed a great deal of patience and understanding of my habitual lateness and my bohemian tendencies; but as time went on, she found it harder and harder to control her temper. I began to lie to avoid scenes and reproach. But that didn't help matters at all.

How many times have journalists or casual acquaintances asked me: "What did Brigitte or Catherine or Jane Fonda see in you?"

For some, the secret was my performance in bed; for others, I was only a vehicle for success; and for still others, I was a Svengali capable of bewitching innocent young girls and molding them as I wished. My reputation is just as contradictory: either I am a cynical, debauched manipulator, a hedonist in search of pleasure or, on the contrary, a man outstripped by the talent and beauty of the women he loves and who, in the end, always abandon him. I have tried to determine the truth, but it is not easy to be totally objective when one is talking about oneself, and self-congratulations are embarrassing.

So why not give the floor to Catherine on this subject? She rarely opened up to journalists, but I did find a few interviews in which she made some disclosures. The compliments paid me do not mean that I didn't *also* have many faults as far as she was concerned. But she never spoke of them to the press, not even after our separation.

*F*ROM *Jours de France,* March 1963:

QUESTION: What was it about Vadim that really seduced you?

CATHERINE: His charm. The quality in a man that affects a woman most. It's an indefinable quality that stems from his intelligence, his smile, his voice. Charm doesn't depend on beauty any more than it does on youth. I think it's what really makes a man attractive.

QUESTION: Which of Vadim's moral qualities most attracted you?

CATHERINE: His generosity. I don't mean his extreme tendency to settle his family's and friends' financial problems, but it was an inner attitude that makes him always see the best in people. Open to everything, he always finds excuses for everyone. He would make an awful presiding judge; he would invent extenuating circumstances for the accused or blindly acquit them.

I don't do anything without asking Vadim's opinion— above all, when it comes to elegance. He helped me to love his favorite colors—white, black, pink, and beige—loose dresses, and raw silk.

Marie-Claire, May 1963:

Vadim is one of the most faithful men I know. It makes people smile when I say that. . . . Some people say, "Poor Vadim, women always leave him. So he's a little scared." I know Vadim. He's not the least bit frightened. I wonder if it's not he who left them. *You know, you can leave someone by doing everything to make them leave you.*

There Catherine showed greater psychological insight than the journalists or the women I had met before her. I suspect that today she has somewhat modified her thinking as far as I'm concerned, but who could resist treasuring such pleasant compliments.

N O one knows (except for the family and our close friends) that we were within a hair's breadth of getting married.

Renée Dorléac had suffered because she had an "illegitimate'' child, and she dreaded the same fate for her daughter. Catherine explained that times had changed, but that didn't reassure the former actress. Her mother's anxiety worried Catherine. And despite her official position as a champion of free love, she was annoyed by people's remarks: "Vadim married Brigitte and Annette. Why not you?" When she joined me on the sets where I was working, she was still the young visiting mistress.

Whatever the reason, whether it was covert or stated, the fact remains that one day we did decide to get married.

I had to leave for Tahiti where Paul Gegauff was to shoot his first film as director. He was anxious and asked me to be close at hand during the shooting. Papeete seemed an ideal place for a wedding ceremony. Catherine agreed that we could not have thought of a more romantic spot.

Our first stop was at a notary's office on the Place Saint-Michel. It was an eerie place, covered with dust and shadows, and crammed full with racks of old files. Mr. Dorléac, Mrs. Dorléac, Catherine and I sat on the threadbare velvet chairs that were arranged in a semicircle in front of the notary's desk.

My future wife's parents had insisted on drawing up a marriage contract. The notary's monotonous voice reciting the inventory had a soporific effect on me, and I dozed off. I vaguely heard them talking about obligatory life insurance, the sharing of property in case of a divorce, of silver and valuables that I didn't own. When I heard the line "In the event of the death of either of the parties, the kitchen utensils will remain the property of the survivor," I woke up with a start. The words "kitchen utensils" were a little too much for me.

"And the ashtrays?" I asked. "You have forgotten the ashtrays."

Catherine, who normally had a sense of humor, gave me an angry look. She hated it when I made jokes at her parents' expense.

I hoped that the Tahitian songs and the emerald water of the lagoons would help me forget about kitchen utensils.

OUR next stop was the Hotel Sherry Netherland in New York—a short business stopover on our way to Papeete. That day it was raining. Catherine was sitting on the bed, taking out of a box a pair of high-heeled shoes we had just bought at Saks. They weren't very practical for walking along coral reefs, but she preferred them to the sneakers that I had suggested. We bought the sneakers the next day. I was looking at the view of Central Park from the seventeenth-floor window when the telephone rang. It was Annette.

"Pipfugl! I know that you love telling your mother the wildest stories. The poor thing believes everything you say."

"What story?"

"The story about getting married in Tahiti."

"It's not just a story."

There was such a long silence that I thought we had been cut off.

"You can't marry that girl," said Annette eventually.

She was convinced that Catherine was living with me only to advance her career, that I didn't love her either and that I had thrown myself into her arms only to get over my separation from Annette. She told me that this marriage would bring me nothing but unhappiness and that she loved me too much to allow me to do such a stupid thing.

"If you marry her," she concluded, "I'll keep Nathalie." (Puce was spending several weeks of vacation with her mother). "I swear that I'm not joking. Even if you're angry now, I know that you'll thank me one day."

I repeated our conversation to Catherine, leaving out certain of Annette's remarks.

"Do you think she'll really carry out her threats?" she asked.

"I'm convinced of it."

Catherine knew how much I cared about my daughter. She suggested that we postpone the marriage until some future date. But I knew she was thinking "forever."

She didn't reproach me, and she seemed unruffled in the days that followed and during our stay in Polynesia. But I believe she never forgave me for the marriage that never took place.

Now, as I examine my own conscience, I realize that I capitulated to Annette's blackmail without a struggle because I was so afraid of losing Nathalie. Parents should never fight over a child. But "the kitchen utensils will remain the property of the survivor" was not totally unrelated to my decision.

☆ *21* ☆

*T*HE years 1962 and 1963 were precarious for the United States. The Cuban missile crisis had brought the country to the brink of nuclear war, President Kennedy was assassinated in Dallas, and the American army was sinking deeper, day by day, into the quagmire of the Vietnam war.

In France, by contrast, these years marked the end of the Algerian war and the nomination of Georges Pompidou to lead de Gaulle's government. It was a period of economic growth and relative stability.

The film industry was at its peak, thanks to the infusion of new blood from the New Wave directors. But the more classical directors were also making excellent films. This variety of styles was beneficial to the French film industry.

Love on a Pillow (Le Repos du Guerrier) was a great success. Brigitte played a more adult character than she had ever attempted before: a respectable, financially well off, middle-class woman, about to marry a doctor, falls in love with an anarchist intellectual who drops out of society and lives like a tramp. Instead of yielding to the lure of the bohemian life and sensual excess to which he introduces her, she domesticates him and makes him marry her on *her* terms. She transforms the dropout into an average citizen.

The last sequence, shot in Tuscany, shows the poet capitulating. He falls to his knees, and she presses his head against her stomach. It is an image of the victorious mother figure. I asked Brigitte to pull her hair back to reveal her forehead for this sequence. I wanted to get rid of the sexy baby-doll look that had been her trademark. But it was like asking a nun to wear a bikini—it was impossible to persuade her.

We had chosen a wonderful location: a sublime sixteenth-century church, overgrown with grass, open to the sky since the roof had caved in long ago. There was a storm gathering, so the producer decided to postpone filming. But I had an idea, and I insisted that we shoot the scene no matter what the weather was. The wind became my accomplice. It blew back Brigitte's famous fringe, giving her face the classical purity that I had been unable to achieve with her hairdresser. She looked quite beautiful this way, and she agreed with me when she saw the rushes.

On the other hand, the spectators booed on the opening night of *Vice and Virtue*. The French were still very sensitive about the Nazi occupation and they didn't appreciate the liberties I had taken with history. Associations of former Resistance fighters tried to have the film banned. I had to wait two years for *Vice and Virtue* to open in art theaters in New York and San Francisco before I received good reviews.

Catherine Deneuve didn't suffer personally from this failure. She was immediately engaged to play in *Les Parisiennes*. But she was mortified that her first important film wasn't a success. Over twenty years later I discovered (in a letter she recently wrote me) that she never forgave me for that unfortunate experience. It's just like Catherine to keep a secret for a quarter of a century.

But the public liked *Les Parisiennes* and began to mention Catherine as a future star.

As a favor to her friend Paul Gegauff, she accepted a role in *Le Reflux*, which he was going to shoot in Tahiti.

Our stay in Papeete (where we would have got married if it hadn't been for Annette's intervention) began badly. Catherine, thinking she was still in Saint-Tropez, sunbathed too long, despite our warnings, and went to bed with a high fever in the evening. A few days later her skin began to peel.

Paul Gegauff realized that he would have to rewrite the screenplay and replace Catherine with a local beauty since the producer didn't have the money to send for another actress from France.

Franco Fabrizi (known to film buffs for his role in Fellini's *I Vitelloni*), Michel Subor (Brigitte's co-star in *Please Not Now!*), and Serge Marquand had the three lead roles. Paul was a bizarre director who seemed more concerned about fishing than directing actors.

The producer was on the verge of hysteria, but it was a wonderful adventure. We slept on a cargo boat that took us from atoll to atoll. On one of them, called Takaroa, there were seventy-two inhabitants. When the Mormons built a superb temple there, sixty-eight Takaroans converted to the Mormon faith. The other four inhabitants remained intransigent Catholics and continued to celebrate Mass in their church, which was a tiny wooden hut surmounted by a cross.

One night a storm came up and turned into a hurricane. The church was blown away, like a wisp of straw, but the temple remained standing majestically. The following Sunday, there were four more Mormons on the atoll of Takaroa.

The night of the storm, Catherine and I were lying on the captain's bed, the only double bed on the cargo boat. The vessel was tossing from side to side. After we made love, she took my head in her hands and looked at me for a long time. She said something, but with the wind making the sides of the old boat creak and the waves dashing against the porthole, I couldn't hear what she was saying.

"What?"

She shrieked, "I'm going to have a baby!"

PREGNANT, Catherine proved to be a woman full of contradictions. One day she got up at dawn, took Nathalie to school, stopped at the studios to kiss me, did the shopping instead of Gustav (the Yugoslav cook who cheated us), tidied the house and watered the plants. Around midnight, when I thought that she would be exhausted, she suggested having a drink at Castel's.

Sitting on a banquette on the ground floor, which was reserved for regulars, she drank with Peter O'Toole, Bob Weber, Elizabeth Taylor, Truman Capote, Françoise Sagan, Quincy Jones and a few politicians on a binge.

The next week she slept until noon every day.

The week after was her shopping period. I hate going to shops, but I accepted this purgatory because Catherine was pregnant. We bought nothing at the maternity shops we went to, but we returned each time with a new pair of shoes.

I didn't lose my bad habits, either. I would often leave the studio bar with Jean-Michel Lacor after a call to Catherine: "I need to relax. I'll be home around midnight."

At one o'clock in the morning, Paul Gegauff or Christian Marquand and I would be at Sexy's on the Champs-Élysées teaching manners to a stripper. At three o'clock, in a bar in Pigalle, after having almost come to blows with a pimp, we settled our differences over a bottle of champagne. At five o'clock, at L'Escargot, we had onion soup and greeted the dawn with the "market porters of Les Halles," giants in white overalls covered with blood who carried entire sides of beef on their shoulders to the meat stalls. Compared to these men a football player looks like a wimp.

Lacor and I congratulated each other for our moral behavior: he had not been unfaithful to Cecile, his wife, nor had I to Catherine.

When I got home, Nathalie had just left for school with the governess. Catherine had made sure that she had put her notebooks and textbooks in her satchel. I found her in the kitchen, washing the dishes from the previous evening.

"You're drunk," she said.

I replied indignantly, "I don't get drunk on a few glasses."

Slow on the uptake, I expressed surprise at her frenzied housework, so early in the morning. "It's Saturday. Gustav doesn't leave until noon. Why are you doing his job for him?"

"I fired him last night," said Catherine.

Gustav had a lover who worked at the post office. Each time they had a fight—which was frequent—Gustav lost control and cut himself horribly as he was preparing our meals. The sink, the oven and even the kitchen walls were covered with blood. On these occasions he would serve lettuce with hemoglobin, or gratin dauphinois a la Dracula. It was very unpleasant, particularly when we were having friends over.

"I'd rather do the dishes than live in an operating room," said Catherine.

W HEN her belly began to balloon, Catherine asked me if it was a good idea to continue making love. "Some doctors are for and others are against. What does the future citizen think?"

"He's for," she said.

W HEN I met her, Catherine had two secret ambitions: to be a mother and to become an actress. Now that she was fulfilled in both domains, her true nature began to emerge; she was made to dominate. She had a very precise view of life to which she expected people and events to conform. Each year this attitude became more and more pronounced until, at the height of success, she proved to be a domestic tyrant. And she has remained so.

She was convinced that she alone was right and capable of making people happy as long as they obeyed her in everything. She was intelligent and lacked neither sensitivity nor humor, and it was easy to be charmed by her before realizing that one always had to say yes, or be excommunicated.

And then there was Aglaée.

Moments of helplessness and sudden moods of despair made this young woman with a temperament of iron appear vulnerable. When her domineering nature began to express itself openly, I became rebellious. I was absolutely intractable, and this created conflicts between us.

I don't know whether Catherine was right or wrong. Truth doesn't exist in these situations. Each person always sees things subjectively. But the fact remained that Catherine had changed. More precisely, a part of her personality that had been hibernating for a long time suddenly awoke.

One day when we were driving to Megève, an argument, begun over our different opinions of an actress, suddenly turned nasty and vicious.

"My God, you take me for Brigitte Bardot," she screamed.

"No danger," I replied. "I can tell the difference between a real diamond and a bottle top."

These were words of anger; neither of us really meant what we said.

She opened the door and tried to jump out of the moving car. I held her back by her skirt.

She sulked for four hours. As we approached the first fields of snow, she said, "Stop, I need to walk."

She got out of the car. Ten minutes later she hadn't returned, and I went off to look for her. I followed her footprints in the snow and found her numb with cold, sobbing at the foot of a fir tree.

"What have you got against me?" she said. Her teeth were chattering.

I carried her in my arms to the car. Her feet were white and frozen. I warmed her against my skin, under my shirt.

"They'll have to amputate and you won't love me any more with artificial limbs."

That made me laugh, and we kissed.

The problem was that we really did love each other.

W HEN I was a child, I used to read a column in *Mickey* magazine called "Truth Is Stranger than Fiction." It's a pity that the magazine no longer exists because I could have sent the following story to the editor.

I was alone in the house when the telephone rang. I picked up.

"Pipfugl! It's your Nenette."

She was back again in Paris and wanted to see me immediately. I was about to leave for an important appointment and suggested meeting the next day.

"You don't seem in a hurry to see me," she said.

"But of course I am. I happen to be busy all afternoon. I really can't cancel."

"And this evening?"

"I'm dining with Paul Gegauff at Serge's place. Where are you staying?"

"At the hotel Prince des Galles."

"I'll call you there tomorrow morning."

She asked after Nathalie, who was doing splendidly. She sent kisses, I sent her kisses in return and hung up.

Serge Marquand lived in the Marais, one of the oldest, most interesting areas of Paris. I arrived late for dinner.

Serge seemed nervous, but Paul, on the contrary, was in a wonderful mood.

"They've been in the bedroom for the last hour," said Paul.

"Who?"

"Annette and Catherine. They're discussing what should be done with you."

I walked into the bedroom.

Annette and Catherine were waiting for me, standing in the middle of the room. I was the accused. They were the jury. I didn't know yet what charges would be leveled against me. I felt uneasy and guilty for not having explained clearly to my ex-wife that we could never return to our past.

Annette: "I'm speaking on behalf of Catherine and myself. You're going to tell us now, immediately, which one of us you really love."

Who had gone crazy? Annette, Catherine, or myself?

"You're joking," I said.

"Not at all, Vadim," Catherine replied.

"I won't accept these police tactics," I said, and left the room.

"So, what's up?" asked Paul, who reveled in this kind of situation. "Were you caught in the act?"

Annette and Catherine joined us a few minutes later. I took Catherine by the hand and left the apartment with her. We got in the car.

"Have you lost your mind?" I asked her.

"If I were not pregnant, you would have stayed with her," she said.

It wasn't true, but I didn't comment. I drove in silence to Avenue Ingres.

After this strange encounter, Annette told me that she wanted to live in Paris for a while to be close to Nathalie.

I rented two apartments on the same floor in a building a few hundred meters from Avenue Ingres. I installed Mother, Mlle. Millet and Nathalie in one apartment and Annette in the other. I sensed—and I would be proved right—that this situation was only temporary.

Catherine didn't forget her career. She met with producers and directors. Her sister introduced her to Jacques Demy and they became friends.

In April, I left for Lapland to shoot the exteriors of my

film *Château en Suéde*, a comedy based on a play by Françoise Sagan.

Catherine, who was seven months pregnant, stayed behind in Paris.

The Italian star Monica Vítti (Michelangelo Antonioni's wife), and Jean-Louis Trintignant were part of the cast. We spent three weeks with a crew a hundred kilometers north of the Arctic Circle.

The nights were short, lasting scarcely an hour, and the air so brisk that we hardly slept. I had already worked with Trintignant on *Les Liaisons Dangereuses* since the Bardot era, and we got along well. We never spoke of Brigitte. Jean-Louis was a remarkable poker player. One night, when he again had won the whole pot, I couldn't help saying: "You're not going to take my money *too*."

He merely smiled.

A FTER shooting the exteriors on location in Lapland, I finished the picture at the Billancourt studio in Paris.

On the eighteenth of June, I was given a message on the set: "Catherine is at the American Hospital at Neuilly." I called her immediately.

"It's due tomorrow," she said.

But three hours later I got another message. "It's a son, Monsieur Vadim. Mother and baby are doing well."

I let Jean-Michel finish the day's work and took off for the hospital.

Catherine was pale and radiant, her hair plastered down with sweat, and she was holding Christian, aged one hour, in her arms.

I already had a daughter, and I was happy that this time it was a boy. I looked at my son in silence. I was moved. Catherine said, "It's a baby. You know, it's the kind of thing that suckles, that always has to be changed, that smells of piss and grows up without asking permission."

The nurse took Christian from her. I kissed his crumpled forehead. "He needs a face-lift," I remarked.

Catherine smiled and took my hand. I sat on the bed. We looked at each other with new hope that made us feel warm inside.

☆ 22 ☆

I never imagined that by the age of eighteen Christian would be exceptionally beautiful, like his mother. He was one of the ugliest babies I have ever seen.

When he was two months old we still couldn't sit him up straight because his head was too heavy and fell forward or sideways or even backward. I was always afraid that it might fall off.

I was reading a novel by A. E. Van Vogt, one of my favorite science-fiction writers, when I heard strange sounds coming from the baby's room. I got out of bed without waking Catherine and opened the nursery door. A ray of light coming from the corridor created strange shadows, and for a second I thought that an extraterrestrial being had slipped into my son's cradle.

The baby was simply trying to push his toes into his mouth.

That night I nicknamed him "the Martian." Catherine, who was blinded by maternal love and thought her baby sublimely beautiful, was furious.

A few months later, the Martian transformed himself into a very handsome little boy.

We were at Saint-Tropez in a house that overlooked the large beach of Pampelone. The July sun and the sea; our friends lunching or dining with us on the terrace covered with Virginia creepers; our boating trips; this baby that Catherine and I adored; the merry noises of little Nathalie, running in the garden filled with roses, daisies and lilacs; and the smell of thyme, mimosa and eucalyptus—all combined to make us happy.

Nevertheless, we had never argued as much as we did then. The hope that Christian's arrival would bring us closer together didn't last very long. Catherine's intellectual and domestic intransigence became more and more unbearable. She reproached me for my lack of organization and my nocturnal outings with friends—which became more frequent. She often called me a liar. Allergic to any kind of Manichaeism and incapable of seeing things as simply black or white, I realize that my interpretation of the word "truth" is rather vague. This annoys many people—especially the women I live with. Catherine and I had totally different temperaments and concepts of life. The legal term is "temperamental incompatibility."

Even when love has vanished, the idea of separation after years of life together is agony. When you are still in love, as was our case, the thought is even more painful. After each quarrel, each misunderstanding, Catherine and I fell into each other's arms. Sometimes she cried, and I did, too, on occasion. But kisses, caresses and tender words could no longer heal a wound that was reopened each day.

Against all evidence, we refused to admit that we were only living out a deferment. In anger, we had threatened to leave one another a hundred times, but we had never calmly talked of separation—until the day of the storm.

I had a boat, Ariston Riva, whose powerful motor allowed us to reach the Levant Islands (50 miles' distance) in less than two hours. Catherine, Paul Gegauff, Pierre Feroz (former secretary to Carlo Ponti), Toni Ades (a young Egyptian producer) and I decided to take the boat to the islands for a day of fishing. The weather was fine and by the end of the afternoon we had caught enough fish for a good bouillabaisse.

Suddenly there was a strong wind from the east. I decided to start back so that we would arrive at Saint-Tropez before nightfall. But Gegauff was, as I have already mentioned, a fanatical fisherman.

"A little longer," he kept repeating. He delayed us until sunset.

On the way back the motor caught fire when we were a little over nine miles from the coast. Ades and Feroz dived courageously into the sea while Paul and I put the fire out with the extinguisher. When our friends were reassured, they climbed back on board. But the motor wouldn't start.

Worried by the winds and the clouds that now covered the horizon, the skippers of all the pleasure boats had long since left for their home base. We were the only ones still at sea. The swell was growing stronger, and night was falling.

There was only one solution: to row the boat ashore. We didn't have any oars so we had to use water skis. After two hours of rowing, we had moved only a few miles. The lights from the coast seemed to be as far away as ever.

The wind was now a tempest and water was flooding the Riva. It began to rain. Flashes of lightning came in quick succession—adventure was becoming disaster.

Paul Gegauff didn't want to give us the fish pail that we needed to bail out the water. "Don't touch my bouillabaisse," he protested.

Finally he compromised and transferred his fish to a picnic basket.

Pierre Feroz was green with fear and couldn't move. Toni Ades, convinced that only Allah could get us out of this mess, had given up rowing and was reciting Arabic prayers. While Paul and I knocked ourselves out getting the boat to move forward, Catherine kept bailing out water with courage and extraordinary calm that filled me with admiration.

Our chances of reaching the coast before a wave upset the boat seemed more and more improbable every minute. But around three o'clock in the morning, we ran aground on a sandy beach a few meters from a large hotel. We were completely exhausted.

Paul still found strength to salvage his fish. The night manager wasn't accustomed to shipwrecked persons as guests, but nevertheless he helped us as best he could. He had a hot bath drawn for Catherine, gave us bathrobes and made us scalding rum grogs.

I telephoned home to reassure Mlle. Millet. She told me that the lifeboat had left the port to search for us. It was recalled by radio.

"Allah heard me," Toni Ades told us.

"Thank you," said Catherine. "It's fortunate that you were with us."

An hour later, sitting next to me in a big armchair, Catherine said, "I really believed we were going to die. I thought about Christian. Nathalie still had a mother, I thought. And then I thought about us. I said to myself, 'If by some miracle we aren't shipwrecked, life will separate us.' Everything was strangely clear. I saw the future as if it was a picture book. I was sad. And I am sad."

A T the end of the summer, Catherine left to make Jacques Demy's *The Umbrellas of Cherbourg (Les Parapluies de Cherbourg)*. I had to go to the Venice Film Festival.

Christian, a delicate child during his first year, had stayed in Paris with his Italian nanny, Bruna, an admirable woman in whom Catherine and I had complete confidence.

On my return from Venice, I spent a few days with my son, then decided to join Catherine in Cherbourg. We spent Sunday visiting the little English island of Jersey, which is very picturesque with its intensely green fields, neatly aligned doll's houses and red brick churches. But the visit was a disaster. For one reason or another, Catherine and I didn't stop fighting.

Discouraged, I left the very next day.

* * *

*T*HE filming of *The Umbrellas of Cherbourg* was a happy and enriching experience for Catherine. She couldn't know that this film would make her a star, but for the very first time she played a character who suited her wonderfully. And Jacques Demy knew exactly how to show to advantage her delicate and romantic physique.

The French cinema needed a new face, less earthy than Jeanne Moreau's and Simone Signoret's and with less aggressive sensuality than Brigitte Bardot's. That was a gap Catherine filled with her very first great role.

When she joined me in Paris, life began again almost calmly. We were like two groggy boxers who had granted each other time out in a round. Catherine spent a great deal of time with the baby, and I worked fifteen hours a day preparing my next film, a remake of *Circle of Love (La Ronde)* from a screenplay by Jean Anouilh.

On December 12, I came home in the late afternoon and found Catherine closing one of her suitcases. It reminded me of something.

"I have to leave," she told me. "I can't take it any more."

She refused to tell me where she was going.

I learned the next day that she had joined Johnny Halliday, who was performing at either Lyon or Evian—I can't remember exactly where.

On December 17, she was back, but she didn't seem happy. She didn't say a word about her lightning journey. When Catherine decides not to speak, it's useless trying to drag the smallest confidence from her. She is sometimes an extraordinarily secretive woman.

On December 21 my friend Olga Horstig (Brigitte Bardot's agent) telephoned to ask if I was free for dinner. "It's a client's birthday. She's alone and I invited her. You know her, I believe."

"Who is it?" I asked.

"Jane Fonda."

THREE

F★O★N★D★A

☆ 23 ☆

*M*AXIM'S has kept the tradition of dinner dancing.

I was dining with Annette, whom I had known for a short time, and several friends, when I noticed Christian Marquand sitting at a table with a young woman on the other side of the dance floor.

"It's Henry Fonda's daughter," one of my friends said to me.

Jane was eighteen years old at the time. I found her pretty, but I would never have noticed her if she hadn't been with Christian. He got up and asked her to dance.

She was wearing a very proper dress with almost no décolletage. It was pulled tight at the waist and reached down to her calves. Her hairstyle, also very proper, reminded me of the young well-brought-up girls one sees typed in American films. The contrast between her and the super sophisticated Parisian women was very refreshing.

Christian and I used to tease each other by pointing out and exaggerating the faults of our new conquests. When he came near us, as he danced with Jane, I slipped a piece of paper into his pocket. I had written: "Have you seen her ankles?"

Jane had swollen ankles that evening. When he got back to his table, Christian read my message, crumpled it up, and threw it into the ashtray. Later on, distracted by someone who had come to speak to him, he didn't notice that Jane had quietly picked up the note. She knew me from photos in the newspapers and suspected that the piece of paper slipped into Christian's pocket had something to do with her. She was curious to find out what I could have to say about her.

This barely civil introduction would have annoyed most women—but not Jane. She told me later that the incident rather amused her.

The next day she left Paris for Los Angeles. And it was there that I saw her again, three years later, and spoke to her for the first time.

A French producer had asked me to try to interest Jane in a role in a film I was to direct. I knew that American actors never commit themselves to a project without having read the screenplay, and the project was too vague for Jane to pay much attention to it. But I was interested in getting to know her. I had other business to attend to, and a week before I was to leave Hollywood I called Jane's agent to arrange a meeting.

She met me one afternoon at the coffee shop of the Beverly Hills Hotel, where I was staying. She had no makeup on, her hair looked as if she'd just run a mile along the beach, and she was wearing blue jeans and a rather masculine blouse. I didn't realize that her appearance had been deliberate. Her agent had said, "Try to be sexy." But she had done exactly the opposite. My reputation as a discoverer of stars and a specialist in eroticism irritated and frightened her. However, if she had hoped to shock me by dressing like that, she didn't succeed. On the contrary, it was her natural look that attracted me.

In fact, when she came to the hotel she had no intention of accepting the role I was going to propose to her. She was merely interested in meeting me. We spoke for at least an hour, and I can't remember a word of our conversation.

Three years later, Francis Cosne suggested that I direct a film based on a best-seller, *Angélique Marquise des Anges*. He wanted Jane Fonda for the role of the adventurous, passionate Marquise. He received a telegram from Hollywood, which he gave me to read: JANE FONDA IS NOT INTERESTED IN A COSTUME DRAMA. SHE ALSO ASKS ME TO TELL YOU THAT SHE WILL NEVER MAKE A FILM WITH ROGER VADIM.

So Cosne signed up an unknown actress, Michele Mercier. The film (which I never directed) was a big commercial hit, even if it was not an artistic event.

It was a few months after that scathing telegram that Olga invited me to her place to celebrate Jane's birthday. On leaving the studio where she was shooting *Joy House,* a film with Alain Delon, directed by René Clément, she had stopped off at her hotel to change her clothes and do her hair. She was charming, and the atmosphere that evening was relaxed and pleasant. She said that she felt lonely in Paris.

"But one reads many things about you and Alain Delon," remarked Olga.

"That's just part of the game, I think," said Jane. "The press agent hints that there's a romance going on between the stars of the film, and the papers leap on the information without trying to check if it's accurate. A denial in this case would only add fuel to the fire. How can you prove that you've never been to bed with a man who has been holding you half naked in his arms on the set in front of sixty people? Alain is an extremely seductive man, and he's good to work with, but I just can't communicate with him. And the director, René Clément, is terribly cold. He's got a heart, I'm sure of it, but he hides it well. Underneath it all he's probably very shy. At the moment, I have only one friend in Paris, but he's a married man with children and doesn't have much free time."

She didn't speak French perfectly yet, but she had no

difficulty expressing herself. It's a pity that her charming accent, grammatical errors and mistakes in using words can't be translated into English. Jane's English is precise and her delivery rapid despite hesitations and intentional pauses. It gives the impression of efficiency and sometimes a certain dryness. In French she speaks in a much more colorful way and her voice is deep and nuanced. The lack of confidence that comes from seeking a word in a foreign language gives her a gentleness which is part of her character, but which, for reasons that I've never understood, she tries hard to hide.

She admitted to us that she had difficulty understanding French, but added, "What I love about Paris is that you can walk in the streets night and day. When you walk in Beverly Hills at night, the police stop and question you."

On the subject of the Californians' excessive dependence on their cars, I told a short satirical story which I had just read in a science-fiction novel. An extraterrestrial being is sent on a mission to study all forms of intelligent life on earth. He arrives in Los Angeles and reports his first finding: "The most evolved inhabitants on the planet have an exo-skeleton, a carapace of metal in varying colors. They move forward on four wheels or more, hold meetings in huge spaces called 'parking lots,' and take shelter at night in individual or multiple shelters called 'garages.' They possess modules operated by remote control which are fragile and supple—in white, black, or yellow—and move rather clumsily on two feet. I am not yet certain of the usage of these things."

I don't know whether or not the story amused her, but she laughed. She told us that she had recently started sleepwalking. "In the summer, I sleep with nothing on, and I have awakened several times completely naked, in the garden. One night I opened the gate. When I regained consciousness, walking along the street, I thought I would die from embarrassment."

The cake with the twenty-four candles was a surprise for Jane. We sang "Happy Birthday to You."

She then told us why she had decided to leave Hollywood to work in France: "I made six films in the states . . . and did three plays on the stage. I received the award for 'Best New Talent of the Year.' But I'm always Henry Fonda's daughter, one of Hollywood's promising new faces. Some journalists nicknamed me the American Brigitte Bardot."

She interrupted herself, smiled and continued, "I've a lot of respect for Brigitte Bardot, but I don't think I'm like her at all. And in any case, I prefer being myself. That's what really got me in Hollywood. I ended up no longer knowing who I really was. I was like a prefabricated product and a prisoner of the system. So I decided to escape all that and get out from under my father's shadow. I agreed to do René Clément's film. Perhaps I'll be able to discover a real identity in France. Everyone told me that I was crazy, that I was ruining my career. Nobody's ever heard of an American actress making a name for herself by taking off for Europe. They mentioned Greta Garbo and Ingrid Bergman, who both came from Sweden to Hollywood; and about Bergman ruining her career by going off to live in Italy with Roberto Rossellini. We'll see."

She had warned us that she had to start shooting early the next morning and had to be home by eleven. "I'm crazy," she said, as she looked at her watch and saw it was past midnight. She left, and I stayed on.

Twenty minutes later the telephone rang. It was Jane calling from her hotel room. She told Olga that the evening she had spent was the best since arriving in Paris.

When Olga put down the phone, she smiled. "You've seduced her."

It was actually Jane who had seduced me, and, in spite of Olga's belief, I didn't dare hope that the attraction was mutual.

* * *

*T*HE producers of *Circle of Love,* Robert and Raymond Hakim, wanted to offer Jane a role in the costume film. I told them about the telegram she had sent to Francis Cosne.

"That means nothing," they asserted. "With actors, you never know."

They submitted an offer to Olga Horstig, and to my great surprise, Jane accepted. The reversal in her attitude was not only due to the evening at Olga's. Jane had decided to work in France. The prestige of Jean Anouilh, the screenwriter, brilliant casting, and the fact that everyone advised her to accept, prevailed over her apprehensions. She didn't think of herself as sexy or pretty and couldn't understand why I was interested in her. She was both frightened and attracted by what I represented—in life, as well as in my films.

At the age of twenty-four, Jane came across in interviews as a young woman sure of herself—of her looks and her sexuality—and convinced that she would soon be a star. She was severely critical of her father and brother, and always ready to shock public opinion.

It was actually very much in her nature to forge ahead and to appear not to care about public opinion, but she was far from being as self-assured as she wanted people to believe. She asked herself many questions about her career, her father and even her emotional life. It seemed to her that she hadn't yet achieved anything, really. That didn't discourage her, but she did find it disturbing.

Every New Year's Eve, Eddy Barclay, the famous music publisher, gave a huge costume ball. Almost all the famous and talented in Paris gathered in the huge reception rooms and the gardens of the Armenonville Pavilion in the Bois de Boulogne. Jane came dressed as Charlie Chaplin, with mustache, bowler hat, cane and baggy trousers. I was an officer of the Red Army.

We played a strange game all evening. She would avoid

me, run into me and avoid me again. Around five o'clock in the morning there were only twenty guests left. Jane was still there.

"You've forgotten the New Year's kiss," I said.

I kissed her on the mouth.

She stared at me and seemed to be on the point of saying something, but she changed her mind, joined her friend, Laurent, and asked him to take her home.

Catherine had celebrated New Year's Eve on her own. I never knew with whom.

A few days later, I went to the Epinay studios to see my friend Jean André, the set designer with whom I worked on all my films. He was supervising the construction of René Clément's sets for *Joy House*. We chatted over a whiskey in the small studio bar. It was raining heavily outside.

Suddenly the door opened and Jane came in. Her hair, which had been styled a few minutes earlier on the set, was dripping with rain. She was shooting a love scene and had put on a raincoat over her nightgown to cross the courtyard. She had been running, and her chest was heaving as she tried to catch her breath. She looked very beautiful arriving out of the night, breathless, dripping wet, her eyes shining, and suddenly embarrassed to find herself standing in front of me.

Someone had told her that I was in the bar with Jean André. On a sudden impulse, she had rushed from the set, fearing that I would leave before the end of the day's shooting.

That instant I knew I was in love.

Two hours later I took her back to her hotel, the Relais Bisson, and went up to her room with her. The windows looked onto the Seine. There was a large bed, visible beams on the ceiling, and a sofa in which we collapsed, as soon as she took off her raincoat.

We kissed tenderly and passionately with the impatience of two lovers meeting after a long separation. I had half undressed her and we were about to make love on the sofa when she suddenly broke away and ran to the bathroom. She came out a minute later, completely naked, and got into bed. I undressed and joined her. But something happened and I couldn't make love to her.

I have read that too much passion can make a man in love impotent, and so I didn't feel discouraged. An hour later, however, I had to face the facts: I was blocked, humiliated and reduced to total impotence.

After the sudden emotional shock in the studio bar and the passionate flirtation on the sofa, I felt that Jane's disappearance into the bathroom and the prosaic way she waited for me naked in bed was somewhat aggressive. The dream suddenly became banal. It was as if she had said to me, "You want to make love? Go ahead."

And that was exactly what was going on in her head, Jane told me later. She felt violently attracted to me and wanted to get rid of her obsession by making love. She refused to fall in love, and felt that once the ritual was over, she would be free. My sudden and inexplicable impotence changed the situation completely.

Around midnight I suggested supper at La Quinta, a small Spanish restaurant near the hotel. We stayed at the Quinta until four in the morning, talking, laughing, and more in love than ever. I drank an impressive number of tequilas, praying that alcohol would drown my inhibitions.

Back in bed—and another fiasco! This time I told myself that too much alcohol was responsible. A few hours sleep and everything would work out.

In the morning I had to stop deceiving myself when nothing happened again. This unexpected situation didn't seem to affect Jane; on the contrary, I think it reassured her. I became more vulnerable and undoubtedly more human in her eyes.

She had to go out to dinner that evening and the next. We decided we would see each other again in two days.

After dining at a restaurant, I took her to a nightclub on the rue de Ponthieu. The several slow numbers that we danced together reassured me about my virility, but back at the hotel it was the same story. It became a recurring nightmare. Besides feeling ridiculous, I felt anxious. Jane was now convinced that I wasn't physically attracted to her. But she enjoyed my company more and more and suggested that we meet the following Saturday.

I had confided in my friend Bourillot, the racing-car driver, who was also a pharmacist. He gave me some pills to take for my next date with Jane.

"Take one after dinner," he advised me, "and one in the afternoon."

Through overzealousness, I swallowed all the pills before arriving at the Relais Bisson. I was sick as a dog all night. Jane looked after me devotedly and took me for a walk in the Bois de Boulogne on Sunday afternoon to get me back on my feet.

This extraordinary business lasted three weeks. I still don't understand Jane's patience with me during it all. She could have said, "Let's be friends. Let's stop playing games." She never refused to let me sleep with her. And I still marvel at my own incredible stubbornness. Any man in his right mind would have put a bullet through his head or given up exposing himself to such ridicule after a few days.

One evening I said to Jane, "I'm going to stay in bed with you until I can make love. One day, two days, a week, a month, a year if need be."

"A year?" she said. "René Clément won't be too happy about that."

In the middle of the night, the curse was broken. I was freed and became a normal man again.

We didn't stay in bed a year, but two nights and a day. I had to make up for lost time.

There was one positive result of this experience, so wounding to my pride: Jane no longer had any reason to be frightened of my reputation.

After my first miserable night with Jane, I had stopped sleeping at home. I saw Catherine and my son in the daytime, but slept in the rue de Bassano when I wasn't spending the night at the Relais Bisson.

Once the situation was "normalized," I stayed with Jane. She was still filming *Joy House* and I was finishing preparations for *Circle of Love*. We saw each other every night.

It was the first time that I had left one woman and fallen into the arms of another without any transition. I hadn't lied to Catherine, and I felt even more affection for her now that we had stopped arguing. She seemed to accept our separation without bitterness. But I believe that she suffered more than I did—not necessarily because she was in love with me, but because she felt that I had abandoned her. Her affair with Johnny Halliday had preceded my meeting with Jane. But she wasn't living with him. I *was* living with Jane. And the fact that I was really in love must have hurt her.

One day, Jane told me that she would be leaving for Geneva for forty-eight hours to see a producer.

I began missing her as soon as she left. Christian Marquand, Maurice Ronet and several other friends helped me forget my loneliness. It must have been almost dawn when we broke up.

I have already said that I sometimes went to the wrong studio. Well, that night I went to the wrong home. The keys to my apartment were in the glove compartment of my car. Instead of going to the Relais Bisson, I went to Avenue Ingres.

I opened the front door and walked to the bedroom, where I got undressed without a sound. Then I got into bed.

Catherine, who was watching me, couldn't believe her eyes.

"Can you explain to me what you're doing?" she asked as I lay down beside her.

It was only then that I realized my mistake. "Sorry," I told her. "I must have come to the wrong address."

Catherine said something but I was too tired and sleepy to listen, and I dropped off before she could finish her sentence.

When I awoke, the bed was empty. Catherine was in the living room. She looked at me in silence, the way one looks at an animal one has never seen before.

"What were you trying to tell me last night?" I asked.

"I was telling you to get dressed and to get out."

"When I went off to sleep, what did you do?"

"I thought of ringing the police. But that wouldn't have worked because it's your apartment. Then I thought of suffocating you with a pillow, but I said to myself that it wasn't worth going to prison for someone like you. And I was too tired to drag you out by your heels. So I went back to sleep."

After a moment's silence, she added, "Aren't you ashamed of yourself, Vadim?"

"Yes, I am ashamed."

It was true.

W HEN Jane came back from Geneva, I asked her, "The man you went to see was your lover, wasn't he?"

"Yes."

"Were you in love with him?"

"I was alone. He was kind, dependable. He helped me."

"Why this trip to Geneva?"

"To settle my problems with him. I also wanted to be away from you so that I could see how I really felt about you."

I began to understand Jane. Her practical side was surprising.

"And what do you feel?"

"I love you."

Later on, I asked her again, "Did you sleep with him in Geneva?"

"Yes. I already told you: I wanted to see what I really felt."

When I got over the initial shock, I felt strangely reassured. It was the first time I had met a woman who didn't lie.

Later on my opinion was to become more nuanced.

*T*HE qualities that attracted me to Jane Fonda were not those everyone recognizes in her today—political courage, leadership, commitment to feminist causes, incredible success in films and business, or the image of an intellectual who sacrifices neither her home for her ideas nor her ideas for her home. It was the vulnerability hiding behind the appearance of strength and self-confidence, her honest search for her true identity and, of course, her face, her body and the fact that we were perfectly compatible physically.

Sexual pleasure, as everyone knows, depends as much on the mind as on the erogenous zones—and even more on imagination and the ability to improvise on techniques of lovemaking. In this, Jane was a total woman. Even to her natural gifts she added a sort of innocence and naiveté which combined charm with pleasure.

I had difficulty placing Jane's IQ, but I was very impressed by her tremendous intellectual curiosity, a rare quality in anyone.

We were very much in love, but Jane didn't have a lasting relationship in mind. She didn't want to become attached to anyone. She felt that she was not at the stage in her life when she should settle down with a man. And she didn't have much confidence in my capacity for long-term relationships.

What was strange in this mutual attachment was the fact that we were diametrically opposed by culture, character, and even by our outlook on life. I was her senior by only ten years, but I had long since analyzed and come to grips with my emotions and my ideas. I had defined my behavior within the confines of society and had set my own rules of the game. I thought I knew myself as much as man is able to know himself, to be aware of his identity.

Jane, on the other hand, at twenty-four, had not yet come out of her cocoon. She was searching for new roads leading to the discovery of her identity. That I was totally different from whatever she had known so far frightened her somewhat, but fascinated her even more. Arriving without a definite form in this new world, she hoped to find in me an answer to the questions her life so far had not provided. I was the door that opened onto the adventure of life.

*O*NCE *Joy House* was finished, production would no longer pay for her hotel accommodations. To save money, Jane and I decided to rent a small apartment.

I found the ideal nest for us at 12 rue de Seguier. It was a narrow street near the Place Saint-Michel, right in the center of the students' quarter, only a few yards from the Seine. It would be impossible to imagine a more romantic spot. There was a huge fireplace, a ceiling with old, craggy beams, and a small staircase leading to a loggia, which took up almost all the upper space. It had been custom-built for the owner, who apparently liked sleeping with lots of people at the same time.

I spent my days at the production office, where I was finishing preparations for *Circle of Love*.

Jane went to museums, took French lessons with Monique Carone, the wife of a photographer at *Paris-Match*, wrote letters to her friends, her brother, her father and her ex-stepmother, Susan (the former Mrs. Henry Fonda), whom she liked very much. She read books, but there were enormous gaps in her literary background, especially when it came to history and politics. I told her to read André Malraux's *L'Espoir* and Gorky's *The Mother* and Machiavelli's *The Prince*. She couldn't finish *The Prince*. She had no interest yet in politics, or rather the mechanics of politics, which was Machiavelli's concern.

Neither of us had been to Holland, so we decided to spend a weekend in Amsterdam. When she saw whores in shop windows in a street known to sailors the world over, Jane had her first spell of militant feminism.

"It's shameful to degrade women like this!" she exclaimed. "A whore is a human being, not a creature that you exhibit like an animal at a fair."

She wanted to smash the windows with the cobblestones on the street.

But my schedule wouldn't allow me the luxury of a stay in prison, and I managed to dissuade her from executing her noble project.

A few feet farther along, I grabbed a pick left behind by the men who had been working on the sidewalk.

"What are you doing?" asked Jane.

I pointed out a young male whore in skintight trousers who was sitting in an armchair, behind a shop window, and making eyes at potential clients.

"It's shameful to degrade men like this," I exclaimed. "I'm going to smash that window."

Then she laughed. In those days, she laughed much more easily than she does now.

*O*N our return to Paris, we were awakened in the middle of the night by the telephone. It was Annette. In a faint voice she told me that she was terribly depressed, that nothing was going right, and that she was fed up with everything.

"I can hardly hear you," I said. "Can you talk louder?"

"No . . . I've taken too much Veronal."

So Annette was going in for it, too.

Half an hour later, Jane and I arrived at the apartment I had rented for Annette ten months earlier. I hadn't alerted my mother, who lived on the same floor with Nathalie, because I didn't think that the situation was really dangerous.

The door was open and we walked in. Annette was a little groggy, but not ill enough to justify calling a doctor. Jane took her into the bathroom to make her vomit, while I prepared a pot of coffee.

Annette had fallen in love with the actor Omar Sharif. With her incredible naiveté, unshaken by experience, she was convinced that he was going to beg her to share his life. In fact, after their first night together in his suite at the Georges V, he had made it perfectly clear to Annette that the adventure ended there.

Omar is a charming man and an excellent friend, but he had a very particular style with women. In spite of the passionate lover that he played on the screen, he was rarely romantic.

Jane knew better than I how to comfort Annette. She spoke in a nice way and succeeded in reasoning with her. She told her that a woman should never put herself in the position of depending on a man, either materially or emotionally.

Annette thanked Jane, cried, kissed her and claimed that she had learned her lesson. From then on she was going to think of her career and her child first. No longer was she going to be a plaything existing just for men's pleasure.

I had never heard Annette talking like this. I was overwhelmed with admiration for the miracle that Jane had just wrought.

Two weeks later, Annette fell in love with a man who owned sugar factories in Casablanca and went off to live with him in Morocco! He was going to be her second husband.

* * *

MAKING a film with Jane turned out to be a real pleasure. She paid attention to directions; she was disciplined, always ready to do better, and punctual; in a word, she was a true professional, which is not always the case with French and Italian actresses.

Jane's professional training was exemplary. A student of Lee Strasberg, the famous founder of the Actor's Studio, she had the opportunity to link theory to practice, thanks to her experience in theater and film. Her directors had prestigious names: Joshua Logan, George Cukor, George Roy Hill, René Clément.

Nevertheless there was something lacking: true spontaneity. She was still only an exceptionally gifted learner, and uneasy about giving free rein to her personality. She analyzed too much. She had met an actor who dreamed of becoming a director, Andreas Voutsinas, who to some people was a ridiculous, grotesque person and to others the devil personified. For Jane, he was a sort of personal guru. She had lived under his influence for more than a year, and the situation seemed to me like Katherine Mansfield's when she was under Gurdjieff's spell. Luckily for Jane, she didn't suffer Katherine's fate and die of tuberculosis having placed too much faith in her Master's omnipotence. Soon after her arrival in Paris, Jane had broken off her relationship with Voutsinas, who returned to the States.

According to Jane, Andreas Voutsinas had aided her a great deal in her profession, despite the resounding failure of *The Fun Couple*, a play he had directed for her in New York. But she finally made up her mind that by dissecting every feeling and analyzing endlessly she was putting her own personality in chains. As a result, she was completely receptive to my advice. All my efforts were directed toward one end: to give her confidence in her looks and in her innermost self. In other words, I wanted to leave more room for her to be spontaneous without damaging her already remarkable acting experience. It was a delicate and subtle task which took several years, because I didn't want to hurt her in any way. I was only the diamond cutter. The diamond already existed and it only needed the extra sparkle that makes a precious stone a unique jewel. She herself (later on, with the help of other directors) covered the distance that led to the supreme consecration of her art: two Oscars as Best Actress.

While we were filming *Circle of Love*, she never imagined that one day she would receive these honors which her father himself had still not won at the time. She often said that she would never be a star.

"I will be a character actress. A very good one. But only a character actress."

I told her that she was mistaken and that for an actor, as for a painter or a writer, at a certain stage one must forget what one had been taught, fulfill oneself and make the transition from being a good craftsman to a genius. A racing-car driver, for instance, becomes a champion after having assimilated the techniques of driving so perfectly that they become second nature to him; he can then trust his reflexes and improvise. It's the same for actors.

The future showed that Jane did benefit from my advice. But she has never been convinced of her real beauty. In my mind, that adds to her attractiveness. There is nothing less seductive than an actress who thinks she's irresistible and confuses the camera lens with a mirror. It's one of the reasons why top models rarely make it in films.

Jane didn't have to take off her clothes in *Circle of Love*, but there was a bedroom scene with Jean-Claude Brialy, who played her lover. The story required that Brialy, wild with passion, suddenly finds himself unable to make love. To express the horror of this sudden failure, he assumed a tragic expression.

"You don't need to make such a face," I told Brialy.

"So how do you want me to look?" he asked me.

"Vadim will show you," said Jane. And she burst out laughing.

I remembered the episode in the bedroom at the Relais Bisson, and began to laugh with her.

No one on the set understood why we were so amused.

*I*T had always been a fantasy of mine to visit the land of my ancestors, but for one reason or another I kept putting off the trip.

One day Jane told me that she would like very much to know Russia, and we decided to go to Moscow the moment the film was finished. We had no difficulty obtaining visas. Thanks to Khrushchev, the USSR was at the height of its de-Stalinization period. Moreover, I was personally acquainted with the Soviet ambassador in Paris.

Our friend Monique Carone agreed to accompany us. She spoke fluent Russian, and we hoped that we wouldn't have to depend on the interpreter provided by the Intourist office.

The Russians had just built a gigantic turboprop Ilyushin, able to fly from Moscow to Cuba without stopovers. We boarded this strange plane at Le Bourget Airport. First we walked through a sort of steamship cabin where twelve perfectly silent men were sitting, all dressed in the same blue suits. Then we walked through a long corridor where there was one compartment after another with sliding doors, rather like the Orient Express. After passing a bar and a kind of restaurant-canteen, we came to an area that reminded me we were actually on a plane: the passengers were crammed into narrow, uncomfortable seats. Finally, there was a section that resembled a luxurious Pullman car, with individual tables and large, very roomy and comfortable armchairs.

"Don't try to tell me that this thing is going to fly," said Jane in a rather worried tone.

"We'll be taking the road to Moscow to avoid radar," I told her.

Against all logic, the enormous machine managed to take off, and despite the eight rather noisy turboprop engines, it was a pleasant flight. The hostesses were completely relaxed and didn't bore the passengers with stupid rules about the position of their seats. They even left the bottle of vodka and the glasses on the table during the landing. I warmly congratulated them.

The first surprise for Jane was that clearing Customs at the airport in Moscow was ten times faster than in New York or Los Angeles.

The brother of Toto Mercanton, the editor of my films, lived with his family in Moscow, and he had a car. He was waiting for us at the airport. As we passed a large residential complex in the suburbs of the capital, Jane noticed a little boy riding around the courtyard on a tricycle.

"Look!" she said with great surprise.

"At what?"

"The little boy. He has a tricycle."

She didn't believe that Soviet kids had toys, and I understood the extent of the gap between the United States and Russia created by each country's propaganda.

For my part, I found Russia exactly what I had expected: little luxury, but no poverty, few uniformed policemen (the police are mainly political, and therefore invisible), tourists complaining of slow service in hotels and restaurants and poorly stocked shops. A new privileged class, composed of Communist party officials, their friends and families, was unaffected by the material problems of the average Russian—like the French kings and the court at Versailles, who were indifferent to the suffering of the peasants. But I also found a warm people who liked to laugh, drink and have a good time. They were critical of their government and the bureaucracy in private, but rarely bold enough to protest in public. On the whole they had adapted to their way of life and were convinced that, despite its faults, socialism was better than the capitalist system. Certain artists, intellectuals and some students who were less vulnerable than the masses to party propaganda, were more recalcitrant and dreamed of Paris, Rome or New York.

Jane had expected to see an oppressed people who were terrified by the secret police and eager to be rid of the Communist regime. This was true for a small part of the population, but not for the average Russian. What finally surprised her most was the cheerfulness of Russian house-wives, called "babas," as they stood three hours in line to buy a scarce product, and the cheerful evenings we spent with families in rather overcrowded apartments. She was also undoubtedly impressed by the broad culture of the students we came across. Those we met spoke fluent French or English and knew the history of the United States and American literature better than Jane did.

I must make it clear that we were in the Soviet Union during an exceptional period. Khrushchev had permitted a certain liberalization, which created a feeling of euphoria among the Russians. But Khrushchev didn't last long.

We were also in a rather special situation to the extent that we didn't need an official interpreter, which made people feel more at ease with us. A tourist who is shunted from hotel to hotel and who depends entirely on Intourist officials has a really miserable time. I wouldn't have lasted two days under those conditions.

The first night we slept in a huge room on the third floor of the National Hotel. Our windows looked out onto the Gorky Prospekt.

Around midnight, a loud, unbearable noise, very much like the rumbling of an earthquake, awoke us. We went to the window. A monstrous procession was coming down the avenue. Behind the tanks, huge green shapes followed one another for more than a kilometer. As tall as a three-story house, these phantoms resembled dead giants under shrouds being led to some apocalyptic cemetery. Next to them the tanks looked like matchboxes, and the huge artillery pieces like children's toys.

I was fascinated. I remembered the Nazi panzer divisions invading the port of Toulon when I was twelve. I turned around, but Jane was no longer at the window. She was sitting on the bed with her head buried between her knees, and she suddenly seemed very fragile, very small and very terrified. For the first time in her life she was confronted with the real image of war. Like most Americans of her age, she knew of war only from films, television and magazines. The shock had unnerved her. She was trembling and incapable of saying a word for about an hour.

"Tomorrow's May First," I explained to her. "It's Russian Labor Day. It's also the occasion for their largest military parade of the year."

I held Jane in my arms and hugged her as one hugs a baby who is frightened of a storm. It was the first and last time I ever saw her so vulnerable.

The next day we watched the parade from a second-floor balcony. Khrushchev, in the government grandstand, faced us on the other side of Red Square.

The camouflaged giants that we had seen passing under our window were Intercontinental Ballistic Missiles with nuclear warheads. They were being presented to the public for the first time. With their shrouds removed, these monsters were just as upsetting, but they had great beauty. Death and art have often made a happy match.

After the military parade, the huge crowd marched, more than a million Russians and Asians displaying all the folkloric richness of a country stretching from China to Europe, and from the Arctic regions to India. After the image of strength and technology in the service of death, there was the colorful disorder of humanity, armed only with silk and cotton and woolen cloth. This motley crowd moved slowly, like a great river, carrying babies on their shoulders and brandishing banners that read "No More War," "Peace on

Earth," "Twenty-Seven Million Russians Died So That the Children of the World Can Live," and so on.

The wish for peace was very evident, but as Jane remarked, "In those twenty-seven million dead, do they include the Russians assassinated by Stalin?"

*H*ENRY Fonda was without a doubt the American actor best known in Russia (I don't include Charlie Chaplin, who was English). He was certainly the best loved. His daughter was warmly welcomed wherever she went.

I had met the actor-director Bondarchuk in Rome, and he invited us to the Moscow studios where, for two and a half years, he had been working on a huge film adaptation of Leo Tolstoy's *War and Peace*, an eight-hour film.

Jane admired the sumptuous sets built on a gigantic lot, and remarked: "It feels just like Hollywood."

Bondarchuk was exhausted and on the verge of a nervous breakdown. "Almost three years on the same film. I can't take any more," he confessed.

He suggested that I finish *War and Peace* in his place. He found the strength to smile, and added, "Don't worry, I'll accompany Jane back to Paris."

Advocates of puritanism in the United States should take lessons in morality from the Russians. In Russia it was forbidden to sleep in the same hotel room if you were not married, unless you were a foreign tourist. Thus, a problem unmarried people of all ages faced was, Where could they make love? In cars? Few Russians had them. At home? The housing shortage made that impossible. The solution was the trains. Public transportation is very cheap in the USSR.

The round trip between Moscow and Leningrad was paradise for illegitimate lovers and people who just liked sex. Jane and I didn't realize this when we took the sleeper to the former capital of the czars. Our compartment resembled a miniroom in a three-star hotel: lacquered wood, a copper lamp on a mahogany table, velvet curtains, a doll's-house bathroom with a shower and toilet.

We spent a very passionate and intimate evening. Late at night, when I couldn't get to sleep, I decided to take a walk in the corridors. I came upon a sleeping car. The first compartment comprised six berths and on each one there was a couple. Twelve people were making love. The rest of the carriage was not quite as active, but I had the impression that people were not bored.

*L*ENINGRAD is a charming city. Despite the horrors of a siege that lasted for more than two years (two-thirds of the population died of hunger or disease or were killed by German bombs in 1941–44), the people of Leningrad have remained more open than Muscovites. The atmosphere was more cheerful and relaxed than in Moscow.

I got permission from the curator of the Winter Palace (constructed by Peter the Great and still in perfect condition) to see the collection of jewelry in the basement, which is normally closed to the public.

Jane was very excited at the thought of seeing these treasures. We ordered several bottles of vodka to go with dinner in our room. Was it a result of the Baltic air, or the excess of pure alcohol? Jane slept so soundly that at eight o'clock, when the curator's secretary called me from the lobby, I couldn't wake her.

I visited the basement of the Winter Palace with Monique. We passed through three reinforced doors, which closed behind us, like Fort Knox. I understood why they took these precautions: we had just entered the cave of Ali Baba and his forty thieves.

I will mention especially the marvelous Hittite jewels, the delicate designs of which could only be appreciated with a magnifying glass. There were the Fabergés: cigarette boxes, animals, daggers, and the ivory revolver inlaid with rubies that had belonged to Catherine the Great. There was a chastity belt given by Ivan the Terrible to a future mistress, who was still a virgin, engraved with these words: "Woman is Desire. Desire is a Dream." We also saw Alexander Nevsky's sword and a ring that belonged to Peter the Great.

The secretary told us the history of the ring. It was on the finger of a Turkish sovereign who had been taken prisoner. "I want it," said Peter, "in exchange for a hundred of your soldiers whom I will free." The Turk cut off his finger and handed it over with the ring to the victor.

"Why did he cut off his finger?" asked Monique.

"I don't know," said the secretary.

"They didn't have soap in those days," I explained to Monique.

What impressed me most and made me fantasize about the robbery of the century was a gift that a Sultan had presented to Alexander the Great. It was the complete riding gear for a horse, woven with golden thread and studded with emeralds: the bridle, the reins, the saddle, the stirrups, and a cover were studded with several hundreds of precious gems.

Back at the hotel, I told Jane about my visit to the Winter Palace in great detail. Even today she hasn't forgiven herself for getting plastered.

The journey to Russia was certainly not responsible for the great turning point in Jane's existence—her political activism. But it did have a psychological effect. It was in Moscow that she began questioning, for the first time, the readymade ideas she had acquired in America and had taken for granted.

And doubt engenders thought.

WITH Annette living her new adventure in Morocco, I could take Nathalie back. The studio in the rue Seguier was too small, and we had to find an apartment. That could have taken time, but my friend and mentor, Commander Paul-Louis Weiller, came to the rescue.

He had turned one of his houses, the Hotel des Ambassadeurs de Hollande, built in the sixteenth century in the Marais district, into a foundation for artists in need. Paul-Louis had a very peculiar notion of artists in need, so Jane and I met his criteria. So did Roland Petit, the director of the famous Ballets de Paris, and his wife, "Zizi" Jeanmaire, a prima ballerina. They occupied the floor above the one assigned to us. Charlie Chaplin, Kirk Douglas and Visconti were often our neighbors when passing through Paris. All these "artists in need" had the good taste to prefer this architectural jewel in the Marais to the Plaza-Athénée or the Ritz. A patron of the arts, Paul-Louis was also an admirer of young flesh, and the garrets were occupied by ravishingly beautiful female dancers and models.

Our apartment included a room with vaults, called the Room of Maps because the walls and ceiling had been decorated by the great artists of the time (1560) with representations of the world as they knew or imagined it. For an American, even a graduate of Vassar, it was impressive.

Nathalie, who was learning geography at school, became annoyed with the fanciful shapes of oceans and continents painted on our walls. Jane caught her one day trying to correct the coast of Africa with a paintbrush. Luckily, Nathalie had used watercolors to modernize these sixteenth-century masterpieces.

Jane got along very well with my daughter. She herself had lived with two different stepmothers, Susan and Afdera, and she never forgot that Susan had succeeded in giving her the warmth and tenderness that she craved at the time. Even though my daughter had the warmth and affection of her father, Jane understood that she needed a feeling of security. She knew how to give her the necessary attention and discipline without brutally imposing her authority.

Even today, Nathalie, who is twenty-six years old, considers Jane more than a mere stepmother.

*T*HE *Umbrellas of Cherbourg* had been given a triumphant reception at Cannes, and two months later it was awarded the Louis Delluc prize.* Catherine Deneuve made two more films, one after the other: *Male Hunt* and *Male Companion*. That year her name and photo appeared in magazines more frequently than Brigitte Bardot's. Brigitte had withdrawn to her villa in Saint-Tropez and consistently refused all scripts offered to her.

Catherine showed no bitterness when journalists asked questions about our breakup. For instance, this interview was published in *Jours de France*, July 4, 1964:

CATHERINE: It's not a question of a real break between Vadim and myself. He's the father of my son. I owe him the greatest happiness of my life. Even though we're physically separated, we're not divided. . . . Vadim and I will never forget each other, no matter what happens.

QUESTION: Would you like to make a film directed by Vadim again?

CATHERINE: It's one of my greatest wishes. No one was more delighted than Vadim that *The Umbrellas of Cherbourg* was such a positive experience for me. He's never been jealous of the success of people he loves. He was delighted that I was making a film with Jacques Demy, and he reassured me and encouraged me when I had doubts. I was not sure I was ready for such an important role. That another director succeeded where he had failed never aroused any bitterness at all in him. Vadim taught me too much for me to deny his influence. My present and my future are a direct result

*The prize given to the first major work of a new film director.

of my past. And my past, from the age of sixteen to twenty-one, was Vadim.

*T*HAT summer, journalists vainly tried to find Jane and me in Saint-Tropez. We were vacationing with Nathalie and Christian in a modest hotel at Claouey (seventy-five inhabitants), on the bay of Arcachon. Our neighbors were a retired police sergeant, his blind dog, an ex-opera singer who was a janitor at the Bordeaux police station and a tax collector who looked like Monsieur Hulot.

Our windows looked out onto an oyster bed. Behind the hotel a pine forest stretched as far as huge sand dunes covered with rushes and wild carnations. From the top of the dunes we had a view of one of the most beautiful and longest stretches of beach in Europe, practically deserted even in the middle of summer. At low tide the Atlantic would recede several kilometers and then suddenly come charging toward the dunes with the speed of a galloping horse.

The former Vassar student, who was used to the luxury of homes in Bel-Air, had some difficulty adapting to the rather dubious comfort of our hotel. There was no room service; there was a common shower on our floor; and the telephone was in the proprietor's office. It was not exactly the lifestyle that she expected from a man whom the press had portrayed as the pope of hedonism. For a child pampered by the luxuries of American capitalism, it was a surprise. But one of Jane's qualities is her exceptional ability to adapt to new situations. Despite her fear of germs—anything not disinfected was dangerous and dirty, she thought—she got used to our rustic vacation. The experience undoubtedly helped her, six years later, when she went to Vietnam.

Accustomed through my upbringing—and the war—to going from palaces to the most modest inns, and not one to associate the pleasures of life only with luxury or comforts, I had no idea what a shock these few weeks in Claouey were for Jane. She didn't tell me about it until many years later.

For my part, I appreciated breakfast on the terrace, which became a raft during high tide; conversations with the other guests, who could have come straight out of a Jacques Tati film; walks on the dunes and the vast beach, sparkling like a mirror; open oysters barely harvested from the sea at low tide; the hunt for shells in the wet sand; and the blissful peace. There was no one talking about films, no journalists and not a single photographer. The children were delighted. And Jane was charming, playing with them and singing happy traditional American songs at the top of her voice on our car trips. Nathalie and I would join in, howling with laughter, because our accents were so awful. I can see Jane now, her head thrust back between the faces of the little boy and the little girl, who were clinging to her shoulders, and all three of them with their bare feet against the car window, tapping the rhythm of the song against each other's toes.

And Nathalie saying, "I *love* your foot fingers."

Jane laughed and asked, "What about my foot fingers?"

"They look like men's feet in museums."

"Museum," said Christian.

"Now he's talking," cried Jane.

"No. He's got hiccoughs,"said Nathalie, correcting her.

For me, it was the picture of happiness. But it wasn't enough for Jane. Something was lacking. A year after the birth of her daughter, Vanessa, she would say, "I reached the age of thirty-two and discovered I'd wasted thirty-two years of my life."

If she had been endowed with speech at birth, she would probably have told the doctor who delivered her mother's child, "I've wasted nine months of my life."

At the time I didn't realize that Jane already showed certain symptoms of a progressive form of American puritanism. She had a deep need to justify her right to exist by influencing or deciding what was best for others for their own good. "A life without a cause is a lost existence" could be her motto. It is a very noble philosophical attitude which I understand to a certain extent. But I can't reconcile myself to the idea of centering life on a "cause." I give the word "life" a broader meaning, which excludes neither pleasure nor time spent (lost, Jane would say) enjoying the amusements that the Inventor of this beautiful planet called earth placed at the disposition of intelligent creatures.

But in one area, Jane's attitude did differ radically from the traditional puritanism she had inherited from the sixteenth- and seventeenth-century Protestants: She never associated the idea of sex with sin. In this she was a woman free from any form of guilt complex.

We were coming back from the beach. Jane was carrying Christian on her shoulders. Nathalie and I were singing "By the Light of the Silvery Moon," out of tune.

A letter from Catherine was waiting for me at the hotel: "You can't help me. But this evening you're the only person I know whom I can talk to as I would to myself, who won't analyze my letter. . . ." It was a long love letter, both an appeal and a farewell, mixing bitterness with sweetness and melancholy, and passionate declarations of love with reproaches. It was signed: "Your mistress—C."

Catherine rarely took off her mask. This letter, which showed her so vulnerable and lonely, upset me.

A memory began to haunt me. I had rented a chalet at Argentière, near Chamonix, in a valley of Mont Blanc. I had left Jane there to go to Italy, where Catherine was making a film. I was going to fetch Catherine.

I remember a strange and passionate night. Neither Catherine nor I expected the explosion of sexuality which took us by surprise, like a sudden illness. No doubt, on that night, for one instant, I had thought that everything would work out with Catherine, that my relationship with Jane was only a dream, and that Christian would grow up living with a mother and father who loved each other.

The following morning we started driving with the baby. And the infernal mechanism started again. We began arguing. It was, once again, a war of words. The old wounds reopened.

When I got to Argentière, Catherine didn't want to get out of the car. I put my suitcase and Christian's on the side of the road and took the baby in my arms. Jane came out of the house and kissed me. I looked back, but couldn't see the expression on Catherine's face. She had done a U turn and had taken off at full speed along the narrow winding road.

*B*ACK in Paris, Jane said, "They're asking me to do a film in Hollywood."

"Have you read the script?"

"Yes. It's a Western. I'm going to say no."

I asked her to let me read the script, entitled *Cat Ballou*.

"It's not a classic Western," I told her the next day. "It's a good comedy."

I knew that she wanted to get back to America and prove to her father and Hollywood that her stay in Paris had been an intelligent move. She was finished with the roles of student and little sensual creature. She wanted to go home with the reputation of a star, which she had forged in Europe. But a Western?

"I like *Cat Ballou*," I insisted. "The woman is courageous, but tender, modern and funny. It's just right for you at this stage in your career."

She hesitated, but finally replied yes to Columbia Pictures.

I had to stay in Paris to be with Nathalie, but I promised to visit her.

The moment she got off the plane in Los Angeles, she called:

"Guess what . . ." she said.

"Me too," I told her.

☆ 25 ☆

THAT October the forest was bursting with yellows, reds and oranges. It was a visual feast.

I rented a car in Denver and drove to Colorado Springs, where Jane was shooting *Cat Ballou*. Her co-star was Lee Marvin. When he was drunk, he would tell me that he hated the French. "But," he would add, "I like you because you're half Russian, even though I hate Russians also."

In fact, Lee Marvin hated anything that wasn't American. But that didn't prevent us from spending a few enjoyable evenings with this fierce xenophobe.

Jane could have changed toward me once she was back in her own country, but nothing of the sort happened. She was affectionate and especially thoughtful, fearing perhaps, that I might feel like a fish out of water on a foreign set. But she was wrong. There is nothing in the world that is more like a film crew than another film crew, whether it's in western Europe, Russia, the United States or elsewhere. And Americans are always open and friendly when they like you.

Nevertheless, I do feel ill at ease on a set when I'm not

working. It's a bit like a captain who's invited on board a ship which he is not commanding. So I stayed on a week.

On my way back to Denver I was stopped twice by the police for speeding. The French feel that laws are made to be circumvented and find it difficult to adapt to American discipline.

I took the plane to New York to meet Raoul Lévy and discuss a project for a film. Raoul was having an attack of megalomania. He wanted to buy Metro-Goldwyn-Mayer and was convinced that Kirk Kerkorian (the owner of a chain of hotels in Las Vegas and chairman of the board of MGM) was paying the porter at the Sherry Netherland Hotel to have him killed. He made me enter and leave the hotel by the kitchens, which became irritating in the long run. Finally I persuaded him to use the hall, like everyone else. That night, unfortunately, a man was killed by three bullets in the head in front of the hotel.

"You see," said Raoul. "We narrowly escaped."

I was condemned again to the kitchen route.

After Jane joined me in New York, we went to live at her father's place on Seventy-third Street near Lexington Avenue. I had met Henry Fonda twice, during the evenings, and we had had an enjoyable time chatting. He was a reserved, polite man totally averse to any allusions to his private life. For instance, if he was asked whether he got up early or occasionally had nightmares, he would feel as uncomfortable as a woman asked publicly whether or not she cried when making love.

My relations with Henry Fonda were superficial but very pleasant. One could say we got along well. I wasn't perhaps the ideal son-in-law, but compared to his daughter's ex-fiancés, he found me reassuring. He had never accepted Jane's affair with Andreas Voutsinas. Thanks to the memory left by Voutsinas, I enjoyed special status from the very beginning. I was the man who had eliminated the perverse Voutsinas from Jane's life. It wasn't true, but I didn't try to change his mind. I accepted the medal for saving Jane without deserving it.

There has been much talk about the crises in Henry Fonda's relations with his children. It seems to me that it was more a problem of semantics.

Jane suffered because of her father's apparent coldness, which she interpreted as a lack of love. One day she told me: "When I was sixteen, I did photo modeling for a month in order to earn money for his birthday present. He said 'thanks' but forgot to open the package. Like a fool, I cried all night in my bedroom."

Her brother, Peter, had more dangerous reactions. When he was eleven, he shot himself in the stomach while playing around with a rifle. People spoke of a suicide attempt.

"I don't think it was that," said Jane. "And perhaps it wasn't an accident, either. Maybe it was an extravagant, romantic way of attracting attention. I really don't know. Peter is a complex man and he needed love."

One thing is certain: The father and his children had the greatest difficulty communicating with each other. Jane and Peter turned the misunderstanding into drama. But drama for an actor is like war for a soldier; it's part of daily life. As for me, I was going to help defuse a bomb which, in any case, would never have exploded. For years, I did what I could to "de-dramatize" relations between Jane and her father.

Henry Fonda had just separated from Afdera, his latest wife. A dark-haired Italian aristocrat, excessive in speech and actions, she was a colorful character and the exact antithesis of her husband. He was not yet living with Shirlee Adams, who was to be the last Mrs. Fonda.

I was sitting in the living room, unconsciously playing with the velvet covering on the chair, which had been torn on one side, when I noticed that four layers of different fabrics had been superimposed on the chair. It seemed rather strange, and when I was alone with Jane I asked her why.

"Each wife has done the house in different styles," she said. "Those are just the covers from each marriage."

One could get an idea of Henry Fonda's marriages the

same way one learns about the different eras of earth's history: by looking at the different strata of the soil.

*M*Y mother liked Jane very much.

They talked about the role of women in modern society, and bemoaned my laxness in the choice of subjects for films.

"She's an exceptional, unique woman," she said of Jane. "She'll be more famous than you, Brigitte or Catherine. She will love great causes and the men who will allow her to have a public persona. Soon, being an actress won't be enough for her. One day she'll want more."

I understood that Jane was looking for her identity, but I thought that a happy love life, success in her profession and perhaps a child would be the fulfillment of her quest. My mother saw further than I.

But there was good reason for my lack of perspective. Jane turned out to be such a perfect, conscientious housewife that I didn't suspect she was, in fact, taking on a new role. It's one of her dominant character traits to be a perfectionist beyond all reasonable limits.

Contrary to what she declared publicly ten years later, I never wanted to turn Jane into a slave of the home. I hadn't done it with my other wives, and I was certainly not going to begin with Jane. I believed sincerely that Jane enjoyed the activities of a housewife, and that was undoubtedly the case. Later on, for political reasons, she spoke of that period of her life as a domestic nightmare. I suspect she has convinced even herself that it was true.

When Jane took it into her head to buy a house in France and fell in love with an eighteenth-century farm near Houdan (about thirty-seven miles from Paris), I knew that she had really decided to live with me.

We had never spoken of marriage, except to agree that it was an old-fashioned formality that we didn't need to be happy.

☆ 26 ☆

*L*OS Angeles is a flat city, an urban paradox. You can define a Parisian, a New Yorker, a Londoner or a Roman, but it's harder to define an inhabitant of L.A. What do they call themselves? Los Angelians? The megapolis is made up of a collection of small towns with radically different ways of life.

Let's talk of the rich. The owners of houses in Beverly Hills and Bel-Air, or in Coldwater, Benedict and Laurel Canyons, are not all film people, but their lifestyles are identical. They meet only at parties or restaurants. They get into their Rolls, Jaguar or Mercedes to get a pack of cigarettes or a quart of nonfat milk. Among the obligatory festivities are countless fund-raising dinners.

"So your government takes no interest in either the poor, the old, the handicapped, medical research, drug addicts or orphans," I said to Jane.

Like a good American with a sense of fair play, she admitted her own faults and those of her compatriots, but she was not very tolerant of sarcastic remarks from foreigners. I never resisted the pleasure of teasing her. For example, stunned by the incredible number of awards handed out each year, I said, "You've turned Hollywood into an Olympic stadium. Everyone here is trying to win a medal."

For professional reasons, Jane and I decided to spend a few months in Los Angeles, at the Bel-Air Hotel. She knew that this kind of existence, however glamorous it might be, would soon bore me. She suggested renting a house on the beach.

Malibu, or more exactly, the beach called Colony, was not as popular then as it is today. One came across writers, artists, singers and film people, many of whom were not yet famous. People like Jack Nicholson, Larry Hagman, John Philips of the Mamas and the Papas, Mia Farrow, Jacqueline Bisset and Bob Towne, among many others, were our friends and neighbors.

I liked the relaxed atmosphere. I wore sandals and blue jeans most of the time. Friends came to the house without making plans a week in advance. I walked to the market, and fished for perch (and, if I was lucky, halibut) for the Provençal fish soup that I served for lunch or dinner. Nathalie and little Christian (he had arrived from France for summer vacation) loved this life.

Until 1970 we spent a few months each year in Malibu. In 1965, the year we rented director William Wyler's house, Jane decided to give a big party for me. Hollywood social events were very compartmentalized in those days. Presidents of studios and stars met at each other's homes—and those who were not yet uppermost had their own parties. We decided that ours would be more democratic.

A young hippie mother breastfeeding her baby sat next to Darryl Zanuck, Paul Newman and Jack Lemmon. Andy Warhol and two actors from his neopornographic underground films drank along with Lauren Bacall, George Cukor, Marlon Brando and Sam Spiegel, while Danny Kaye gave a Pop artist his recipe for spaghetti a la carbonara. Warren Beatty, surrounded by young actresses, explained that he had become suddenly impotent and would be leaving for India the next day. (It was of course a lie—sometimes

Warren loves to mystify people.) One particularly cheerful group included Jack Nicholson, Peter Fonda, Dennis Hopper, Bobby Walker and Terry Southern, who would make a splash in a few years with their film *Easy Rider*. Then there were Sidney Poitier, Gene Kelly and Natalie Wood, who gave tap-dancing lessons to my daughter Nathalie and two friends she'd picked up on the beach.

During the evening, everyone at the beach joined the party. We had installed a dance floor and a huge tent there. The Byrds, one of the most famous rock groups of the day, played and sang until dawn. We also had a big fireworks display.

Jane was better than a perfect hostess. In one night she had brought Hollywood up-to-date.

As in a film by Antonioni or Fellini, when day broke the workers took down the tent and the dance floor while a few millionaires and stars, overcome by exhaustion, slept on mattresses on the terrace and couches in the living room.

The sun was high in the sky. I was sitting on the edge of the wet sand with my arm around Jane's shoulders. We watched a little seal playing in the waves. I kissed her. That kiss had the delicious taste of success, madness and the California sun seasoned with the capricious wind from the Pacific. It tasted of Jane and the happiness we shared.

*J*ANE would get up at six in the morning to go to the studio. When she got home, around seven in the evening, she would find me in the kitchen supervising Roberto, our Cuban chauffeur, houseman and cook, or at the bar in the living room having an evening whiskey with friends.

Sometimes she asked my advice. When she did, I was very careful. Each film director has his own conception of his film, and nothing is more unbearable than an actor or actress arriving on the set with ideas that have been suggested by someone not associated with the film.

When Jane was not going to the studio, she made lists. She was an uncontested champion at list-making: she would make shopping lists, lists of bills to pay, lists of meetings, lists of letters to write, etc. . . .

But at that time she still knew how to relax. A few hours of idleness was not a mortal sin. She liked rock music, Bob Dylan and Joan Baez. She made collages and during the summer began preparing papier-mâché ornaments to put on the Christmas tree.

Every week Larry Hagman organized processions on the beach, a sort of carnival in which everyone let off steam. People disguised as gorillas, confederate soldiers, Texas tourists, Roman whores, or even as themselves, followed the American flag brandished by Larry. Then we all met in the Jacuzzi back at his pleasant home, which was always filled with children. The bad guy of *Dallas* is one of the friendliest and most charming men I have met in America.

Jane and I were rarely seen in fashionable restaurants or at parties in Beverly Hills.

During the day, but mainly at night—I'm a nocturnal writer—I worked on my film projects.

Sometimes Henry Fonda came to see us, and it was then that I met Shirlee Adams. Shirlee, who is still as ravishing as she was then, was always in a good mood, completely devoted to Henry and clearly in love with him. She organized the famous actor's life with great sensitivity and skill without ever giving him the impression that she was dominating him. She was neither his slave nor his master; she wanted only his happiness. Taken in hand, pampered, gently and firmly reprimanded when necessary, Henry had finally found the woman he needed.

Shirlee suffered from a habit that is common to many Americans: She couldn't stop herself from telling you the price of every new object or piece of clothing she bought. I teased her often about it. When she was eating a piece of New York steak, I would say, "Fifty-five cents, Shirlee. Seven twenty a half pound at the Farmers Market."

She had a good influence on relations between Jane and her father. One day Shirlee told me, "Jane thinks that I live with her father because of his name and his money. Men much younger and a hundred times richer than Henry have asked me to marry them. I love that man, Vadim. I really love him."

When Jane was convinced that Shirlee really loved Henry, she softened up and gradually accepted her.

I remember a conversation Jane had with her father:

"She's too young for you. She'll drop you."

"No one ever drops a Fonda," said Henry.

Jane looked at her father and smiled.

"No one ever drops a Fonda." She would not forget that phrase.

*C*IRCLE *of Love* was a well-written and well-acted comedy. It was perhaps a little subtle because it wasn't aimed at highbrows, and it lacked the simplicity that could please a larger public. It was too Parisian. Even though all it talked about was love and sex, it was not an erotic film. Jane revealed only her shoulders.

That didn't stop the American distributors of the film (Joe Levine's company) from putting up a giant poster of Jane, completely nude, in Times Square. She took it badly. What shocked me personally was that the poster was extremely ugly.

Jane began a lawsuit, so they covered her backside with a black rectangle, which added bad taste to pornography.

I was once again a victim of the preconceived idea that my films were meant to scandalize people. Contrary to what the majority of distributors think, you can't fool the public. There's nothing worse than selling a product under a false label. *Circle of Love* had been well received in Europe, but it irritated the critics here, who believed the publicity.

Jane was not yet a star in America despite the commercial success of *Cat Ballou*. The star of the film was Lee Marvin's horse, who would go to sleep when his rider was sleeping off a drinking bout. Marvin himself said that the horse deserved the award when he accepted it at the Oscar ceremony.

*S*AM Spiegel offered Jane the lead role in an ambitious film, *The Chase*. The cast (Marlon Brando, Robert Redford, E.G. Marshall, Angie Dickinson) held out great hopes for the film. Lillian Hellman had collaborated on the screenplay. The director was Arthur Penn.

But Jane, quite rightly, was worried about the film's future. She knew that Marlon Brando was bored with the film, and one night she did a brilliant imitation of Marlon, in his role as sheriff, taking two minutes to answer yes to a simple question. Seated at a desk, she sighed, scratched her nose, failed to find a philosophical answer worthy of a Californian sheriff, tilted the chair back, belched without making noise. She then looked at the sun through the window, trying to remember the exact distance between the earth and the sun, and having failed, scratched her nose again, touched the lobe of her ear. She thought about the question, closed her eyes, opened them, threw back her head as if about to laugh, but didn't laugh. Picking up a nickel on the desk, she stared at it as if the reply to the fundamental question "Who created God?" was engraved on the coin. Finally, she turned to the one asking the question and said, "Yes."

Jane's imitation, in a sense, was as brilliant as Marlon's performance when he played all the roles in *A Streetcar Named Desire* on the Champs-Élysées.

*I*N 1965, the majority of Americans were not aware that their government had created an infernal machine in Vietnam which was getting harder, day by day, to dismantle. When I told Jane the process triggered in Indochina was repeating itself for the second time, she didn't believe me.

"Your war was a colonialist war," she replied.

"And what's the difference between that and a capitalist war?"

"We're not defending our economic interest, like the French did. We're there to tell the Communists: Stop. That's enough."

"You're right," I said. "The only good Communist is a dead Communist. But I hope that more Vietnamese will survive in Vietnam than Indians in America."

It was a joke, but she took my remark seriously.

"I hate what we did to the Indians," she said. "But that genocide has nothing to do with Vietnam."

I had invited my mother to spend a few weeks with us in Malibu. She brought me French magazines and newspapers. They talked about *Viva Maria*, which Brigitte and Jeanne Moreau were making in Mexico under Louis Malle's direction, and Catherine Deneuve's romance with David Bailey, the star photographer of fashion models, who had just broken up with the famous and ravishing Jean Shrimpton for Catherine.

There was no apparent reason for the sudden decision Jane and I took to get married.

Biographers of Jane Fonda have written, "Vadim insisted that she marry him. She ended up saying yes." I neither insisted, nor even suggested that we legalize our union; it shows a lack of understanding of Jane to imagine that she would be capable of taking such an important decision through weakness, weariness or simply kindness. She has never let anyone make the important decisions in her life for her.

It was also speculated that I was seeking a publicity coup. If so, why a secret marriage improvised at the last moment and practically unmentioned by the press, which had been informed too late? The only journalist present was Oriana Fallaci, who was there only as a friend and didn't write a word about the marriage. If Jane or I had wanted publicity when we got married, nothing would have been easier.

In fact, we did everything we could to avoid it. Only a few very close friends were told about it—and only three days before the ceremony. We chartered a private plane. In Las Vegas, Jane did not come with me to City Hall to buy the license and sign the papers, so there was no risk of a journalist's catching on to the reason for our trip to that city.

The ceremony took place on August 14 in our room at the Dunes Hotel in the presence of eight witnesses who hadn't breathed a word about the event to anyone. Most of my friends and family in France weren't even told until the day after.

Those who took the trip with us, in addition to Oriana and my mother, were Christian Marquand and his wife, Tina (daughter of the actor Jean-Pierre Aumont), Peter Fonda and his wife, Susan, and Dennis Hopper and his wife, Brooke Hayward, who was Jane's best friend.

The judge who married us was so tall that he could barely get through the door. He was upset when he discovered that the future spouses hadn't thought about the rings.

"It's the best part of my speech," he complained.

In order not to disappoint this excellent fellow, Christian handed me his wedding ring, and Tina lent hers to Jane. Unfortunately it was too big, and Jane had to hold her finger up in the air throughout the whole ceremony. (Her gesture looked like the classic "Fuck you," and we found it hard to keep straight faces.) Despite that comic incident, Jane was overcome with emotion and began to cry.

She was the first to be surprised by her unexpected reaction. These tears meant that she attached more importance to the symbolic meaning of marriage than she cared to admit.

We spent the evening and part of the night mingling with the other tourists in the hotel. We were happy. We didn't dare to pronounce the word "forever," but we sincerely hoped that life would allow us to grow old together.

I won two thousand dollars at a baccarat table, and the next day the same little plane that brought us to Las Vegas set us down in Burbank. Mr. and Mrs. Plemiannikov's life returned to its routine, without any apparent change.

But the question remains: Why did we get married?

Perhaps Jane already wanted to be a mother and thought that it would be better for a child to have married parents.

She was irritated by the image of Vadim-Svengali adding a naive American to his list. By marrying me she gave our relationship a moral dimension. It was a way of saying, We love each other like everyone else. We want to be happy like everyone else. We want to be a family.

There is also in Jane a basic wish to carry things to the limit. Marriage reinforced her conviction of the moment that she would be an ideal wife and mother.

I must mention that Jane was always more sensitive to public opinion than her often provocative statements to the press would suggest.

As for me, I was happy at the idea of marrying Jane. Although I did not attach undue importance to marriage, I did feel more at ease in the United States in the position of a husband rather than that of a lover who was part of a famous actress's baggage.

For most people marriage is an end in itself, a social contract necessary for the couple's happiness. For us, on the contrary, it was a distortion of our principles. But isn't the act of rejecting a rule a way to establish one?

Without realizing it, we had started an epidemic. Five days later, Catherine Deneuve married David Bailey in London. In December, Shirlee Adams became Henry Fonda's fifth wife.

I was expecting Shirlee and Henry to get married, but Catherine's marriage surprised me. She had declared a hundred times to journalists that she was against the archaic formality, that true love did not depend on legal contracts, and that, in any case, she had always refused to marry me!

Perhaps she felt a sort of need for taking her revenge on destiny; she would succeed with another man where she had failed with me. The parallel with my own life was evident. I had fallen in love with a famous American actress, and she had fallen in love with a famous English photographer. I spent part of my time in the States. She settled in London. I married my American. She married her Englishman.

Was it a coincidence?

☆ 27 ☆

*T*HE farm that Jane had bought at Saint-Ouen-Marchefroid (one hundred and two inhabitants), about thirty-seven miles from Paris and three miles from the little town of Houdan, was in the heart of the countryside. Woods of beech and oak trees, about an acre of which belonged to us, covered the low hills of the Ile de France. To the west and to the north, stretching as far as the eye could see, were fields, dotted here and there by rows of tall poplars, where hare, wild boar and partridge ran free. To the south, a few houses, hidden by clumps of trees, formed a gentle, restful landscape, bursting with color in spring and summer, clothed in haze in autumn and silent and white in winter.

In France Jane was free from all professional obligations most of the time. She made only two films in five years there after her sketch in *Circle of Love*. With her usual energy and efficiency she devoted herself to renovating the house, designing the garden and putting in plants and flowers. To cover the muddy surface of the courtyard, we bought from castles nearby eighteenth-century paving stones, still marked by the wheels of carriages belonging to princes of the time. A winter conservatory, a henhouse, a badminton court, swings, a toboggan and an automobile track for the children were constructed in the garden. The pony that Columbia gave Jane when *Cat Ballou* opened had its own private stable. Nathalie rode it to school and to fetch milk and cheese from the neighboring farm.

We began to work to transform the outbuildings into editing rooms and guest rooms, and the granary into an indoor swimming pool and a projection room.

I shared the considerable cost of these renovations as far as my means would allow. Jane and I never had arguments over money. I earned a good living, but it's common knowledge that actors' salaries are much higher than those of film directors, and that they can make many more films a year. Between the choice of a subject, work on the screenplay, preparing and shooting a film and post-production work, I rarely made more than one film every two years.

Jane asked for my opinion, but I tried not to influence her too much in the organization and decoration of her new universe. Nevertheless, I did offer a few ideas of my own. Monique Carone had sold us her car, a 1937 Panhard Levasseur, a collector's item which had only one defect: It didn't work. I had it cut in two lengthwise with a blowtorch and welded it together again around a birch in the middle of the garden. No one knew how the tree had managed to grow through the car. In time it became a valuable sculpture. The new owners now show it off to their friends. My other idea was of a more intimate nature. I had a wall between the bedroom and the bathroom replaced with a huge window that could be hidden behind a curtain.

Jane ordered truckloads of trees to plant in the garden. As the months, then the years wore on, this became a disturbing habit, an obsession. The garden was filled with pine, birch, bougainvillea and beech trees, and even a cedar from Lebanon. She bought larger and larger trees. The cost of this forest, growing less than a hundred meters from the real forest, was astronomical. I didn't realize it, but I was copying one of Oscar Levant's phrases when I remarked, "If God had a bank account, he would have created that garden."

No doubt Jane was suffering from homesickness and was trying unconsciously to create roots in France.

An Italian family, father, mother, daughter and son, came to live with us at Saint-Ouen-Marchefroid (we were always looking for a name for the house but never found one, so it was called simply "the house" or "the farm" or "Houdan"). The Italians shared the household and kitchen chores among themselves, looked after the garden and fed the animals. Four people to look after a couple and a child (Nathalie was eight years old), make life very comfortable. Jane had perhaps become chief of operations in the house but certainly not a housewife tied to the stove and vacuuming the carpets.

She made more and more lists, argued with the plumber, the carpenter, the stonemasons, and the painters, gave instructions to the staff, went to Paris twice a week for classical ballet lessons and read screenplays that her agent sent her from Hollywood. Sometimes she shut herself in the kitchen to make one of her favorite dishes—New Orleans-style ham or turkey with pineapple.

We entertained a lot, and Jane was always the perfect hostess. I would actually have preferred that this perfect wife give herself a little more free time. But she only allowed herself to do nothing when we were on vacation.

In the courtyard alongside the house we had planted sunflowers, which went crazy. Like Jack's giant beanstalk, they never stopped growing, and their magnificent corollas soon reached beyond the roof of the farmhouse.

"What have you done to them?" I asked Jane.

"I know the magic formula that makes everything grow," she replied.

Christian was listening to us. He was only three years old, but he was already very interested in money: material concerns occupied an increasingly eager place in his mother's life, and that had obviously affected him. He gave Jane a flowerpot, in which he planted a ten-franc note.

"Say the magic formula that will make it grow," he demanded.

"*Break abbrak badabbrak*," said Jane.

During the night I planted a twig in the flowerpot and attached five or six ten-franc notes to it. When Christian awoke, he ran to the flowerpot. He stared at his "money plant" in wonderment. When he went back to his mother in London, he told her that he'd found a way to become "very very very rich."

Jane reprimanded me for playing this trick, which she considered immoral and against her educational principles.

"You allow children to believe in Santa Claus," I said. "Why not in the Holy Dollar?"

My wife did not appreciate this kind of humor.

*A*S Jane had predicted, *The Chase* was not a success. She had then made *Any Wednesday* with Jason Robards and Dean Jones, a charming comedy well received by the public and critics.

At the beginning of 1966 I finished the screenplay of *The Game Is Over (La Curée)*, a modern version of Emile Zola's famous novel about the middle-class milieu and the sharks of the world of finance in later nineteenth-century Paris.

Jane had played both serious and light characters, but they were all monolithic—by that I mean characters that didn't really develop as the story unfolded. With *The Game Is Over* I was offering Jane the role of a woman who is transformed between the beginning and the end of the film.

Renée, a young girl from a good family and educated in a convent, marries a rich and powerful man, a shark of the business community. He's twenty years her senior but very seductive. The character of Sacquard was played by Michel Piccoli.

The fashionable, superficial young woman, who is treated

like a precious doll by her husband and is, without realizing it, deprived of true love, which she has never known, discovers the passion of her life when Sacquard's son by a first marriage, played by Peter McEnnery, returns home to his father, having just completed his studies.

Love transforms Renée, who blossoms. She asks for a divorce so she can go and live with her young lover. But Sacquard won't stand for this assault on his pride. Besides, he has already decided to marry his son to a young heiress, hoping that the alliance will save his financial empire from collapse. By subtle and diabolical means he slowly drives his wife to madness.

At the end of the film, Renée, who has cut her long hair to satisfy her lover's whim, definitely goes mad during a masked ball held to celebrate the engagement between Sacquard's son and the young heiress. I am not the only one who thought Jane was sublime in this last sequence.

Some critics reproached me for my not remaining too faithful to Zola's text. But in France, in other parts of Europe and in many other countries, the film was, on the whole, a critical and commercial success, as well as a personal triumph for Jane. She had won her wager. She had proved that she could be a star without waiting for consecration by Hollywood. Her first Oscar would come a few years later.

I'm still surprised by the obsession of journalists and some members of the public with eroticism and nudity in my films. In the one hundred and ten minutes of *The Game Is Over,* I counted only three and a half when Jane is seen partly naked (she is never completely naked). These few scenes were spoken of as though Jane walked around naked throughout the entire film. Where does this fixation come from? The Biblical symbol of Eve and the serpent is more profoundly embedded in our unconscious than we believe: A naked woman must remain innocent. When she discovers sexual pleasure she unleashes on the world all the evils that plague mankind.

In *Coming Home* there are love scenes that are much more graphic than anything in *The Game Is Over*. But nobody was offended because the heroine Jane played had an excuse. The sexually explicit lovemaking scenes were allowed in order to prove that the hero was still a man despite his paralyzed legs. It was a good deed. I must add that those scenes were shot with a body double.

But in general, sex for pleasure, sex without moral or medical excuses, sex without the notion of guilt is still not accepted—at least, not in the cinema. If it is, it must be tinged with sadism—but then we are talking about disturbed people—or it must make people laugh, as in sex comedies. To cleanse oneself of the pleasure of loving pleasure for its own sake, you have to take offense, criticize or laugh at sex, as if sex wasn't meant for us. In this domain, when will we return to a more natural and accurate perspective, like the Greeks of the Athenian republic?

When I came into the world I must have come to the wrong civilization.

I introduced Jane to a great friend of mine, a truly exceptional man. Roger Vailland had belonged to the Surrealist and Dada movements before World War II. A hero of the Resistance who had fought with the Communist network, he broke with the party in 1950, disgusted by the French Communist leaders' submission to the Stalinists in Moscow.

He became famous with his best-seller *Drôle de Jeux,* a novel based on his experiences fighting against the Nazi Gestapo, and a few years later he won the Goncourt Prize for his book *La Loi*. Vailland was the last representative of this race of men who had brought the philosophical values of the eighteenth century to modern literature. A libertine and a moralist, he applied his intellectual theories rigorously to his life. He was a man of character.

His very handsome, ascetic face was lined with wrinkles of pleasure. A man who loved life, was a loyal friend, and never made concessions to hypocrites and snobs, he went to bed with princesses and prostitutes, always treating women and their sex with respect.

This famous writer lived in a pleasant, modest house in the country. He only came to Paris for his work or a few times a year to have fun. We had become very close during our collaboration on *Les Liaisons Dangereuses*.

Politically, he helped Jane to see that the world was not black and white with the good guys, the democratic nations, on one side, and the bad guys, the socialist countries, on the other. His anticommunism was not like American anticommunism, which is based on fear and lack of knowledge of its ideological adversary. He understood perfectly the mechanism that led from Marxist philosophy to totalitarianism, as well as the excesses and logical consequences of capitalism: the dictatorship of money.

He was also a theoretician of freedom for the individual. He rejected, with equal rigor, Judeo-Christian puritanism and communist hypocrisy when it came to sex and man's right to pleasure. "There's only one thing that's missing from the Declaration of the Rights of Man or the American Constitution," he said. "The right to happiness without the right to pleasure is a lie." This statement of belief, coming from a man of such integrity, who had never hesitated to risk his life for his ideas, couldn't fail to impress Jane.

When I arrived with Jane in Roger Vailland's garden for the first time, the sun was breaking through thick clouds. We had tea on an iron table near a Giacometti statue, surrounded by hollyhocks. (Vailland didn't allow himself his first whiskey until nightfall.) Elisabeth, his wife for fifteen years, told Jane a story.

"The old Catholic Italian families are very strict with their daughters," she said. "They're terrible. A kiss at a dance means dishonor and shame. When I came out of the convent, where I was educated, I thought you lost your soul if you made love to a boy before marrying him. Yet I detested the nuns and the priests. . . . I'll tell you about it one day. When I met Roger and ran off with him, he thought I was still not liberated from the principles inherited from my parents. One day he dragged me into a church. During Mass, in a nook behind the fount, he asked me to lift up my skirt and we made love standing up. 'Now that your Christ has blessed our union,' he told me, 'we can get married.' Which we did, and which allowed us to leave Italy without being stopped by the police.''

Elisabeth was a remarkable woman. Thin as a rail, strong as an oak, with black hair and black eyes, she was luminous with love for her husband, and she was always considerate of people's happiness as well as their weaknesses. Her face combined the strength of a peasant with the delicate features one expects from an aristocrat. You didn't think, Elisabeth is beautiful, or Elisabeth is ugly. Elisabeth was Elisabeth.

Elisabeth caressed Jane's face and said, ''I like your third eye.''

What she meant by ''third eye'' was one's vision of the universe. A superior dimension. The power to transcend oneself. Grace.

Roger Vailland said that there could never be true love in a relationship without freeing oneself from a sense of ownership and, above all, from jealousy on the sexual level. Not only did Elisabeth accept his extramarital affairs, she often introduced him to young girls or women capable of pleasing him. They never lied to each other.

''And if your wife made love with another man,'' Jane asked Vailland one day, ''would you be jealous?''

''That's completely forbidden,'' Roger told her.

''Why?''

''Because she would stop loving me.''

''Is that true?'' Jane asked Elisabeth.

''Yes,'' she replied. ''I would lose respect for him if he allowed me to come in the arms of another man.''

''That's not fair,'' said Jane. ''I don't call that freedom.''

"Perhaps. But freedom is not always a mathematical equation. Roger and I have found our freedom and we're happy."

One day Jane, in her own way, would go to the limits of freedom.

That night, in the narrow bed of the guest room, after we had made love, Jane asked me, "Do you agree with Roger's theory?"

"No," I told her.

"Why not?"

"Because you're not Elisabeth."

I kissed her and we went to sleep on a reply which wasn't a reply at all.

I would be able to give a reply today, but I couldn't at the time.

I had lived with three women and had played by the rules—meaning that I attempted conjugal fidelity; yet temptation was often stronger than the attempt. But I never spoke of these emphemeral adventures. Brigitte, Annette and Catherine, in turn, had kept theirs secret as long as it had been possible. The results had not seemed convincing. There is a dangerous limit to a couple's sexual routine.

After three years of living with Jane, I had convinced myself that the solution was to be found in sexual freedom based on reciprocal honesty. Sex being only one of the pleasures of life—although perhaps the most important—it should not be invested with greater moral value than, say, gourmandise or the joys of jogging. When I made love to another woman, I talked to Jane about it. With time, I went further. I brought home some of my conquests—sometimes even into our bed. I did not demand that Jane share in my frolics; I desired that she be my accomplice. This complicity in no way altered my attachment to my wife; on the contrary, it maintained and exalted it.

I was convinced that our erotic relationship was intelligently balanced between tenderness, an essentially monogamous passion, and flights of great fantasy, which never became a form of addiction. I knew that couples whose need for fantasy becomes routine risk trouble in their relationships as much as couples who succumb to monotonous repetition of the conjugal act.

Jane seemed to understand, and as always, went all out—all the way. Yet I did not know that she was suffering, probably because she didn't want to admit it to herself, thinking she was wrong to hold on to the rules of a traditional morality which, I told her, was outdated. But the truth is that she simply wasn't made for that kind of freedom. She recently confided to me that she had felt humiliated, diminished and even guilty about being a woman. With little self-respect, her respect for me was equally diminished.

As for Jane, she did not allow herself extramarital escapades. This should have opened my eyes. I was heading down a one-way street. Thinking I had found the secret formula for happiness, I was rushing toward an impasse.

Later, Jane would react, would acknowledge her desires in arms other than mine. There were pangs of jealousy, but no apprehensions, since she, too, told me everything. It still had not dawned on me that by finally accepting her sexual freedom, she also was about to distance herself from me, to escape.

There were some mitigating circumstances for my blindness: The very peculiar ambience of the late sixties, the mutation of Western society, the new theories of sexual freedom and the rights of women, all helped to create an aura of intoxication. Ancestral rules were on shaky ground. Old walls were crumbling, but no one knew yet how to rebuild.

Jane and I were the guinea pigs of an unstable era, and we did not know it.

☆ 28 ☆

I have said that Jane was ultimately more attached to secular values for a couple—fidelity, a traditional sense of family—than to the libertine philosophy of which, in truth, I had been the proponent and example. But, like all exceptional beings, she was, of course, not cut from only one kind of cloth. She was a woman who in no way was lacking in contradictions.

There was something pagan, an almost mythological quality in her. I take the word "pagan" from something Romain Gary confided in me one day when speaking of Jane.

"I saw her on the beach at dawn. She was a glorious, naked pagan goddess, followed by a nymph and two fauns. It was an image of the beginning of the world. It was youth, boldness and freedom."

I can still hear this famous writer's words and his serious, melancholic tone of voice. He was in Saint-Tropez for the weekend at the Tahiti Hotel on the Pampelonne beach, where Jane and I were spending our vacation. An insomniac, he was leaning out his window waiting for the sun to rise, when he saw a scene that was not meant to be witnessed.

Jane was running naked toward the sea, laughing. Behind her were a woman and two men, also naked. All four of them threw themselves into the water, swam to the Riva anchored about fifty meters from the shore, "and disappeared toward the horizon, as if the Mediterranean was their garden, pleasure their right, and nudity their wedding costume," concluded Romain Gary.

The evening before, Jane and I had been visited by two friends. He was intelligent and shy, rich, a handsome young man with a very personal, very black sense of humor. His wife had the proportions of a Rodin sculpture, and eyes sparkling with life—the kind of beauty that causes a person to look even if his back is turned. They were on their way to Rome and had made a detour to Saint-Tropez to have dinner with us.

After a candlelit dinner on the terrace of our suite, facing the sea that was hardly rippling that night, they decided it was too late to resume their journey,

"You can sleep on the couch-bed in the living room," I suggested.

At dawn we were still in the living room, talking. We should have been exhausted, but we felt like running. We rushed from the room onto the deserted beach. That was the scene Romain Gary had seen from his window.

The period of our life in which we indulged ourselves to the fullest was set in New York toward the end of the sixties: Pop art, Andy Warhol, the Village, the rejection of traditional morality in all its manifestations, the joy of living, and world-weariness, also.

New York was giving birth to a style that would break Europe's monopoly on newness. New York celebrated sex without guilt. This mini-society didn't represent the majority of Americans, naturally, but the search for new frontiers in art, pleasure, sex and morality was in itself a totally American sociological and cultural phenomenon. The goals were original and surprising in a country with Puritan traditions, but the dynamism of the phenomenon was worthy of the legendary pioneers.

Jane and I spent a fair amount of time in New York during that era. We took in everything, from the famous Max's Kansas City to the extraordinary studio of the painter Roy Lichtenstein, and from Andy Warhol's Factory to the warehouse on Tenth Street that served as a theater for a young troupe of actors. There the audience was seated on different levels of scaffolding, like swallows on telegraph poles. There was no stage. The actors, all naked, performed in the center of the warehouse and sometimes went off the walk among the audience. So you had the lead woman (a ravishing redhead) or one of the male actors suspended in midair above you, and if you raised your head you would find a male or female sex organ a few centimeters from your face. It did not claim to be an erotic show but a philosophical work with rather obscure symbolism. It was about the birth and life of a tyrant. I was told that the political content was obvious. That aspect of the play completely escaped me, but I had an excellent evening, balanced on my wooden plank.

It was that very night, in a very noisy and exciting nightclub (I forget the name), that Jane and I met E. They danced together and one didn't have to be a clairvoyant to see that they were attracted to each other. When they came back to our table, where I was with a friend of E's, a very pretty, rather intelligent brunette, Jane said to me, "E has suggested kidnapping me."

E was a few years younger than Jane. Well proportioned but not tall, he had very blond hair and was strikingly handsome. His face had the delicate features, the innocence and sublime purity of an archangel. He was, however, a completely amoral person.

Jane and I never spent more than a few weeks at a time in New York. And E came and went in our life like a charming and perverted elf.

Yes, I remember those days like a dream. And certain

images still haunt me, like the illustrations in a book of fairy tales that one sees as a child, before being able to read.

The Jane of those days and the Jane of today no doubt still have the same soul, but they are not the same people. One has reincarnated into the other without going through the process of death and birth.

☆ 29 ☆

*T*HE note, badly written in Italian and full of misspellings, went like this: "If you don't come to the corner of the Piazza Navona and the avenue at midday on Sunday, then I think Mummy will kill Daddy. My name is Stefania. I will be there."

Like most famous people, I received a lot of letters from crazy people. But this note was obviously written by a child. So I went to the Piazza Navona on Sunday at the set time.

A young kid pulled at my shirtsleeves.

"*Dottore* Vadim." (In Italy film directors are given the honorific title *Dottore*.)

"Yes."

"It's me who wrote to you."

"Are you Stefania?" I asked in astonishment.

"No," replied the boy. "But I thought you might not disturb yourself for a boy."

Only little Romans could have such an idea.

"So what's your name, Stefania?" I asked, rather amused.

"Franco."

"Okay, Franco. What do you want? Money? How much?"

"I won't say no to money," said Franco. "But most of all I don't want my mother to kill my father."

"And what have I got to do with that?"

"You . . . nothing, *Dottore*. It's your wife . . . la Fonda."

I bought Franco an ice cream from one of the wandering merchants of the Piazza Navona. We sat on the edge of the famous fountain and I listened to his story.

The subject of the twist of fate that might make Franco an orphan was a letter that had arrived a year earlier at my home in Malibu, addressed to Jane Fonda. Jane had read it, crumpled it up and thrown it into the wastebasket. I didn't make a habit of asking my wife questions about her mail, but I felt a queer impulse to do so this time.

"What was it?"

"An Italian producer, Dino de Laurentiis. He offered me a role in a film based on a comic strip."

"Can I read it?"

"Of course."

I took the letter out of the wastebasket, smoothed it out and read it. The film in question would be based on a French comic strip I knew well. The heroine was named Barbarella. Dino's first choices had been Brigitte Bardot and Sophia Loren, who had both refused. They had the same reaction as Jane: "A comic strip character? He can't be serious." The fad for movies like *Star Wars, Superman* and *Raiders of the Lost Ark* had not yet arrived. But for a long time I had dreamed of directing a film based on science fiction or a comic strip.

I explained to Jane that cinema was evolving and that the time was approaching when science fiction and galactic-style comedies like *Barbarella* would be important. She wasn't really convinced, but she realized that I had a passion for the project and she replied to Dino de Laurentiis's letter.

Dino asked me if I would direct the film, but it was clear that after Bardot's and Loren's rejections, if Jane had also refused the film would never have been made.

It was the second time that Jane had based an important decision in her career on love. Two years earlier, the producers of *Doctor Zhivago* had offered her the role that David Lean had finally given to Julie Christie. Jane had turned down the offer because she didn't want to spend seven months in Spain, away from me, although she was dying to work with the famous English director.

I N August 1967, I started the cameras rolling on *Barbarella* in de Laurentiis's studio in Rome.

The titles unfolded over the image of Barbarella taking off her astronaut's costume and floating, completely naked, between the fur-lined walls of her space ship. This futuristic striptease in a state of weightlessness has become a classic.

The chief makeup artist, who covered Jane's body with foundation makeup every morning, became ill. He was replaced by his assistant who, one evening after some heavy drinking in a bistro, began boasting that he had caressed the buttocks, the breasts and the inside of the divine Fonda's thighs.

Echos of this story reached the wife of the assistant makeup artist, a Calabrese as jealous as a tigress. She bought a revolver and told her eldest daughter that she intended to turn her unfaithful husband into a sieve. Terrified, the daughter spoke to her brother Franco, who decided to write to me.

I asked the boy what I could do to help him.

"Speak to my mother," he said.

He took me to a church on the Trastevere where we waited for the end of the High Mass. When the faithful came out of church, he introduced me to his mother. She was a domineering woman with an intense, severe look in her eyes, and I believed her when she said that the only reason she had not killed her husband was because she couldn't find any ammunition for her weapon. She added that despite the respect she owed my wife, all actresses were whores, and all directors were Satan's emissaries. I promised her that her husband would be assigned to make up only the extras, that very Monday morning, and she agreed to postpone her family vendetta.

When we said goodbye, she asked me for my autograph. "For Maria," she said. That was her first name.

I didn't tell Jane about this incident because it would have upset her. Besides, the chief makeup artist was back at work on Monday morning.

Unlike Brigitte Bardot, who had no problems with nudity, it upset Jane to undress on the set. Not for moral or even political reasons—her incendiary statements about the media's exploitation of women's bodies would come later—but simply because she did not feel that she was well shaped. People who have had the chance to admire the perfection of her body in *Barbarella* will find it difficult to believe this.

*T*HE shooting of *Barbarella* was very painful to Jane for physical reasons. She was put in a steel corset and suspended ten meters above the ground by a metal arm; she was attacked in a cage by hundreds of crazed birds; bitten by cannibalistic dolls, and she was locked up in a pleasure machine. The costumes were often more than uncomfortable; her breasts and waist were pushed into a transparent mold. But she showed courage and patience beyond belief. Thanks to her, the ambience on the set was, right until the end, exceptionally friendly. That is rare in a film where one encounters innumerable technical problems every day.

We had rented a house on the Via Appia Antica, a road that had witnessed the passing of Roman legions and the death of thousands of Christians on their crosses. The house was the oldest inhabited dwelling in Rome. The tower above our bedroom dated from the second century *before* Christ; the west wall of the living room dated from the second century *after* Christ. The rest of the house had been built in the fifteenth century. In the baroque park, which was overgrown with weeds, the tomb of a patrician of Nero's time was to be found next to an oval basin which had been dug in 1938 by one of Mussolini's cousins who apparently loved water lilies and goldfish.

When we were in bed, we would hear strange sounds— thuds at regular intervals, and sometimes groans—behind the walls and above our heads. The first night, Jane thought that a woman had been locked in the attic and was being tortured and raped by sadistic criminals. She decided that we should go to help her. Since we didn't have any weapons, I suggested calling the police.

"They'll arrive too late," said Jane.

We walked to the top of the tower, but found no door. All the exits leading to the attic had been closed off for centuries. We decided the noises and the groans were probably ghosts or protoplasmic entities who didn't need a door to take refuge in the attic.

Back in our bedroom, I pulled off Jane's nightdress under the pretext of checking her to see whether or not she was a ghost. We fell into bed laughing. Soon our sighs of pleasure drowned the laments of the wandering souls.

A few weeks later we were entertaining friends at dinner when a gray bundle dropped onto the plate of the American writer Gore Vidal. It was a baby owl.

"May I have the recipe?" Gore asked Jane without flinching.

Three little owls, who had come out of a hole in the wall adjoining the old tower, flew around the living room. We now had an explanation for the lugubrious howls and noises that sometimes woke us at night: A particularly neurotic family of nocturnal predators was living in the attic.

On Sunday morning Jane and I were awakened by the echo of an incredibly pure voice. We got up, walked along the corridor, went down the stairs of ancient stones worn by footsteps like rocks by the waves of the sea and walked into the kitchen to find Joan Baez singing as she prepared bacon and eggs for the actor John Phillip Law. In the film, John played a blind angel who recovered his life force after making love with Barbarella. In life, he was an excellent friend, nothing more. He did not like the hotel, so he was living with us on the Via Appia Antica. He had invited Joan Baez for the weekend.

I was present in the kitchen when Joan and Jane met. They liked each other, but neither of them imagined that two years later they would find themselves leading a crusade which, in a certain sense, would change the course of history.

The future political heroines spoke of Rome, music and films. John Phillip joined us and we devoured Joan Baez's eggs, which were delicious.

*O*NE evening Jane handed me the telephone and said, "It's someone who knows you well."
 I took the receiver and immediately recognized the sensual voice with its childlike intonations.

"Vava? It's your ex-wife. We're neighbors, you know. I've just rented Lollobrigida's villa on the Via Appia. Guess what stupid thing I've done again."

"You're remarried."

"I've been Madame Gunter Sachs for the last year."

"It's hard not to be aware of it."

I hadn't seen her since her marriage to the famous German millionaire. The marriage had surprised me. Brigitte was allergic to celebrity and power. She hated all the consequences of success: social climbing, vanity, lies and often cruelty. She didn't want that for herself, and she was wary of it in others. She had always fallen in love with unknowns.

The exception to the rule was Gunter. A rich playboy for

some, and the last of the great lords for others, everyone will agree if I say that Gunter had style. It was not the kind of style that would impress Brigitte, however. He seemed to be the exact antithesis of the kind of husband I had imagined for my ex-wife. But he was generous and romantic, in his own way. Brigitte, tired of her young lovers' jealousy and egoism, undoubtedly felt in need of a man who would take charge and protect her. An extravagant wedding was held on July 14, 1966.

"Not because my Teuton is interested in the storming of the Bastille," Brigitte told me, referring to the French national holiday on the same date, "but because his lucky number is fourteen."

With Gunter, Brigitte led the life of a star for the first and last time: she traveled on a private Boeing to Las Vegas and Monaco, and the Jet Set was there to meet her. Gunter gambled for high stakes, and he won with style, always betting on number 14.

One day Brigitte said to him, "Bet on number twenty-eight, it's my birthday. You'll win double." Gunter followed her advice and lost over one hundred thousand dollars that night. To show that he didn't bear her any grudge, the next day he gave his wife a jewel worth the amount he had lost.

The papers spoke of the ideal marriage. I suspected that behind the screen of happiness, things were not quite that simple.

Gunter and Brigitte had both asked me to come to see them. I was very busy shooting *Barbarella,* but one Sunday afternoon I found the time to go to their house on the Via Appia. The villa that Lollobrigida had rented to Mr. and Mrs. Sachs for two months was large and luxurious. The butler said that the master was showing the park to some guests, but that madame was in the living room on the ground floor. He led the way.

Brigitte was in the middle of a huge room, wearing blue jeans and a T-shirt; her little silhouette seemed to be lost on the marble floor among period furniture that wasn't built to her scale. She was standing near the bar, drinking red liquid from a cocktail glass with a straw. She appeared bewildered and, above all, very lonely. When she turned toward me, I saw tears running down her cheeks. It had been ages since I had seen her cry.

She smiled. "My Vava, I'm a little sad."

She dried her tears with the back of her hand and kissed me. She remained in my arms for a long time. When she broke away, she had regained her composure and her sense of humor.

"I have a butler, three maids, four gardeners, a chauffeur, two duchesses, the ex-King of Greece or Spain—I don't remember any more—the second in command of the Mafia in Nevada, friends like Serge Marquand, the prince of Savoie, Paul Newman, Visconti, Ava Gardner and a husband who spoils me . . . and I'm bored. I'm bored like I've never been bored."

Then she complained that, with Gunter, she always had to be on the move, always traveling. She couldn't stand the casinos any more.

At that instant, Gunter and his guests walked into the living room. He greeted me warmly. Then he saw his wife in blue jeans and a T-shirt.

"Haven't you changed yet?"

"What's wrong with my blue jeans?" asked Brigitte, suddenly irritable. "You don't like the way they stretch over my ass? I thought you liked that."

Before leaving the living room she turned around and said to me: "Vava, come and help me choose a dress. At least you know how to dress women."

"And undress them," added Gunter, to make the guests laugh and ease the tension.

I followed Brigitte into her bedroom. Still furious, she threw her shoes, her jeans, her T-shirt and her underpants across the room, swearing as she did so.

When she calmed down, she went to the wardrobe

and opened the door. Then she saw her reflection in the mirror.

"I expect you've already seen naked women," she said, smiling. "In any case, we'll end up together when we're old."

She was over thirty but her body was as supple and firm as when she was twenty. Her breasts were a little heavier, but that suited her.

Is Gunter really in love with her, I wondered, or fascinated by her image? I knew that Gunter, who was very aware of the impression he made on others, believed he had found in Brigitte a star in the true sense of the word: that is to say, a glittering object, inaccessible and admired by the whole world. But, in fact, all that star longed for was the peacefulness of a warm, friendly little house where she could indulge her habits and feel protected from the rest of the world. That disturbed Gunter's plans.

Brigitte took out a simple but clinging jersey dress from the wardrobe. Despite Gunter's insistence, she rarely bought clothes from the great couturiers.

"Do you think it'll be all right?" she asked me.

"I'll tell you when you put it on."

She slipped on the dress, which was very sexy and exactly her style.

"Superb," I said. "And very pretty. It's a pity I'll have to wait until I have white hair to have another chance with you."

Brigitte laughed. "You shouldn't complain. Your wife isn't bad at all."

She looked at herself again in the mirror and sighed.

Two days later Brigitte made her first escape. Before the end of the year she decided to get a divorce.

She refused the money that Gunter offered her and returned almost all the jewels. Nevertheless, they remained on good terms. Brigitte said later that Gunter had told her, "You're like a superb sailing boat in the middle of the bay, whose sails sway back and forth. If there's no wind to blow, the boat will remain there without moving." And she added, "That wind, it has to come from somewhere. The drama of my life is that I can't seem to blow any wind my way."

J*ANE* received a letter from Andreas Voutsinas that seemed to worry her. I only knew Voutsinas by reputation. According to Henry Fonda he was a manipulator and a social climber, who had been one of the worst influences on his daughter. According to Jane, he was an intelligent man with a personal vision of acting which had helped her a great deal professionally.

Andreas Voutsinas's life was falling apart since he left the set of *Joy House* to return to the States. Having failed to find work, he was broke and deeply depressed. Jane asked me if it would upset me to ask him to Rome and give him some work on my film. *Barbarella*'s cast included actors of many different nationalities—Italians, French, Germans—and I needed a coach to teach them the English text. I thought it very nice of Jane to worry about her ex-companion's problems. I like people who are faithful to their friends. I agreed to let Andreas come, on the explicit condition that he did not take it upon himself to make her rehearse her role or undertake any analysis of the character she was playing. I couldn't see Barbarella being reviewed by Freud or Strasberg.

One fine morning in August, Andreas Voutsinas arrived with his bags at our place on the Via Appia Antica. He seemed mannered and affected in his behavior and evidently infatuated with his little person. With his meticulously pointed beard and sparkling black eyes, he reminded me of a sort of Mephisto straight out of a comic opera.

But Andreas was intelligent and did not lack humor. I eventually got used to his presence and became quite friendly with him. He told me that I had saved his life, that I was his friend forever and that he hoped to prove to me one day that when a Greek feels gratitude he means it.

*I*N order to direct *Barbarella*, I had to postpone the shooting date of another film, *Spirits of the Dead*. We knew when we signed our contract with Dino de Laurentiis that we would have to leave Rome in a hurry, immediately after the last sequence of *Barbarella* had been shot. We spent only twenty-four hours in our house at Houdan before leaving for Roskoff in Brittany, where the crew of *Spirits of the Dead* was awaiting us.

The film was structured as a triptych: three short stories by Edgar Allan Poe brought to the screen by three directors— Louis Malle, with Brigitte Bardot and Alain Delon; Fellini, with Terence Stamp; and me. My two lead actors had the same name: Fonda. One was Peter, the other Jane. It was the first time—and to this day, the only time—that brother and sister made a film together. The film was original and interesting, in my opinion; it is often shown on television and in art cinemas all over the world. I didn't think of it at the time, but it must have been very strange for Jane to go without any transition from her futuristic costumes to medieval robes. In fact, my episode in *Spirits of the Dead* was adapted from a Gothic short story, "Mezergenstein." It's also the only film in which Jane appears in period costume.

Peter was an almost perfect specimen of the New Wave young Americans of the sixties. He loved rock music, political singers like Bob Dylan, grass and psychedelic mushrooms, and he knew all the hippie slang. His respect for the dollar and his practical business mind were reconciled with his pacifist philosophy and spiritualist attitude, which was vaguely tinged with Hinduism. Peter was the instigator and the catalyst of the very popular film *Easy Rider*. He worked on the screenplay for this film on my set, in between takes, with Terry Southern, author of the erotic bestseller *Candy* and co-writer of *Doctor Strangelove* and *Barbarella*. The evenings at Roskoff during the shooting of *Spirits of the Dead* were too enjoyable for us to ruin them by working.

Peter liked to play the guitar. With the appearance of a big, rather lost adolescent and a disarming smile, he charmed everyone, including the technicians and, above all, the pretty young girls who played the ladies of the court.

Andreas Voutsinas had followed the family. He kept his position as coach, and I also gave him a role in my film. He played the traitor, and with great ease, I must admit.

The landscape of Brittany is harsh and dramatically beautiful. The moors, covered with heather and lavender, end at the edge of the black granite cliffs. One of the most murderous seas in the world crashes furiously against the rocks. It is a landscape evoking the end of the world, a landscape of legends, especially in winter, when the wind is howling and when dark, twisted clouds spread out and regroup a hundred yards from the ground as if they were a backdrop for some mad opera.

On Sunday, I had taken Jane for a walk on the moors near the bay of Trepasses. She was shivering, not because it was cold—she was warmly dressed—but because the suggestive power and mysterious beauty of the place opened the doors of her subconscious to the terrors of childhood that she thought had been buried long ago.

She remained silent for over an hour. When it began to rain we took shelter in a little *crêperie*. There, in front of a cup of hot wine and a crêpe made from wheat flour, Jane seemed to return to reality. She told me that she had been thinking a lot about her mother recently.

"Perhaps because I'm thinking more and more seriously about having a child," she added.

Jane was still very young when her mother began to suffer from chronic depressions. Her condition became serious and she had to be hospitalized. With the cruelty that is natural to children, **Jane**, instead of trying to understand, bore her mother a grudge for what she considered a betrayal or a defection.

"I must have been twelve. My mother was in the hospital and I hadn't seen her for a few weeks. I looked out of the window and saw a car being parked in the courtyard. My mother stepped out. She was accompanied by two nurses. I didn't want to see her. I didn't want to speak to her. I was frightened and angry. She had been under psychiatric care for a long time, and I practically never saw her any more. Children are quite unforgiving when it comes to absence. But at the same time I loved her. I was upstairs with Peter, whom I didn't allow to leave the room. For an entire hour I heard my mother calling us, but I didn't budge. Finally one of the nurses told my mother it was time to go back. 'Oh, no,' my mother said. 'Not yet. I must talk to her.' And she cried out my name again. I left my hiding place and watched out the window as the car made a U turn and disappeared. It was not very long after that, on her birthday, that my mother committed suicide in her room at the hospital. They told me the next day that she had died. It was only years later that I learned the truth: that she'd slit her throat."

Jane naturally felt guilty over the memory of this last meeting with her mother, which never took place. What did her mother want to tell her? Was it a call for help? Had she already decided to die? If Jane had spoken to her, would it have changed anything? So many questions that would never be answered.

After devouring her second crêpe, Jane confided, "I've watched the way you behave with your children for several years. And you've given me confidence. I'm not frightened any more, I think, of having a baby."

As you know, Nathalie lived with Jane and me. She sometimes visited her mother during vacations. Catherine Deneuve, on the other hand, had kept Christian. But he spent a lot of time with us. He was still very young, and the problem of sending him to school had not yet arisen.

"Do you want us to have a child?" Jane asked me.

"I'd be delirious with joy."

"That would make three kids in the house. Perhaps a little too many," she worried.

"We have five cats, six dogs and four Italians, so we might as well have three kids," I remarked.

A FTER the shooting of *Spirits of the Dead,* we decided to spend Christmas in Megève. Jane didn't particularly like skiing but she knew it was my favorite sport—a sport I had practiced since I was seven. So each winter she took lessons. She was not very talented at skiing, but with willpower and work she made decent progress.

On Christmas Eve I became ill with a fever and a sore throat. Having to stay in bed made me furious. Jane left in the morning with her ski instructor, and on her return she told me about her skiing achievements. She didn't enjoy playing cards and didn't understand the different chess moves. Television was practically nonexistent in France at that time (and it is hardly any better now). This limited the range of possible distractions in a hotel bedroom. We had the choice of reading or making love—but reading gave me a headache.

It was, I believe, three days after Christmas. It was snowing outside when Jane walked in with her woolen Norwegian bonnet on her head. Her cheeks and nose were red from the cold. She kissed me and undressed without speaking. She was completely naked, and I smiled because she had forgotten to take off her woolen bonnet. We made love on the carpet, then on the sofa, and later on, in the middle of the night, in bed. Jane was very tender and intense . . . languorous and serious at the same time.

I know that it was on that day, or night, that Vanessa was conceived.

☆ 30 ☆

CATHERINE Deneuve's marriage to David Bailey was like Brigitte's to Gunter—ephemeral. The two actresses were not alike, but they did have one thing in common: both of them could not bear to be contradicted. They had become accustomed to having their every wish and desire pandered to on the set—so wouldn't it be the same at home? The men they lived with had to adapt to their outlook on life and accept their judgments and decisions. This led to a dilemma: Either the man had a weak personality and obeyed without complaining or he refused to let himself be regimented—but that created friction, and then arguments, which finally led to a break.

During the time I lived with them, neither was really a star and they were both still very young. But even then, I noticed their growing tendency toward domestic tyranny and their need to give orders and to surround themselves with yes-men and yes-women.

Jane was very different on this score. She was hard on herself, but she knew how to be understanding of others. No one exercised dictatorial authority in our home. I was a little more capricious than she, and she was more nervous than I, but in general the authority was shared. That doesn't mean Jane showed less strength of character or personality than the others—on the contrary, as the future showed. But her goals were higher, more ambitious and also less egotistical. She made a cult of hard work, which was not the case with both Brigitte and Catherine. For them success had come without much effort, and when they were *very* young. They seemed to have forgotten that luck was a factor and thought that the world owed them everything. Since they had always succeeded easily in everything, they deduced that they were always right.

I don't mean that they didn't suffer like every human being. They had their moments of great confusion, difficulties in love and personal dramas. During the summer of 1967, a terrible misfortune occurred in Catherine's life. Her sister Françoise who, with Christian, was the person she loved most in the world, died a terrible death in an automobile accident. Françoise had left Catherine, with whom she had been spending the summer at Saint-Tropez, to take a plane at Nice. Before arriving at the airport, she lost control of her car, which skidded off the road, rolled over, landed in a field and suddenly caught fire. She couldn't undo her safety belt in time and was burned alive, jammed under the wheel.

The two sisters had just made a musical comedy together, *Les Demoiselles de Rochefort*, with Jacques Demy, the director of *The Umbrellas of Cherbourg*.

I wasn't in France when I heard the tragic news, but I didn't have to speak to Catherine to imagine the depth of her pain and sadness. Even today the wound has not healed. And it never will be.

That very year was to bring new success to Catherine's acting career: she incarnated the heroine of Luis Buñuel's *Belle de Jour*. The old master had not made a mistake when he chose her to play the character of Séverine, a middle-class woman with a cold, pure face, who lives out her erotic obsessions in her head. Every star—rightly or wrongly—

becomes identified with a film and a character. For Catherine it will be *Belle de Jour*. The film was a worldwide success and remains a classic, but when it opened in Paris the French critics were unimpressed and unfair. A more perceptive journalist wrote, in *Positif*, "The brilliant brains of our critics manifested in chorus the disappointment caused them by *Belle de Jour* . . . thus proving the softening of their own cortexes."

I remember a completely dismayed Catherine showing me the reviews that she had cut out of the papers. Nevertheless, the public lined up outside the cinemas where *Belle de Jour* was being shown. That day remains in my memory for another reason. As the maid and the nanny were out, I had offered to look after Christian. After Catherine had left for a meeting that evening with a man whose name I forget, I asked my four-year-old son whether he would like to watch television, play cards or have something to eat.

"All three," he said.

So we did just that. We ate in front of the television set and played Battle.

"What a lot of forbidden things," said Christian in ecstasy.

"What do you mean?"

"With Mummy, everything's always forbidden. You don't eat in the living room, first of all. You're not allowed to eat while watching TV. And you don't play cards while you eat."

After dinner, Christian, who was furious that I had won at cards, suggested a game of hide-and-seek. I wasn't thrilled at the idea, but since I had not seen my son for several weeks, I decided to go along with him. I will pass over the moment of panic in the kitchen when I grabbed Christian just as about two-thirds of his body was about to disappear into the empty automatic waste-disposal unit. For my intention is to speak of my surprise on opening Catherine's wardrobe where the little boy had hidden. He was sitting in an ocean of shoes of all shapes and colors and nationalities.

Christian saw that I was impressed by that army of shoes and dragged me to two other cupboards where there were moccasins, high heels, flat heels, pointed shoes, boots, short boots, ballet shoes, sandals and tennis shoes. I estimated over two hundred pairs of shoes in all, without counting the slippers.

It was almost midnight and Christian refused to go to sleep. I had perfected a few games for children who didn't want to sleep. That evening, I decided to use the method called "the hypnotizer hypnotized." I warned Christian that I was going to hypnotize him, and, as expected, hypnotic passes, counting backward, had no effect.

"I can't do it," I told him. "But you can perhaps put me to sleep."

He passed his hands in front of my eyes, counted to ten and was delighted to find that he had actually hypnotized me. He wanted to wake me up to tell me about his success but I kept my eyes closed. Since he had no one to talk to, he lay down on his bed, put his head on the pillow and went straight to sleep.

Catherine came home at two in the morning.

"What time did he go to sleep?" she asked.

"Around ten o'clock," I lied. "How was your evening?"

"Very enjoyable," she said.

She rarely spoke to me about her private life. She took off her shoes.

"Is it true that Jane's pregnant?" she asked suddenly.

"Yes."

She made no comment.

We kissed each other and she closed the door of the apartment behind me.

I had parked the Ferrari in the street. I got in and started off in the direction of the Point de Saint-Cloud. At that hour of the night, the western freeway was practically deserted. I drove to Mantes-la-Jolie at more than a hundred miles an hour. I took the highway and then the secondary road 311. I knew each bend by heart. In less than half an hour after leaving Catherine, I arrived at the house in Houdan. Jane was asleep. I got undressed and slipped into bed. She woke up, kissed me and held me in her arms. She was now four months pregnant and her stomach was getting round. I couldn't sleep. I was thinking about something that Louis Schwartz had said a month earlier.

Schwartz was my doctor and an old friend. During a conversation I told him that Jane had had the mumps a few weeks after the beginning of her pregnancy.

"If the mother contracts mumps a short time after she conceives," he said, "there is the risk of giving birth to a mongoloid child. It's a slight risk."

"Slight? Can you be more precise?"

"Certainly not more than one in five hundred," said Dr. Schwartz.

One in five hundred . . . what did that represent exactly? And doesn't one run the risk of being hit on the head by a brick or a falling flowerpot, or being run over while crossing a street, or catching a fatal illness, or drowning, or having a car accident? When I thought about it, it began to seem that, in essence, the very principle of life was a lottery in which you could draw the wrong number at any moment. To live is to take chances. I finally decided that one chance in five hundred was an acceptable risk.

Schwartz suggested an abortion, but Jane refused. I agreed with her. But I was often plagued with doubts: Had we made the right decision?

*T*HE strange revolution that erupted in the spring of 1968 in Paris, which nowadays people euphemistically call "the events of May," surprised everyone by its suddenness and the way an initially unorganized, makeshift movement spread in a few days. It all began with a simple student revolt at the University of Suresne and the government's clumsy, excessively violent reaction to what was not a very serious incident. Within a few days the whole of

Paris was in the streets, behind barricades, fighting with the police and the CRS (Corps Républicain de Sécurité, the equivalent of the National Guard in the United States). The provinces followed suit, and a general strike, which affected the whole country, was organized by the trade unions and the political parties of the left, which had decided to leap on the bandwagon of the revolution.

Jane, who was almost five months pregnant, could have remained quietly at our home in the country with no more knowledge of the events than what was said on the radio. But a totally unexpected circumstance had placed me at the very heart of the struggle and had thrust heavy responsibilities on me during this troubled period.

I had molded several assistant directors on my sets who were now considered tops in the profession. These Young Turks of the left, led by Jean-Michel Lacor, decided to break the political yoke imposed on the technicians' union by the Stalinist old guard, which had been in control since the end of the war. They asked me to be a candidate at the next union presidential elections. I had the greatest chances of being elected in opposition to the Communists because I had no political label, but I had always defended the union interests of the workers and technicians. Political power didn't interest me in the least, so I firmly rejected the idea.

Nevertheless, I spoke about this to Jane, who told me that I was wrong to shy away from it. My duty was to do what I considered to be best for the profession in general. I admitted that the Young Turks were right. It was high time to shake the jammed wheels of the union machine.

"So, don't hesitate," said Jane.

Caught in the crossfire of the studio and the bedroom, I finally decided to accept.

The vote was taken at the general meeting. I received 99 percent of the vote.

Three days later, the May revolution erupted with the suddenness of a flash of lightning in a cloudless sky. During those few historic weeks, without wanting to, I would preside over one of the most important CGT* unions in the country.

In the days that followed the events took a more violent turn. Barricades were erected everywhere. Trees were cut down and pavement pulled up; cars were burned and shop windows shattered. One heard the frequent sirens of the police cars, ambulances and fire engines, the explosions of tear gas, and sometimes shots. Paris was overwhelmed by the blackish smoke of fires and the white smoke of tear gas. At night flames lit up the clouds of ashes skimming the rooftops. Jane liked to accompany me to union and inter-union meetings. A relay radio kept me informed of the dangerous spots, and when I was with Jane, I took routes that were theoretically calm. Despite my efforts, she had occasion to see Parisians fighting on the barricades several times.

I had made my own analysis of the situation and discussed it with Jane.

"The government will be overthrown," Jane concluded after having listened to me attentively.

"I'm convinced of the contrary," I said. "The Communists have mobilized their troops and joined the students' camp in order to take control of the situation and nip the movement in the bud. They can't accept a revolution that outflanks them on the left. The Communist party will not admit it, obviously, but it is the government's best potential ally."

Few people made the same political calculation as I did. Even the president of the Republic, General de Gaulle, believing his government had lost the battle, left Paris secretly by helicopter to get the support of the French occupation army in Germany.

During that time, Jane went through a radical political metamorphosis. She, who in her mind had always refused to see any connection between the French war in Indochina and the American war in Vietnam, realized, through talking

*C.G.T. General Confederation of Labor.

to a number of committed Frenchmen of politics and literature, that it was fundamentally the same war, even though the vocabulary and the justifications used in America were different. She suddenly understood the essence of the Vietnam peace movement which was taking on new dimensions in her own country.

Oddly, this newfound political conscience—for which I was largely responsible—did not bring us any closer. Quite the contrary. Jane was now traveling down a road that was very different from the one I had followed since childhood.

It is probably quite difficult for the American reader to conceive of the sum total of experiences and data on human behavior a child could absorb during the Nazi occupation of France and the immediate postwar years. I saw priests inform on Jews and Resistance fighters, I saw men I looked up to tremble in abject fear during bombardments, I saw the power of money, political hypocrisy, pure sadism and stupidity. I also saw heroism and self-denial on the part of plain and modest people of whom one would never have expected such a show of courage. During the liberation, I saw hapless people, whose sin had been to do business with the Germans in order to feed their families, shot without a trial. I saw women with shaved heads being spit upon and mercilessly heckled by a mob because they had succumbed to the charms of German soldiers. And I saw true collaborators of the Germans, shielded by fortune or social rank, regain power and respect once the war was over. I saw the selfsame crowd that had applauded Field Marshal Pétain (the head of the pro-German French puppet government) four years earlier, scream and howl with satisfaction when those less lucky than their neighbors were dragged off to prison or the firing squad.

The war over, I saw the great ideals again subjected to politicians and political reality. And the same ones in power again, and the same ones leading a herd without memory. Later—I was a very young journalist—I learned that the same Russian heroes who had helped defeat the Nazis were now massacring Hungarians in Budapest. And there were the wars in Indochina and Algeria.

At sixteen, I had established a rule for myself: In order to avoid cynicism, and worse, causticity and bitterness, I was going to take the best from life. Its pleasures. The sea, nature, sports, Ferraris, friends and pals, art, nights of intoxication, the beauty of women, insolence and nose-thumbing at society. I kept my ideas on politics (I'm a liberal who is allergic to the words "fanaticism" and "intolerance"), but refused commitment in any form. I believed in man the individual, but had lost my faith in mankind at large.

Jane, on the other hand, had faith in mankind and a strong belief in political action and allegedly worthy causes.

This spring and summer period of 1968 was also a turning point for the woman in her.

She had always been afraid to assume her femininity. She equated anything purely feminine with weakness. Between her mother, destroyed and propelled beyond the brink of madness by a process beyond her grasp, the sex-object ideal generally prevalent in America, and Hollywood in particular, she could not help having a devastating image of her female identity. This was the very reason she had always put off the time of motherhood, while desperately longing for a child. Recently she said to me, "With this baby growing in me, the belly getting bigger and rounder, with the world seeing my condition, I was suddenly proud to be a woman. My fears, my hangups . . . they just vanished!" Even before being born, this child had given birth to a woman.

A S a result of some evenings spent with several children of the Kennedy clan, I had made the acquaintance of Sargent Shriver, the American ambassador to France. We became friends, and he ended up being the godfather of our daughter.

On the night of the vote that would decide which Democratic nominee would be running against Richard Nixon, Jane and I were in the salon of the ambassador's residence on Avenue Gabriel. We were watching the proceedings on television. The final race was between Eugene McCarthy, a strong advocate of the Vietnam peace movement, and Hubert Humphrey, a politician of the traditional party mold. When Humphrey carried the vote over McCarthy, Sargent Shriver said, "They just put Richard Nixon in the White House."

There was an additional twist to that evening: Interrupting the coverage of vote proceedings, the television cameras went to the outside of the building, where massive demonstrations on behalf of McCarthy were taking place. Using clubs, the Chicago police brutally charged the demonstrators. Blows, screams, bloody heads and faces. Among the forefront of the demonstrators—and hence most exposed to the brutalities—a young man, looking particularly fierce and fiery, stood out. Jane, of course, did not know that she was looking with a mixture of apprehension and admiration at the man who, five years later, would be her husband. And the TV reporters, who didn't know him either, had not mentioned his name: Tom Hayden.

*I*N France, as I had foreseen, the working classes, influenced by the Communist party, let the students down. With the end of the general strike the revolution fizzled out as quickly as it had caught fire. De Gaulle returned to Paris, and order was reestablished.

Jean-Michel Lacor and his friends were now firmly installed in the union's executive committee, so I could resign.

In June I left with Jane for Saint-Tropez, where we had rented a villa with a large terrace overlooking the sea. Nathalie and Christian were with us. Jane's belly got rounder every day. After the stormy spring months, we could really appreciate a few weeks of peace and relaxation in paradise.

☆ *31* ☆

*E*XCEPT for the unhappy episode of mumps, the nine months of Jane's pregnancy went as well as possible. She remained active right up to the end and took great care of her body. I helped her to apply natural products with a hormonal base to keep her skin supple and avoid stretch marks.

Jane was convinced that her child would be a boy, but we had nevertheless thought of a girl's name in case her instinct was wrong. I liked the name Vanessa because it was one of the only names that can be pronounced the same way in English, French, Russian and most other languages. Jane had thought of it because of her friendship at the time for the actress Vanessa Redgrave.

One night, rather late, Jane had an attack of abdominal pains. I suggested taking her to the hospital, but she said that it was a digestive problem, only cramps. Her insistence astounded me. Nevertheless, I decided not to take any risks. The hospital was an hour away by car. There was no question of taking a woman about to give birth in a Ferrari. I used our second car, a DS Citroen, which had a supple, comfortable suspension. On the way, Jane decided that the pains were not cramps caused by a digestive problem.

"I think I'm going to have the baby in the car," she said.

I was prepared for that eventuality, but I was hoping that I wouldn't have to act as a midwife on the shoulder of the highway. We arrived at the maternity clinic at Belvedere around four in the morning. Susan, Henry Fonda's third wife, was waiting for us. We had telephoned her before leaving the house.

Jane was still a teenager when her father introduced her to a ravishing young woman, Susan Blanchard, who was ten years older than she. Susan gave Jane a lot: understanding, tenderness and advice. She was able to understand the problems that existed between her stepdaughter and her husband, and the void that had been left by Frances Fonda's suicide. I had met Susan in New York and had been instantly engrossed by her tenderness, her charm and her natural optimism tempered by a rather caustic wit. Susan had arranged to be in Paris when Jane would be giving birth. I was grateful to her. In this important moment of her life, Jane would not be totally cut off from her birthplace and her family.

Finally, I was the one whom Susan had to support and comfort most of all. Jane's pains returned almost every twenty minutes, and between spasms Jane chatted with her ex-stepmother. She had learned the exercises for painless childbirth.

"It doesn't seem to be working very well," she said. "I must not have exercised seriously enough."

Finally she had to be given anesthesia. The gynecologist arrived around five in the morning. Jane left for the delivery room, apparently very calm. After examining her, the doctor sent word that nothing would happen for several hours. He would keep her under observation in the delivery room. Susan and I decided to take a walk to relieve the tension of waiting. She understood that something was bothering me and skillfully led me to reveal it. I told her about the mumps and what Dr. Schwartz had said.

It was daybreak and a bistro at the Porte de Saint-Cloud was opening its doors. The regular riders of the first subway train, who were on their way to work, leaned on the counter and ordered the usual coffee with cream and croissant. For Susan and me it was hot chocolate and half a buttered baguette. I noticed the post office calendar on the wall; the waitress, a dish towel on her arm, was tearing off a page to reveal the day's date: Wednesday, September 28.

"Look," I said to Susan. "It's Brigitte Bardot's birthday."

At six o'clock, I called the clinic. They gave me the doctor who wanted to speak to me.

"I'll be frank," he said. "I'm worried. Your wife's water broke a few moments ago. And there was blood."

"What does that mean?"

"I don't know yet. Perhaps it's simply an intra-uterine vessel that's exploded. In that case, it's nothing abnormal. I'll keep you informed. But I won't have any more news before eight o'clock."

The gynecologist was trying not to alarm me unnecessarily. I knew that he wanted to spare me too violent a psychological shock in the event that the baby was deformed. If a quick decision had to be taken, it was better for me to be in condition to think. When I rejoined Susan at the table, I was very pale.

"Is something wrong?" she asked worriedly.

I couldn't get the words out. Finally I said, "The doctor will wait for us at the clinic in two hours. Everything's fine."

But less than an hour later we were back at the Belvedere clinic. Nothing is worse than waiting when you know you are helpless and useless. I understood the clichés of a certain kind of literature: "each minute appeared to be a century," and "the seconds of agony." At 7:45 a nurse walked toward us in the waiting room.

"The baby and mother are doing well. It's a girl."

Later, the gynecologist said to me, "It went well. But I was really worried."

We joined Jane in her room. She was pale and her eyes had rings under them, but they shone with intense brightness. I had already seen that luminous smile which comes from within a mother who holds her newborn baby in her arms.

I heard little tappings on the windowpane and turned around. The room was on the first floor and it looked onto hospital grounds. Nathalie was standing on a chair, behind the window. She was looking at Jane and the wrinkled little thing that was her sister. She understood Jane's happiness and my own joy, and she knew that something was going to change her life. Children were not allowed to enter a room when a newborn baby was there. I joined my eldest daughter on the grounds.

"You won't love me any more," she said.

"Don't be silly, sweetheart," I told her. "Did I love you less after Christian was born?"

She smiled. I took her in my arms and she rested her head on my shoulder.

☆ *32* ☆

*J*ANE breastfed Vanessa. Motherhood suited her. She had never been more beautiful. I had more experience than she with babies and taught her many things which usually only mothers know. Jane appreciated the fact that I knew how to change Vanessa's diapers, that I knew the amount and the right temperature for the supplementary bottle, and that I could differentiate among the baby's various cries: "She's got a stomachache." "She must be in a bad mood." "She must be irritated. We'll have to change her." "She's had a nightmare." Yes, there was a baby language that Jane could not yet decipher. For her, every tear was a cause for alarm. She read every imaginable book on the education of children, modern pediatrics, etcetera. Jane never did anything by halves. She went for theory, while I was more for empirical methods. We complemented each other perfectly.

In November, *Barbarella* was released in Paris and was hardly noticed. Neither the public nor the French critics were used to this kind of futuristic fantasy. We had to wait a few months for the opening abroad before the film had any success. In spite of the often divided reviews, the film was an event. *Barbarella* was several years ahead of its time, but it was one of those films that do not disappear after a few months. Fifteen years after the opening, *Barbarella* is still shown in cinemas all over the world and regularly on television.

Dino de Laurentiis and Paramount presented the film as a uniquely erotic product. That was a mistake. For a while it created a misunderstanding on the part of the public and encouraged Jane to fulminate against her role and this film, which she would later tell the press "presented me as an erotic object." That was during her "hard" feminist phase when she used anything and everything to fuel her political position. Nowadays she has gone back on this rather sectarian view. She realizes that I had great fun creating the first galactic heroine. After all, the costumes of Superman, Buck Rogers, Flash Gordon and many other masculine characters of futuristic mythology were sexy and erotic. Why should women be treated differently? The fact remains that Jane is strikingly beautiful in *Barbarella,* and this image, which has nothing sexist or derogatory about it, will remain with us for a long time, I hope.

A few weeks before Christmas Jane was offered a role by the producers Irving Winkler and Charles Chartoff: the part of Gloria in an adaptation of the Horace McCoy novel *They Shoot Horses, Don't They?* Strangely enough, I had written an adaptation of McCoy's novel for Brigitte Bardot in 1953, when I was still only a beginning screenwriter. But the producers were afraid of the story, which they found to be too pessimistic. Later, famous directors like Charles Chaplin were tempted by the same project, but they all abandoned the idea.

Jane accepted on the condition that she have approval of the final screenplay, and we decided to leave Houdan for California at the end of January. I understood from Jane's mood swings that, despite her efforts to adapt to the French way of life, she couldn't do without the land of her birth. She remained an American above all.

She suggested finding a school for Nathalie in Switzerland during the filming of *They Shoot Horses, Don't They?*. I didn't really like the idea of leaving the child alone after the birth of a new baby. But most parents are obsessed with the problem of finding the right school, and they give it priority over everything else. Jane was no exception.

"I don't want her to lose one whole school year," she said.

Theoretically she was right. So we left for Switzerland by car in search of the best possible school.

We were driving along the hairpin bends of Combes Pass when I suddenly stopped the Ferrari on the side of the road. The sky had that tender, blue purity characteristic of alpine climates. Glittering in the distance was Lac Leman mirroring the tall mountains with their snow-covered peaks. Everything was beautiful, vast, noble and calm. The struggle for success, the thirst for money and power by men, these small ants in the valley ten kilometers below, seemed on this scale derisory, or even abstract and remote.

We got out of the car. Jane leaned her head on my shoulder and put her arms around my waist. Tears were running down her cheeks. Jane cannot be reproached for lacking character, but tears do come to her easily. Emotions always act on her lachrymal glands. I wondered why she was crying. The beauty of the landscape had never particularly moved her before. I now know that she was crying about the end of something. It was not yet clear in her mind, but she suspected that the future would not be the one we had imagined together. No doubt she was a little frightened.

P ELICANS, not yet decimated by pollution, were diving into the water like Stukas, and were surrounded by squawking, always hungry sea gulls. A couple was running on the wet sand. Near the rocks, to the north of the beach, three surfers wearing rubber suits were waiting for the seventh wave. "Monday, Monday," of the Mamas and the Papas, could be heard over the roaring of the ocean. Someone was giving a party and the loudspeakers were going full blast. Malibu hadn't changed.

The house that we had just rented had a terrace overlooking the beach, a large bar in the main living room, a huge kitchen, a guest house in the garden, and a bedroom on the first floor with a bed that was greater in width than in length, from which there was a superb view of the ocean when the shutters were opened. Two or three times a year, when the air was exceptionally clear, you could make love looking at Catalina Island. The decor and furniture were simple, pleasant and in good taste. There was a lot of light and sunshine; it was a house made for happiness. We had turned one of the bedrooms into a nursery for Vanessa, who was now four months old. Her nanny, Dot, a charming old English lady, spoke with a Cockney accent which I found delightful. She resembled a character from a Bernard Shaw play. Dot had been dresser to many stars of the theater for over forty years, before beginning to take care of children.

Nathalie was in boarding school in Switzerland. It was one of those institutions more like a three-star hotel than a school.

A few days after our arrival, I was taking our Italian greyhounds, Mao and Lilliput, for a walk on the beach when I saw a man kneeling in the sand, staring at something. As I got closer, I realized it was Jack Nicholson. He had a twenty-four-hour beard, and I wondered how long he had been without sleep. In the palm of his hand he was holding an orange that had been washed up by the ocean and was stained with tar. It looked like a globe of the world. He placed a finger on one of the tar stains.

"There's Europe," he said.

He pointed to another stain.

"There's Asia and there's Africa."

Something seemed to be bothering him.

"The American continent isn't there," he said.

He thought for a minute and said, "If the American continent doesn't exist, that means we don't exist either. If we don't exist, what are we doing here?"

"I've arrived from Paris," I replied. "And I didn't notice that the United States did not exist."

"It's jet lag," he explained.

After a long silence he said, "The state of nonexistence can enable one to understand many things. For example, that the world is an orange covered with tar stains . . . even Einstein didn't foresee that."

He looked at me with a provocative, disarming smile that was also a little diabolical. He seemed to be making fun of himself or others—probably of himself *and* others.

I suggested moving from the "nonexistence" of the beach to the "nonexistence" of bed, and he agreed to follow me to the house. I put him in one of the bedrooms, and he woke up twenty hours later, even more bearded and disheveled than before. But he was in an excellent mood. He thanked Jane for building a house around him.

"When I fell asleep there was only sand everywhere and stars above my head. They've taught you good manners in France," he added, with admiration.

Jane laughed.

Jack asked, "Which year are we in?"

"1969," said Jane.

"Shit! I'm late," said Jack.

He asked if he could borrow a slice of bread and a piece of Swiss cheese, and he left us.

Dot entered the room with Vanessa. "Supper time," she said.

Jane sat on one of the armchairs on the terrace and undid her blouse. She took Vanessa in her arms to breastfeed her. But the little one began playing with the nipple instead of feeding. She took it between her fingers, pinched it and burst out laughing, showing her gums where her first teeth were coming through.

"She's inherited her father's bad habits," said Jane to Dot, smiling.

*I*N *The Game Is Over,* Renée, the character played by Jane, cuts her hair to please her lover. I had filmed the locks that fall under the scissors as a symbol of love destroyed. But I had used a wig. For *They Shoot Horses, Don't They?* Jane cut her real hair. A coincidence? That very day, for the first time, I had the vision of Jane leading her own life on one side, and of myself leading my own separate life on the other. There are always moments of doubt, arguments and threats of divorce . . . that is part of a couple's life. Things sort themselves out in a few minutes, a few hours or, at worst, a few days. But now I knew that the disintegration of our love had started. And it was an irreversible process.

Nothing dramatic had occurred. Jane's obsessive commitment to her work and her lack of warmth in her daily contacts bothered me, but it was the symbol of the cut hair—the desire for a new face and the desire for change—that gave the truth away. I opened my eyes to a reality that unconsciously I had refused to accept.

I myself was less in love with Jane. Her perpetual need for activity and her need to take everything seriously began to tire me. I had fallen in love with an ambitious, dynamic woman, gifted with great sense, but vulnerable and capable of irrational, spontaneous moments, of being playful, and of doing silly things. I found myself with a monster of efficiency who often made me think of a robot. Of course I am exaggerating, but it's only to make myself better understood.

I have never kept a diary but I have begun several. I found the first lines of one of those attempts that covered no more than two pages. The date: 20 May 1969. "She came back from the studio at eight o'clock. She kissed me and asked how Vanessa's day had gone. She spoke about an alcohol solution for the gums of the child, who was cutting a new tooth. Two weeks before she began filming, Jane stopped breastfeeding Vanessa because she had no milk left. Jane spoke with Dot in the kitchen as she ate a few leaves of lettuce and a piece of Gruyère cheese. She drafted a long list. Now she's in the bedroom working on her lines for tomorrow. She's perfect, she's sublime. What's she so frightened of that she has to throw herself into work like this? There's a limit to efficiency. I think it's time for me to learn to stop loving. . . .''

I had invented the word *desaimer* for this circumstance. I prepared myself sensibly for the inevitable, unable and unwilling to change. I could not say that Jane was *another* Jane because part of her personality had taken the upper hand and was submerging the rest. She was evolving. She was moving unsteadily toward the future, but it was precisely the submerged part of Jane that I loved. Living with the new Jane interested me less. I knew, however, that the separation would be long and painful despite my exercise in emotional anesthesia. In addition to *desaimer,* I also called this process the yoga of the pessimist.

But something in the relationship was unusual. We still understood each other well sexually. And I don't think that Jane was pretending, even through kindness; she's not a hypocrite.

She, no doubt, would have liked *me* to change. With hindsight, when I consider her ideal man, the man of her life would be Tom Hayden, her present husband. It's evident that I had no hope of making that kind of metamorphosis within myself, so I don't feel any retroactive regrets.

JAMES Poe had written the adaptation of *They Shoot Horses, Don't They?* and convinced Winkler and Chartoff to produce the film, which he wanted to direct. He also had the idea of proposing the role of Gloria to Jane Fonda. Poe was a reserved, almost shy, man. He lived with one of the queens of the horror films of the time, the amazing Barbara Steele. He seemed to get on well with Jane. However, just before shooting began, he was fired and replaced by Sydney Pollack when Jane gave the green light to the producers.

The future showed that this choice was not a mistake, but the principle of firing a man who had been at the origin of the project, and of snatching his brainchild from him, seemed to me to be a little barbarous. I wasn't really surprised by the producers' decision; but I was by the fact that Jane agreed with them. I couldn't understand that attitude coming from a woman who was so sensitive to social injustice, to the corrupting power of money and to the lack of humanity in Hollywood's moguls. I refrained from criticizing or even judging Jane. This incident, however, revealed to me another side of my wife's character: her ability to forget compassion when it was a question of better results. Efficiency came before all else.

Jane and Sydney Pollack met every day to talk about the changes that had to be made in the screenplay. Sydney was a determined but pleasant man. His energy and time were all concentrated on his work. In that he got on very well with Jane.

The action of the film, set in the Depression, took place during the course of a dance marathon; these were quite common at the time. For a few dollars, Gloria, the heroine of the story, pushes herself to the limit of her strength, and finally dies. Jane became completely absorbed——I would even say possessed——by her character, once shooting began. She often slept in her dressing room at the studio and kept on her makeup from the previous evening to give more reality to Gloria's progressive exhaustion.

Sometimes, I would take Vanessa with me to visit Jane at the Warner Brothers studio where the film was being shot.

* * *

DURING this period the relationship between Jane and her father seemed stable and happy. Jane was married, she had a child, and she was orienting her career definitely toward Hollywood. She had not yet made her public stand on Vietnam. Henry was satisfied. After the shooting of the film, life seemed to take on a more normal rhythm.

AND there I was, hoping again that everything might yet work out for us. Hope, that incurable condition which clings to a man when everything seems lost, did not spare me.

During a party given in Roman Polanski's home in Benedict Canyon, Jane disappeared for over half an hour with J, a very handsome man. When she reappeared her hair was disheveled and her skirt slightly crumpled.

"I was in the bathroom when J joined me," she told me. "He asked if he could help me."

J had locked the bathroom door and had tried to "help" Jane as best he could. A few minutes later, the housekeeper began knocking on the door.

"What's going on in there?" she screamed. "Open the door!"

That woman had taken it upon herself to look after the morals of the Polanski household. She had her work cut out for her.

Interrupted in the middle of their flirtation, Jane and J had to leave the bathroom reluctantly.

When Jane got through her story, she added, "I hate it when something's half finished."

Jane was particularly beautiful that evening. Cheerful. Very self-assured. The butterfly had emerged from its chrysalis and was spreading its wings. She hadn't kept her prematurely interrupted adventure a secret, but it became clear to me that I was no longer her accomplice. I remember suddenly feeling a great chill.

*A*T the end of June we packed our bags and stored some boxes and my fishing tackle in the garage of Henry Fonda's villa in Bel-Air. The house at Malibu was returned to its owner.

We took the plane for New York with Vanessa, Dot and the two Italian greyhounds. A week later, we embarked on the S.S. *France* for Le Havre. Andy Warhol had come to say goodbye to us in the suite that we had reserved for our Atlantic crossing. It was neither the Dom Perignon nor the caviar nor the extraordinarily luxurious cabins that impressed him, but the fact that the steward brought us Coca-Cola in the old glass bottles. He made us promise to bring him back several dozen.

The captain of the *France* invited Jane and me to join him on deck. It was a wonderful way to leave the United States. On the way to the deck, I made a friendly gesture to the Statue of Liberty which had made the same journey, but in the other direction, eighty-three years before.

☆ *33* ☆

THE atmosphere in our house at Houdan was both rustic and modern. The country furnishings blended with the comfortable sofas and the latest stereo system. Jane had managed a happy mixture of styles.

A few days after our return from the United States, she decided to begin work on a project we had often discussed: the transformation of the barn into a winter swimming pool and a projection room. Did she want to ward off fate by beginning construction just when the future of our marriage seemed uncertain?

On July 21, 1969, the arrival of the first American astronauts on the moon was televised. The event was scheduled for 4:00 A.M. French time. The first steps of man on another celestial body was not only a miracle of intelligence and technology but also a poetic and philosophical symbol. I thought that the human race had experienced nothing more exciting since a biped living in a cave hit upon the idea of using a shinbone to make a weapon. I never understood why Jane didn't wake up to watch the astronauts on television, one of the most exalting adventures in the history of mankind. Still, fifteen years later, she would travel from Los Angeles to Cape Canaveral to watch the departure of the first woman astronaut. But in the latter case Jane participated in the event. The papers would publish her photo and comment on her presence. It was a political gesture.

Vanessa, then ten months old, was crying in her room. I went to get her and sat her against the wall in the living room next to the television. Fascinated by what I was watching, I had forgotten my daughter. Armstrong walked down the ladder of the module and planted one foot on the lunar dust. A second later, he put down another foot. Then, unsteadily, like a baby, he took his first steps and began to walk. At that very moment I thought I was seeing double. There were two Armstrongs. I realized that the second astronaut was Vanessa standing on her legs. She had chosen the precise moment when Armstrong was walking in space, 221,600 miles above the earth, to try her first steps. Covered with Pampers and cotton overalls, her silhouette resembled that of the American hero. After taking four steps, she fell on her behind. Armstrong, however, continued walking.

*I*F one compares the end of a love affair to an illness in its terminal stage, one can press the analogy and speak of a remission. I remember the two weeks that we spent at the end of September in Saint-Tropez as being the last truly happy days of our marriage.

We were living in a hotel on the beach. The weather was exceptionally good. I filmed several of these privileged moments. The Riva ride along deserted creeks, the pure, transparent water, the white sand, Jane naked in the sun, Vanessa laughing in her little dinghy. On September twenty-eighth on the hotel terrace, the cake with one candle... Vanessa celebrated her first birthday. Jane took photos and burst out laughing when her daughter, having covered herself with chocolate mousse from head to toe, decided to eat the candle. The film is silent, but one can imagine what Jane is saying from the movement of her lips: "You can see that she's got Russian blood." I remember having replied, "But Russians don't eat candles." "Yes, they do," said Jane. "It's a well-known fact."

I discovered Andreas Voutsinas's treachery when I returned to Paris. As soon as he had realized that my marriage to Jane was in difficulty he rushed into the breach. With the duplicity worthy of a modern Iago, he devoted himself to disparaging me in Jane's mind, using truths, bogus truths and unfounded gossip.

I thought of our meeting in Rome when he claimed that I had saved his life, of his professions of friendship and eternal gratitude. Thus, it was Henry Fonda who had judged him best. Fortunately Andreas's activity didn't bother me. Jane might be momentarily troubled by the games of a skillful manipulator, but I knew that she wouldn't allow herself to be truly influenced. Her existential problems were on a higher level. She still had no answer to the question, "What do I need in my life for fulfillment?" She searched . . . and searched. . . .

India and its promise of spiritual tranquillity had been made fashionable by the hippie movement. A potpourri of psychedelic hallucinations, Gandhi's nonviolence movement and the Oriental mystics' meditation and search for truth had created this new mirage: India, humanity's promised land. For anyone searching, the answer was to be found in the land of gurus and wise men.

A college friend of Jane's who was stopping off in Paris en route to Bombay played the role of catalyst. Jane decided to accompany her. She hoped she might find the answer to her identity problem there. I think that she also wanted a few weeks' solitude, time to think things over far from me and far from Hollywood.

Dot, Vanessa and I waited quietly in Paris for the explorer to return. I received a few brief reports of her journey, which gave me no real sense of her psychological state. But a month after her departure a long letter arrived. A love letter. Jane said that she loved me, and that the journey had opened her eyes: What she truly wanted was to be with Vanessa always. She would never leave us. She could hardly contain her impatience to return to us soon. This letter should have pleased me. But it worried me. Such a declaration of love was not Jane's style. It seemed to me that she was trying to convince herself. Mail between India and France takes a long time, and Jane came back only three days after I got her letter.

She was slightly thinner and didn't seem to have found peace and wisdom. If India had fascinated her, it was because of its incredible poverty, the skeletal children who were sometimes too weak to beg for food, the dead collected from the pavements each morning, the contrast between the upper and lower castes, rather than its fakirs and gurus and the serene and awesome beauty of the Himalayas. The beauty of the palace of one thousand and one nights of the King of Sikkim, where she was warmly received (the queen, American by birth, was her contemporary), made her feel even more deeply the terrible deprivation of the many millions of Indians. This journey didn't provide Jane with an answer to her personal problems, but it did help her to take a great step towards social awareness. She understood that the struggle against social injustice is not waged by meditation or saving one's soul. Still troubled, she was, nevertheless, much closer to her moment of truth than she imagined.

I wanted the Irish novelist Edna O'Brien to write the screenplay of my next film. It was the story of the emotional and political education of a woman of thirty-five by her seventeen-year-old stepdaughter. Edna accepted, and Jane and I went to London to meet her.

Jane got along very well with Edna O'Brien. This great writer was living proof that a woman can be independent in every domain and yet remain tender, romantic, warm and—in the best sense of the word—feminine. Through her own crises of growth and independence, Jane had become more and more interested in the problems that women face in a society dominated by men. Edna was one of the pieces of the puzzle that helped to clarify my wife's ideas.

We spent only two weeks in London before leaving for California. This time we didn't rent a house. It was a significant detail. I had reserved a suite at the Beverly Wilshire for Jane and myself. Vanessa and Dot were staying with Henry and Shirlee Fonda.

Knowing that our separation was merely a question of time, I could have made the decisive step myself and taken responsibility for the breakup. But I decided not to for several reasons—above all, in order not to damage Jane's ego. It's always harder to be the one who is left than the one who decides to leave. I didn't want to provoke bitterness or bad feelings toward me, especially because of Vanessa. Still present in my mind was Henry's phrase that Jane repeated one day: "One never leaves a Fonda," and the expression on her face when he said this. Another more frivolous reason was that in the final analysis the situation didn't upset me. I'm in no way a masochist, but it is part of my nature to like ambiguous, complicated, unclear situations. It was a change from the routine of love. It wasn't as disagreeable as one might think.

Jane was not seeking a new love affair. She wasn't leaving me for another man, but for herself. She told a journalist later, "Vadim is an intelligent man, he respects people, but he wasn't prepared for what happened. He would better understand a woman who leaves him for another man than a woman who leaves him for herself." If that is really what she thought, she was completely mistaken. The truth is that I much preferred to see her taking off on the chariot of politics, at war against war, to her leaving me for another man. I found this to be loftier as well as much easier on my ego.

She had found her way. The time had come to shed the old skin, to transform, to change.

It was in the room at the Beverly Wilshire that she finally said the words that I had been expecting to hear for months: "Vadim, we must separate. I still love you very much but I need my own time, my life and my freedom."

I remained silent for a while and asked, "And Vanessa?"

She was immediately on the defensive. The child was a sensitive issue which touched both of us. Her tone became aggressive. "It's a problem, I know. But I can't do anything about it. We'll decide on the conditions later."

It wasn't the moment to provoke a crisis, and even less to open hostilities. I replied that I had hoped to spend the rest of my life with her, but that I knew it was a dream, and I was a little sad.

"A little sad? Is that all you can find to say?"

She looked at me as if I had arrived from Mars or some far-off corner of the Milky Way. Actually, I was suffering a great deal, but I couldn't bring myself to say so. I have never been able to talk about my great hurts to my friends, my wives or my mother. It's the same with physical pain. I will complain about a headache or a burn on my finger but not a broken ankle. In French one calls that *pudeur*—the word doesn't exist in English.

There was no surgical separation. We left the Beverly Wilshire for the guest house of Henry Fonda's villa in Bel-Air.

One evening, in our little living room, I was listening to a Rolling Stones song for the seventh time.

Jane screamed from the bedroom, "That's enough! Change the record. I can't work."

I turned off the stereo and walked into the bedroom, which Jane had transformed into a hippie den: Indian fabric covering the bed and walls, soft lighting, candles, red and blue light bulbs, incense burning on a low table. She put down her pencil, which she was using to underline some sentences in an article about Vietnam, and said, "Listening to the same piece of music over and over is a sign of depression."

I was unaware of that. For more than a year afterward, in order to avoid such nervous depression, I refrained from listening to the same piece of music twice in succession.

FOUR

DIALOGUE WITH THE STARS

☆ *34* ☆

I had just spent a month with my children in my house at Malibu.

We fished, sailed, dined in the Magic Palace, visited the wax museum and Marineland. We got lost in Disneyland. And, above all, we religiously paid homage to the modern world by absorbing hundreds of hours of junk TV without even complaining of sore bottoms. For Christian's seventh birthday, I gave a big party with elephants, three ponies, a thousand multicolored balloons, two clowns and a magician. We were all satisfied and in agreement on one point: If God existed, he should not allow this kind of life to come to an end.

But the day came when I had to send each of my children back to their respective mothers.

Nathalie had to go back to Rome to Annette Stroyberg, who had been engaged for two years to an American millionaire of Greek origin.

Christian had to go home to Catherine Deneuve in Paris.

Jane Fonda was waiting for Vanessa in London.

In those days, in Los Angeles all the flights for Europe left from the same building. Vanessa was handed over to an air hostess. Christian, who was used to Paris–L.A. flights, hugged me and slipped between the legs of the other passengers. Nathalie, who was more sentimental, almost missed her call. The departures were all scheduled to leave at almost the same time. I found myself "orphaned by my children," as Christian said, and walked to the exit. I was about to leave the airport building when I heard my name: "Roger Vadim is asked to present himself at the Air France office."

The Air France tickets all carried the name "Child Vadim" followed by an initial. Two of the tickets had been endorsed by Pan Am and TWA. A little distracted, as usual, I had sent the wrong child to the wrong mother.

Nathalie, who was due to return to her mother in Rome, was on her way to London, where Jane Fonda was waiting for Vanessa.

Vanessa was flying to Paris, where Catherine was awaiting Christian.

I spent the whole evening and night on the telephone to the three capitals telling the mothers that they would not be receiving the right child,

I have tried to clarify the reasons that determined Jane Fonda's political vocation. It is not my intention to discuss her activities in this area. That is something that concerns her and the American people.

I may have given the impression that our divorce was solely due to this metamorphosis. That is perhaps not quite fair. I have my own weaknesses and faults, which certainly contributed. But I don't wish to talk about them. Self-critical public sessions are not my style.

Life with my "ex-wife" at Henry Fonda's house was not unpleasant, but when a couple decide to separate, it is, generally, with the intention of no longer living together. So I rented a house on the beach in Malibu and moved in with

Dot and Vanessa. Jane, who was taken up with her political activities, traveled a great deal. She was happy that I could look after our daughter. Nathalie, who hated her school in Switzerland, came to live with us.

The film project I had planned with Edna O'Brien didn't materialize, so I agreed to direct *Pretty Maids All in a Row* for MGM. The story was set in a high school in Beverly Hills. Rock Hudson, Angie Dickinson, Telly Savalas and fifteen of the prettiest, youngest actresses in Hollywood were part of the cast. The evenings at Mailbu were joyous, and I suddenly discovered a great number of friends. I had little time to think about my destroyed marriage.

I had spent some hours with Jane and Angela Davis, who seemed to be a reserved and intelligent woman. I was surprised to learn, a few weeks later, that all the police in the United States were looking for her. Two FBI agents came to see me on the set at MGM. They asked me if I knew where she was. They asked me if Jane Fonda knew where she was hiding out. I didn't know. They asked me questions about my wife's political activities (we were not officially separated). I told them that they certainly knew more than I did on that subject. It was the truth. But naturally, if I had known anything that might hurt Jane, I wouldn't have told them.

Jane began to travel endlessly. It's a habit that has remained with her. Women's lib, American Indians, Black Panthers, oppressed minorities and, above all at that time, the movement against the war in Vietnam, took up all her time. She often stopped off in Malibu for a few hours, kissed her daughter and then left for the beach to give a TV interview. Vanessa sat a few yards away on the sand and listened to her mother talk about the destiny of the world. She would have preferred to have been sitting on her mother's knee.

Having finished the post-production work on *Pretty Maids All in a Row*, I decided to return to Paris, For a newly divorced man, I had just spent several particularly distracting months, but the wound caused by Jane's departure was still open. I thought France would be a good place to let it heal. At moments in life when one feels fragile, the instinct is to return to one's roots.

Jane had not abandoned her career for her new political activities; far from it. She was preparing to film *Klute*, which was to be the peak of her career as an actress: her first Oscar. The new man in her life was her co-star and companion in the political arena, Donald Sutherland.

We decided that Vanessa would follow me to Paris. The decision was made for practical reasons—Jane had too little time to devote herself to her daughter—but also, I would like to make clear, she respected my attachment to Vanessa and knew that the little girl adored me. Even when she was in full political frenzy, denouncing the oppression of women by men, who have all the power, Jane never exploited the rights over her child that society conferred on her as a mother. She always showed concern *above all* for the emotional realities involved in the problems concerning the custody of the child. One can't say the same about the majority of divorced parents.

*I*N her frenetic desire to break with anything that might remind her of the material reality of her life as a wife at home (and what was she so afraid of?), Jane decided to sell the house in Houdan. She sent instructions from Los Angeles. In the process of this long-distance sale, many of my personal belongings were lost or stolen. I missed my seventeenth-century chess set and my collection of first-edition science-fiction books—a collection which now would be very rare; but above all, I was upset about losing my souvenirs from childhood—letters, drawings, photos, my first manuscripts—not to mention official documents. For years I had problems with the tax authorities because I couldn't justify anything retroactively. And everyone knows what that can cost.

Jane had every right to erase thoroughly a whole period of her life, but not to blot out traces of *my* past at the same time. On the financial level we had no problem. I received the amounts of money I had invested in purchasing and improving the house—but she could have kept it all.

I had to find a new place to live in Paris, so I rented a ground-floor apartment with a garden on Avenue Foch. Vanessa loved her new home, which was only a few steps from heaps of sand, the lake of the Bois de Boulogne where ducks swam, little cars with pedals that one could rent, an underground gallery known to all the kids in the neighborhood for its toy shops, and a cinema where they showed Walt Disney's *The Aristocats* all year long.

Dot had returned to London to resume her career as a dresser for the theater, which she missed. I had inherited a new nanny, hired by Jane. Suzy, very tall, with very red hair, was quite nervous and always certain that she was about to be raped. Suzy and Vanessa often returned home out of breath, having run all the way to escape sexual perverts, who, as we all know, wait for unfortunate American female tourists on every street corner in Paris. It was as good a way as any to jog. Yet, Suzy was not very pretty—not at all the kind of woman to arouse the beast dormant in every man.

I decided to spend a few days' vacation in Venice. Vanessa remembers, in particular, the pigeons of Saint Mark's Square who mistook her woolen hat for a latrine. I gave Suzy two days off to chase—or flee—the rapists in the labyrinth of canals and narrow streets. That very evening I found her at the hotel in tears. She had met an Italian man on the Vaporetto. He was thirty-five years old, short but handsome. They discovered that they both loved art and beautiful objects, and the man invited Suzy home to admire his collection of etchings. She accepted, thinking that at the last moment, when he suddenly would jump on her, she would have time enough to decide whether to submit or scream rape out the window. But nothing happened; he really wanted to show her his etchings. After a glass of port, he accompanied her politely back to the hotel.

Having never succeeded in being raped—either because she ran too fast, or because she had come across the only true amateur etcher in the world—Suzy decided to return to the United States. Jane sent me another nanny, Elizabeth, who was about thirty, with a rather classically beautiful face. She was a woman of quiet behavior and made an excellent impression on me.

I was making a film in the French Alps near Megève. Elizabeth, as usual, had fallen asleep in a field after eating. While waiting patiently for her to wake up, Vanessa was watching the insects in the grass at her feet. From a distance, I saw Elizabeth stand up and stagger as she walked. She hasn't woken up yet, I thought. Vanessa took her hand and made her stop at the side of the road. After a truck passed by, the little one made sure that there was no oncoming traffic. Then, still holding on to her nanny's hand, she made her cross the road.

I thought that Elizabeth was using her own method for teaching Vanessa to cross roads. When I spoke to my daughter, who was only three, she said, "When I let her cross the road by herself, she gets us run over."

I discovered that Elizabeth was an alcoholic. I spoke with Jane about it over the phone. It was clear she was reluctant to accept my judgment about Elizabeth.

A few days later, Jean-Michel Lacor discovered Elizabeth was putting whiskey in Vanessa's night bottle to help her sleep. This time I took matters into my own hands and sent Elizabeth back to the United States. Jane still didn't believe me.

Six months later Jane finally discovered the truth. "You were absolutely right," she acknowledged.

One of Jane's great qualities is her ability to acknowledge a mistake.

* * *

*T*OWARD the end of my filming in the Alps, Jane arrived in France to discuss a film with Jean-Luc Godard. But first she visited Vanessa.

Having learned that Jane had serious doubts about the screenplay—she didn't agree with the political content—Jean-Luc lost no time in sending his associate, Jean-Pierre Gorin, to meet her. Two hours after Jane's arrival in Megève, Gorin was in the living room of the house I had rented for the summer, submerging her in political/artistic explanations of the profundity and historic significance of the story, *Everything's Okay*. Jane, who had just arrived from Geneva, hadn't slept for twenty-four hours and was suffering from jet lag. She was surprised and a little irritated by the almost hysterical insistence of Godard's emissary.

"If you don't mind, I will put my daughter to bed now," she said. "I haven't seen her for two months."

After she had kissed Vanessa and sung her a lullaby to put her to sleep, Jane came downstairs, hoping to nibble on a piece of celery and a little cheese in peace. But Gorin was waiting for her, firmly planted in front of the refrigerator. He harassed her for three hours. Jane was so exhausted she hardly had the strength to reply. He threatened to destroy her political image if she refused to make *Everything's Okay*.

"Godard will take the wind out of your sails. You'll have no political respect anywhere any longer. By refusing to make his film, you'll be making a mistake that we'll make you regret for a long time."

He was talking so loudly that I heard a good part of the conversation. I was indignant at this way of badgering a woman on the verge of complete exhaustion. Around two o'clock in the morning, I decided to interfere in a matter that was none of my business. I walked into the living room.

"No third degree in my home," I said to Gorin. "Find another place for it."

He pretended to believe that I was joking. Jane threw me a grateful look and went off to bed.

Fearing Godard's retaliations, she finally agreed to make *Everything's Okay*. As she had predicted, it was a commercial disaster, and its political opportunism annoyed hard-liners.

I mention this anecdote because I witnessed it—but Godard was not the only one who would use Jane's political image and her extraordinary impact on the media for their own ends.

I would never have imagined that I would fall in love again a year after my separation from Jane.

Catherine Schneider was twenty-eight years old. She was tall, elegant, and had a great deal of charm. Her blue eyes were irresistible. But she had a very cruel sense of humor. She was renowned for her beauty and the way she played with men's hearts. Heiress to one of the richest families in France, she had no ties to the cinema. She liked to see films, but that was as far as it went. She had two boys from a first marriage.

Our affair surprised many people, but we got along very well. Under an almost cold exterior, Catherine was actually romantic and passionate. (I have the impression that I'm writing the same sentence for the second time!) She had no intention of becoming an actress; the very idea made her howl with laughter.

At the beginning of the winter of 1972–73, she and I went to Røros, in Norway, where Jane Fonda was making *A Doll's House* under the direction of Joseph Losey. We planned to spend a week there before going back to Paris with Vanessa, who had been staying with her mother during the filming.

The weather was beautiful the day of our arrival. The countryside and the streets of the small town were covered with snow. Jane was friendly to Catherine.

''Vadim told me that you get along very well with my daughter.''

''She's unique,'' replied Catherine. ''I adore her. By the

age of nineteen I already had two babies. But they were boys."

I knew Joseph Losey and went to see him.

"You lived with Jane Fonda for six years?" he asked me.

"Yes."

"Nevertheless, you still seem to be in good shape."

His rather sarcastic comment was, in a certain sense, justified. The actress Delphine Seyrig, also a member of the cast, was rather like a French Jane Fonda; she was politically active and a champion for the women's liberation movement in France (the MLF). Losey could have perhaps survived one or the other, but the alliance of these two superfeminists was too much for him.

"They discuss each shot," he complained. "The other day Delphine told me that the way I asked her to drink tea was sexist. Sometimes I just feel like leaving the set and taking a walk in the snow until I am completely exhausted and have forgotten everything." He laughed at the idea and helped himself to a large glass of Aquavit.

That evening Jane arranged to be alone with me. "I'm pregnant," she said.

I didn't know whether to congratulate her or appear surprised.

"I've decided to get married," she added.

"That's an excellent idea."

"Only I can't."

"Why not?"

"We're not divorced."

I had forgotten that detail. Since there had never been any financial problems between us, or any disagreement over the custody of Vanessa, we had overlooked the formalities necessary for a divorce.

"Who's the father?" I asked, unable to resist teasing her.

"Tom Hayden."

Of course I knew. For several months now, the American press had been speculating on the nature of the Jane Fonda-Tom Hayden connection. Tom was then one of the notorious Chicago Seven. One might be tempted to think that the encounter between these activist leaders, these two spearheads of the peace movement, would at least have been tumultuous and storybook-like. Not at all. Always captivated by paradox, I loved that they had met under the auspices of a—slide show. Tom had heard that Jane was having a public showing of her photographs from Vietnam, and he invited her to his place to see his own slide show on "the history and culture of Vietnam." This method of seduction revealed itself to be highly efficient, since they are still living together fourteen years after the fact.

"Why marry him?" I asked.

"I have never been particularly anti-marriage, have I?" She replied smiling. "Besides, one of the reasons I'm marrying Tom is that I don't want to hurt his mother. She'd never understand that the parents of her grandchild aren't married." Unarguably a good argument. I, myself, have married for equal—and lesser—reasons.

"Fine," I said. "Let's get a divorce. Just tell me what has to be done."

*T*WO months later I found myself in the Beverly Wilshire Hotel with Catherine Schneider. She had accompanied me to Los Angeles, where I was to settle the formalities of my divorce.

Jane's attorney and mine were on the verge of a nervous breakdown, and with good reason: We were in total agreement about everything. After we had signed the papers, my attorney said in a lugubrious tone, "It's the first divorce of its kind that I've encountered in my entire career. If you and Jane start a trend, it's the end of me. It'll be my ruin."

A few weeks later Jane married Tom Hayden.

*W*ITHOUT realizing it, I had followed a cycle that was as regular as the changing seasons: every five years I had become the father of a child by a different woman. A girl—a boy—a girl—and in 1974 it was the turn of a boy.

Two months after the birth of Troy (Jane and Tom's son), Catherine Schneider gave birth to a boy whom we called Vania. Before the end of that year she became the fourth Madame Plemiannikov. We bought an apartment at 6 Avenue le Play, overlooking the Champs de Mars, that immense garden dominated by the Eiffel Tower extending from the Seine to the Ecole Militaire.

Jane stayed with us when she passed through Paris. In this very luxurious apartment, my ex-wife received activists from the extreme left, like Regis Debray, former colleague of Che Guevara and today counsel to French president Mitterrand. In another living room in the same apartment, Valéry Giscard d'Estaing, then president of France, sipped tea with my new wife. He was a cousin of Catherine's and always showed her a great deal of affection.

"Who is visiting Jane Fonda?" asked Giscard.

"A terrorist, a Maoist, and the president of the Trotskyist movement," she replied, pouring a drop of milk into her guest's teacup.

On her return from her famous and controversial visit to Hanoi, Jane spent two nights at our apartment with Tom Hayden and their son, Troy. President Giscard d'Estaing visited us after an official dinner at the Élysée. He spoke to Jane and seemed to be very interested in what she had to say about the war in Vietnam and her meetings with its leaders. Tom came back from the kitchen with a chicken thigh. He sat on the floor and began eating the chicken with his fingers. I saw the terrified expression on Catherine's face as she stared at the drop of fat that was about to fall onto the superb Kenneth Noland carpet we had bought in New York a month earlier. While listening to Jane, Giscard watched the scene out of the corner of his eye, surprised by Tom's extreme nonchalance and secretly amused by Catherine's agony.

"Those young American politicians are completely relaxed," he said after Tom had gone to bed.

One thought seemed to bother him. "Do you think he'll be President of the United States one day?"

VANESSA was growing up. My relationship with Jane remained excellent. Our daughter divided her time between California and France and became completely bilingual. But when she was nine years old, Jane and I decided that she couldn't continue changing schools during the year.

Having just got divorced again,* I decided to settle in California. I took a house not far from Jane's in Santa Monica. Thus Vanessa could continue to divide her time between her father and mother. We have spent several Christmases together, as a family, in the mountains—once with Robert Redford, a great skier, in Sundance, his Utah ski resort, and another time in Canada at Panorama, renowned for its "helicopter skiing," where a chopper drops one off on a summit as high as 11,500 feet. The cold is intense, and one must immediately protect oneself from the icy, powdery snow that is whipped up by the helicopter as it takes off. After that it's a dream: endless virgin slopes; glacier crevices, which the guide shows how to bypass; sudden change of snow texture; danger of avalanches; rocks; then skiing through the pine forests; and finally down an icy trail to your destination, the valley. The whole thing is certainly not for beginners. I was mesmerized by Jane's courage and determination. She was obviously out of her league, but came out of it with flying colors.

Vanessa also managed to finish the course. I'll confess to a little cheating: I carried her on my shoulders several times.

Last winter we were in Aspen with a few of the Kennedys, who are all remarkable skiers.

---

*I had hoped that by marrying a woman who was not an actress I would have a chance to settle down. I was wrong.

* * *

*S*YMBOLIZING the dream of modern woman is a heavy responsibility. Being a political figure, an exceptional businesswoman, an active supporter of her husband's career, a conscientious mother, a producer, a writer and an international star is a bit much for one person. Actresses have cracked up completely simply because they have become stars. As for me, I don't think I could survive one day in the current life of Jane Fonda.

When Jane arrives after 11:00 P.M. from New York, Chicago, or Kansas City where she has been on business she opens her mail, calls her husband in Sacramento (elected Assemblyman Tom Hayden has to spend several days a week in the capital of the state of California), and then prepares work for the next day. In bed, she tries to read an article or a screenplay and falls asleep on the page.

At 6:00 A.M. she is up. There is no maid in the house. She drinks fruit juices and nibbles on something as she takes notes for her next book or lecture. Then she runs a few kilometers, mingling with the dawn joggers. At 8:00 A.M. I meet her with Vanessa at SMASH (Santa Monica Alternative School) for a meeting with the teachers. Jane is worried about her daughter's repeated latenesses and asks if the school report can be done twice a week, not monthly. The woman director agrees. The teachers are pleased with Vanessa. Like many gifted children, she tends to use her gifts to do as little as possible, but her reports are excellent—"A" in every subject. At 8:30 A.M. the meeting is over. Jane's mind is at ease.

"I'm a little annoyed," she tells me, half-smiling. "Apparently Vanessa is more punctual when she sleeps at your place."

"Because she doesn't rely on me to wake her and make her hurry. Usually I sleep in the morning."

Jane leaves the school at the wheel of her Volkswagen

(she has a big station wagon for her trips to her ranch in Santa Barbara). At 9:00 A.M. she goes to the workout center. There, for an hour, like a good student, she tortures her body, which refuses to grow old. She goes home, takes a shower, does her hair and makeup lightly and makes ten telephone calls.

At 11:30 she is in her office. With Debby, her secretary, she settles a few personal matters, signs checks and the letters of the day. Then she confers with aides about production problems. Around 1:30 she has lunch—an extremely light lunch in the studio canteen—with the screenwriter on her next film.

The afternoon is no less heavy. There's an interview for a future television show, and a meeting with a friend who is responsible for struggling against the new laws of the Reagan administration that are slowly eating away at all the social advantages women have gained over the last twenty years. Around 6:00 P.M. she goes home, spends a little time with her son, gives instructions to the gardener, and phones her stepmother, Shirlee Fonda, with whom she is very close. Then she heads for the kitchen-dining room to prepare dinner. Healthy, simple food is her diet, to the great despair of Vanessa, whose French chromosomes have given her a definite taste for more sophisticated fare.

Tom Hayden arrives from Sacramento. After dinner there is a meeting with Tom's staff to discuss and define the strategy for the November elections.

It's 11:00 P.M. Jane quickly packs a small case. At 7:48 the next morning she flies off to Miami.

I don't know whether or not Jane would appreciate this portrait of Superwoman. Nevertheless, it *is* a typical day in her life. Fortunately there are breaks. She takes time to see friends, not all of whom are part of her political entourage. She goes to rock concerts and takes the children to see movies. Occasionally she had dropped in on me for one reason or another (to give a book to Vanessa for instance) and chatted for two hours, forgetting to feel guilty. Two hours doing nothing is an unheard-of luxury for her. She gets up suddenly and says, "I've played hooky again."

For some people, Jane is a dangerous extremist, a fanatic feminist, and for others she is a committed woman struggling against social injustice in all its forms. But everyone asks the same question: "Does this surprising machine, successful in everything, have a heart?"

I will reply by speaking of Jane's love for her father. Henry didn't have a very expansive temperament, but as he got along in years he opened up more to his daughter. For thirty years Jane had been waiting for that miracle, and in the last years they became very close. But destiny didn't seem to want her to know true peace in her relationship with Henry. Jane suffered in body and soul from the long, incurable heart disease that took her father away. By looking at Jane's blue eyes and the expression on her face, I could guess Henry's state without having to ask.

Her grief when he died, discreetly held back, but profound and tragic, was the grief of a woman who knows how to love.

One day when Jane and I were walking in the hills of her ranch I said, "You've succeeded in practically everything you've attempted in your life. If you could have one wish, what would it be?"

She stopped and sat down near a brook to think. Then she said: "To grow . . . not on the surface, but in myself. I would like to grow in depth. I'd like to understand things better within myself."

ALTHOUGH Catherine Deneuve is French and we have a child together, I had fewer occasions to see her than to see Jane Fonda.

The last meeting with her that left me a truly pleasant memory was over ten years ago. Catherine was seeing a lot of Marcello Mastroianni, who was very much in love with her, and one evening the three of us had dinner together in a nice restaurant on the Left Bank in Paris. All the men in Catherine's life since her divorce from David Bailey have been pleasant, without much personality. Obedient, devoted and well brought up, was how they impressed me. But I liked Marcello very much. I found him attractive, funny and charming, not to speak of his talent. I was delighted that Catherine's relationship with him gave me the chance to know him better.

We drank a great deal that evening at the restaurant. Catherine was at her best—gay and amusing. Before leaving I insisted that the owner of the restaurant sell me the huge bouquet of flowers on the bar and I presented them to Catherine. Marcello was peeved that he didn't think of it first. "You're taking the flowers from my mouth. It's not fair," he said.

All three of us got into my car and Catherine asked me to drop Marcello at his hotel. I did so. Then I drove her home and kissed her goodbye.

If her intention was to tease Marcello and make him a little jealous, she succeeded. The next time I saw him he told me that during dinner he had suddenly felt that he was in the way.

"You were like old lovers . . . laughing, understanding each other implicitly. For a moment, I thought that she was still in love with you."

I assured him that if he ever had reason to be jealous, it would never be because of me.

Marcello said that women always got rid of their men, and he told me what happened to him and Faye Dunaway. They were in love and were living together in New York. She kept saying to him, "I'm not at ease when I'm not in my own home."

To make her more comfortable, he decided to rent her an apartment.

"Now I was living in her home," said Marcello. "But

nothing had really changed. A few days later, she stopped me in the hall and showed me my suitcases in front of the door. She never told me why I was so suddenly sent away."

He sighed. He was convinced that Catherine would throw him out one of these days.

"I admit that I am not always an angel," he said.

My son Christian also liked Marcello a lot. "One day," he told me, "I heard people shouting. He was arguing with my mother again. The door slammed. I heard the car roaring off. He never came back."

I asked Christian if he knew why Marcello and Catherine had split up.

"No," he said, "but they argued more and more."

Marcello had a child with Catherine: Chiara. She is one of the prettiest little girls I have ever seen.

WHEN Christian came to live with me, his mother slipped a detailed list of all his clothes into his suitcase. If a sock was missing when he returned, she would scold him and complain that I was encouraging his untidiness. So my son and I made a habit of not opening the bag any more. On his arrival, we slipped it under the bed and went off to buy clothes for him.

Why is it that with Catherine I always have the feeling that she is somehow sitting in judgment over me?

A few months ago, and for the oddest of reasons, I found an answer to this question. As Uncle Sam personifies the USA, a female bust named Marianne has been the symbol of the French Republic since the revolution of 1789. It can be found in every city hall or mayor's office in the country.

In the early sixties it was suggested to endow Marianne with Brigitte Bardot's features, and thousands of statues with BB's face were cast in plaster and sent across the land to replace the old ones. Virtuous citizens cried heresy, but by and large the French found the idea quite charming.

Then, early in 1986, I found myself in the city hall of a

small community on the outskirts of Paris where a friend of mine was getting married, when suddenly I had the feeling that somebody was staring down my neck. I turned and discovered the bust of the French Republic as it gazed at me with plastery eyes. It was no longer Brigitte Bardot; it was Catherine Deneuve. Was I hallucinating or had Catherine ousted Brigitte in the role of Marianne? A surprised whistle escaped my lips, which was quite incongruous with the solemnity of the mayor's address. "Excuse me," I said mentally to Catherine the Republic. "I promise never to whistle again during a marriage ceremony."

Having just arrived from a long stay in Los Angeles I did not know that after two decades some highly placed officials had decided to bring Marianne's profile up to date. Many famous women had been considered to replace BB, but *shobiz oblige*, and the decision had finally gone to Catherine Deneuve.

If one considers that Jane Fonda symbolizes tomorrow's woman, and that in 196 years Brigitte and Catherine were the only women to have lent their faces to the French Republic, it would be difficult to deny that I seem to have a strong propensity for banner-carrying ladies!

W*HEN* I'm with Brigitte Bardot I still have the feeling that I'm with a child who needs protection. She still hasn't made the transition from childhood to maturity. She has gone from her collection of stuffed animals to animals of flesh and blood. For twenty years the papers have talked about her crusade on behalf of abandoned dogs, laboratory monkeys and all those creatures who suffer but can't talk or complain. She refused fortunes to make films in Hollywood because she didn't like traveling; but she has gone to Alaska to try to save baby seals. She fights for her animals with the same sincerity and energy that Jane Fonda uses on behalf of mankind.

Ten years ago, when she suddenly gave up films, most people didn't believe it. But I knew she was sincere. She was unable to become, even on screen, a real grownup person with real adult problems. She hasn't betrayed the little Brigitte. She said goodbye and bowed out while there was still time.

I saw her last year in Saint-Tropez where I was spending the summer with my ex-wife Catherine Schneider, and with Vania, Christian and Vanessa. (Nathalie, my eldest daughter, was detained in New York by a film project.) I called La Madrague, Brigitte's house. She recognized my voice and cried out, "It's you, my Vava." Her voice was warm and friendly. I asked her when I could see her.

"Not this evening, I'm answering letters. Over two hundred. And I have no secretary. It's tough but I've got to do it. They're not autograph hunters who are writing to me, but friends, friends whom I don't know, but who understand me. They encourage me in my war for the animals. Tomorrow evening, okay? You'll take me out to a restaurant."

The next evening at the agreed time I rang the bell at the gate of La Madrague. A chorus of barking dogs answered. The caretaker opened the gate. He told me that Brigitte was still at the Petite Garrigue, an isolated house in the pine forest, a "secondary retreat," as she called it. Around nine-thirty an old Renault station wagon pulled up in the courtyard. The legend, wearing blue jeans and a T-shirt, was in the driver's seat. She got out of the car, her hair disheveled and her face and arms covered with dried mud.

"Sorry I'm late," said Brigitte. "They've just played a dirty trick on me. The caretakers of the Petite Garrigue left without telling me. I had to clean up, water the plants, *and* feed the pigeons and my guests." She laughed despite her bad mood and fatigue. "Do you like me like this? What I don't understand is why they took the new spare wheel out of the MiniMoke."

We sent into the house, which hadn't changed in fifteen years. The furniture, the objects and the size of the rooms were all on a human scale—comfortable, simple and very personal.

"I'll go scrub myself clean and change," said Brigitte, leaving for her bedroom. "Help yourself to a drink."

I found a small empty space on the couch that was not occupied by any of the eleven cats and eight dogs, and I sat down.

We decided to dine at the Auberge des Maurea, an old Saint-Tropez restaurant on a narrow street far from the crowds of the port. They had reserved a garden table for us, isolated by a few climbing plants. Brigitte was wearing trousers, a blouse with rolled-up sleeves and an embroidered waistcoat. Her hair fell freely over her shoulders.

We ordered a bottle of wine and they brought us some anchovy croutons to conform to tradition. Between true friends it always seems as if there has been no separation. The conversation began as if we had seen each other the day before.

"So are you happy?" asked Brigitte.

I told her a little about my life. "And you?"

It wasn't anguish but a sort of silent questioning that I read in her eyes.

"In a way, I'm happier than before," she said after a short silence. "I have what I want. Peace. Are you afraid of growing old?"

"The idea doesn't thrill me," I said. "But my mind still functions, I leave behind many twenty-year-olds on the ski slopes, and there are even women who find me attractive."

She laughed. "It's funny, isn't it? When we met I believed that a woman had really had it after the age of thirty-five. I'm approaching fifty and yet many men find me still not bad. That doesn't mean to say that I respond to their advances, but still, it makes me happy."

She spoke to me about the man who had been sharing her life (more or less consistently) for the last few years.

"I get along rather well with him. There's a sort of gentleness that I'd never known." She laughed again. "I must say that my emotional life has always been rather chaotic."

Some customers were walking toward the exit. A woman with a pleasant face came up to our table.

"Mademoiselle Bardot, I admire you so much. Could I have your autograph?"

"Oh, no, madame," said Brigitte. "I'm not an actress. I don't give autographs any more."

"Excuse me," said the woman. "You know you are... very beautiful." She walked off.

"She was going to say: You're *still* very beautiful," remarked Brigitte.

*B*RIGITTE has opened a boutique on a small street that leads from the port to the citadel—a thirteen-by-nineteen-foot cubbyhole loaded with knickknacks: an old bicycle, postcards, autographed photos (she does not give autographs, but she sells the past), a dress from *And God Created Woman*, ballet shoes from *A Very Private Affair*. Only Brigitte would surrender the froth of her legend to the public, as in a flea market.

The shop enables her to help friends who work there to earn a livelihood. I doubt if it provides her with even a modest income. But the idea of such a boutique is indicative of the value she attaches to her years of fame. She abandons the masks with which she had been disguised in spite of herself. It is as if she is saying to people, "My image as an actress was only a dream. Come. Enjoy yourselves with these bits of the material that you used to tear from my body. They're not worth much, I tell you. Reduced prices."

Nevertheless, the minister of culture, Jack Lang, has just given Brigitte the Legion of Honor. The insolent girl who said no to all the taboos would have burst out laughing if anyone had told her that one day a cabinet minister would give her a medal which only honorable citizens and good soldiers normally receive.

Today, Brigitte Bardot is fifty years old. I wonder what she thinks of it?

Epilogue

THE MARTIAN

*M*ANY people keep telling me, "You should make a film starring all your ex-wives."

It's an amusing idea but impossible for reasons one can easily imagine. Once, however, chance brought all these goddesses together, at the peak of their beauty, on the same set.

I had just met Jane Fonda and was making *Circle of Love* with her at the studio in Saint-Maurice.

I was showing Serge Marquand how to fall from a window onto the pavement of a street during a fight scene. But my demonstration was too realistic and I broke my shoulder.

Annette Stroyberg, who was passing through Paris, had come to see us on the set. She was present when I had the accident. Jane, told of the incident in her dressing room, ran over immediately. The two women supported me and did their best to comfort me while we were waiting for the ambulance.

It so happened that Catherine Deneuve was rehearsing on another set. She heard about my accident and came to find out how I was.

When the ambulance arrived, Jane, Catherine and Annette got in with me. By extraordinary coincidence, Brigitte Bardot was driving into the courtyard of the studio as we were leaving. You wouldn't dare allow this kind of coincidence to happen in a novel or screenplay—but in real life such things do occur.

The guard asked Brigitte to make way for the ambulance and told her the name of the patient. In a panic, Brigitte got out of the car and jumped into the ambulance.

I saw the anxious faces of four women leaning over me, and despite the terrible pain in my shoulder I was able to savor that moment to the fullest.

"He's completely green," worried Brigitte.

"That's normal for a Martian," explained Catherine.

They all looked at me for an instant—Brigitte, Annette, Catherine and Jane—and burst out laughing.

PICTURE CREDITS

Bardot

1—Pictorial Parade
2—Neal Peters
3—Sygma
4—*Paris-Match*
5—*L'Express*
6—Sygma
7—Pictorial Parade
8—Sygma
9—Roger Vadim
10—Pictorial Parade
11—Memory Shop
12—Roger Vadim
13—Memory Shop
14—Memory Shop
15—Neal Peters
16—Sygma
17—Pictorial Parade
18—Sygma
19—UPI/Bettmann
20—Sygma
21—UPI/Bettmann

Deneuve

1—Pictorial Parade
2—Sygma
3—Sygma
4—UPI/Bettmann
5—Sygma
6—Sygma
7—Sygma
8—Wide World
9—Sygma
10—Sygma
11—Sygma
12—Pictorial Parade
13—Gamma
14—Memory Shop
15—Lester Glassner Collection
16—UPI/Bettmann

Fonda

1—Pictorial Parade
2—Pictorial Parade
3—Sygma
4—Hughes Vassal/Gamma
5—Neal Peters
6—Pictorial Parade
7—Roger Vadim
8—UPI/Bettmann
9—Pictorial Parade
10—Roger Vadim
11—Gamma
12—UPI/Bettmann
13—Roger Vadim
14—Apis
15—Roger Vadim
16—Pictorial Parade
17—UPI/Bettmann